Gazing on Secret Sights

GAZING ON SECRET SIGHTS

Spenser, Classical Imitation, and the Decorums of Vision

THERESA M. KRIER

Cornell University Press

Ithaca and London

First published 1990 by Cornell University Press.

International Standard Book Number 0-8014-2345-7
Library of Congress Catalog Card Number 89-28299
Printed in the United States of America

*Librarians: Library of Congress cataloging information
appears on the last page of the book.*

⊖ The paper used in this publication meets the minimum requirements of the American National Standard for Permanence of Paper for Printed Library Materials Z39.48—1984.

For my parents

Contents

Acknowledgments

Spenser begins the most grateful stanza of *The Faerie Queene* by asking, "And is there care in heauen?" It seems to me likely that there is, when I consider my good fortune in friends and colleagues who have great funds of energy and intelligence. Barbara Bono, T. V. Buttrey, Helen Cooper, Joseph Loewenstein, Paolo Visonà, and the readers for Cornell University Press helped me to work out ideas large and small and rescued me all too often from witlessness. Carol Kaske took endless pains to keep me honest—many clarities of the book are due to her—and I hope I learned from her example. (To her I owe the felicitous suggestion of the Chaucerian adjectival form "venerean.") Heather Dubrow and Shirley Scott sustained from a distance with unflagging expressions of confidence. Alyson Hayes was a source of cordial comfort during an unexpectedly rough period. Notre Dame's College of Arts and Letters becomes an increasingly exciting and, well, *collegial* place to work, thanks in part to Dean Michael Loux and my colleagues, among whom Joseph Buttigieg, Christopher Fox, and especially Gerald Bruns and Stephen Fallon must stand for many others. It is due entirely to the wryly tolerant patience of typists Nila Gerhold, Nancy Kegler, and Cheryl Reed, and to their unblinking acceptance of final draft after final draft, that this book appears now, rather than some years from now. Bernhard Kendler and Marilyn Sale of Cornell University Press, and their copy editor Jackie Wehmuller, applied all their resources of tact and good will to the long process of book production.

Financial assistance for late revisions came from the National Endowment for the Humanities and from Notre Dame's Institute for Scholarship in the Liberal Arts. An earlier version of sections from Chapters One and Two was published in *Spenser Studies* 7 (1987); reprinted with the permission of AMS Press, Inc. Parts of Chapter Four went into an essay in *Modern Philology* 84, 2 (November 1986). I am grateful to the University of Chicago Press for permission to reprint. Quotations from Spenser's works are taken from the Variorum edition published by the Johns Hopkins University Press; Vergil's *Aeneid* is quoted from the Latin edition of R. A. B. Mynors (Oxford University Press, 1969); texts from Ovid are reprinted by permission of the publishers and The Loeb Classical Library from Ovid's *Metamorphoses*, Volumes III–IV, Books I and II, Cambridge, Mass.: Harvard University Press, 1977. Permission to use these texts is gratefully acknowledged.

I've dedicated this work to my parents, who gave "gentle noriture" to my "tender youth."

THERESA M. KRIER

Notre Dame, Indiana

Gazing on Secret Sights

Introduction

The Pampered Eye

In 1813, Robert Southey praised Spenser with the happy embrace, not to say the sentimentality, characteristic of other writers in the period:

> Yet not more sweet
> Than pure was he, and not more pure than wise;
> High priest of all the Muses' mysteries![1]

William Hazlitt, Southey's great antagonist, was also an admirer of Spenser, though for other reasons. In his essay "On Chaucer and Spenser" he quoted Southey's lines in order to disagree with them: "On the contrary, no one was more apt to pry into mysteries which do not strictly belong to the Muses."[2] This was not the

---

[1] Robert Southey, "The Lay of the Laureate," Proem 18. From *The Poetical Works of Robert Southey, with a Memoir*, 10 vols. in 5 (Boston: Houghton Mifflin, n.d.), 136.

Greg Kucich documents responses to Spenser among writers of the eighteenth and nineteenth centuries. See, e.g., "Leigh Hunt and Romantic Spenserianism," *Keats-Shelley Journal* 37 (1988), 110–35; "The Spenserian Psychodrama of *Prometheus Unbound*," in *Nineteenth-Century Contexts* 12 (1988), 61–84; *Keats, Shelley, and Romantic Spenserianism*, forthcoming from Pennsylvania State University Press.

[2] William Hazlitt, "On Chaucer and Spenser," in *Lectures on the English Poets*, in *The Complete Works of William Hazlitt*, centenary ed., ed. P. P. Howe (London: J. M. Dent, 1930), 5.19–44 at 40.

first time that Hazlitt had rebuked Southey's terms of praise for Spenser. In the essay called "On the Character of Milton's Eve," published the previous year in *The Round Table* (1817), he had quoted Southey's lines and had suggested a crucial distinction between Milton's methods in his chaste envisionings of Eve, and the methods of writers like Spenser "who have pampered the eye and fed the imagination with exuberant descriptions of female beauty." Milton has "tempered" his descriptions with "moral severity": "There is not a line in his works which tends to licentiousness, or the impression of which, if it has such a tendency, is not effectually checked by thought and sentiment.... Spenser, on the contrary, is very apt to pry into mysteries which do not belong to the Muses. Milton's voluptuousness is not lascivious or sensual. He describes beautiful objects for their own sakes. Spenser has an eye to the consequences, and steeps everything in pleasure, often not of the purest kind."[3] Hazlitt uses Southey's excessive warmth partly to score a point for his own self-presentation of urbanity and dry wit; but the transformation of Southey's vague and glowing "Muses' mysteries" into specifically sensual, passionate, and erotic mysteries that edge the limits of poetic decorum is also a palpable hit, at Spenser as well as Southey. The tone of urbane discernment emerges again in the offhand appearance of the casual idiom "has an eye to," here cannily describing Spenser's habit of going out of his way to depict objects of visual and sensual pleasure.

Hazlitt's fine remark about Milton's Eve rather oversimplifies the case of Spenser. Because Hazlitt's interest here lies chiefly in the morality of eroticism in the two authors, his brilliant contrast of their handling of description and desire stops short of remarking on their shared epistemological and representational problems. But Hazlitt's choice to compare the two poets on this issue, in the context of Milton's Eve and of female beauty more generally, is acute, as is the open-ended suggestiveness of those "consequences" to which Spenser "has an eye."[4]

---

[3]"On the Character of Milton's Eve," in *The Round Table*, ibid., 4.105–11 at 110.
[4] Milton anticipates the narrative difficulties of depicting to postlapsarian perception the prelapsarian nakedness of Eve by foregrounding the problem: he announces her freedom from shame while also giving her a traditional, and problematic, shamefastness. He thus provides her with both modesty and the candor of her nakedness, as in *Paradise Lost* 4.289–92, 312–20, 705–19; 5.377–85. Milton also chastens the

This book is about the prying into mysteries and the pampering of the eye, and the consequences of these activities, in Spenser's work. It is about the relationships between vision and purity which concerned Hazlitt, about what can be known through vision, about the social dynamics and decorums of vision. It is also about Spenser's handling of these subjects through myth, specifically through the imitation of Vergil's and Ovid's great mythic works.

It is worth glancing at a couple of Spenser's characteristic episodes here, in order to frame the questions that I ask of his episodes throughout the book. One comes from the sixth canto of *The Faerie Queene*, one from its penultimate canto. In each of them a beautiful female character—one a woman, one a goddess—has chosen to seclude her beauty from the world at large; in each of them she is exposed to view against her will. Each episode is set in a wood densely populated by nymphs and other nature spirits; each depicts the gaze of a horned god who traditionally has various associations with natural eros. Each owes something not just to ancient myth generally but to Ovid's mythic works.

While Una wanders through the wilds of Book 1, seeking the Redcrosse Knight, she is overtaken by Sansloy, who attempts to rape her:

> Yet for to feed his fyrie lustfull eye,
> He snatcht the vele, that hong her face before;
> Then gan her beautie shine, as brightest skye,
> And burnt his beastly hart t'efforce her chastitye.
>
>   (1.6.4)[5]

Nature is so shocked by this perfidy

---

response of the reader to these visions of Eve by attributing to Satan, or to nonexistence, the visually inflamed and epistemologically flawed passions of envy, despair, and the hunger of the have-not. See, e.g., *Paradise Lost* 5.443–50. These delicacies about the aesthetics and the ethics of vision Milton shared with Spenser and seems to have studied in Spenser's work.

For a discussion of the problem of Eve's modesty, see William Kerrigan and Gordon Braden, "Milton's Coy Eve: *Paradise Lost* and Renaissance Love Poetry," *English Literary History* 53 (1986), 27–51. For brief suggestions of Milton's debt to Spenser in handling readers' entrances into paradises as privileged and purified viewers of the erotic, see Isabel MacCaffrey, *Spenser's Allegory: The Anatomy of Imagination* (Princeton: Princeton University Press, 1976), 258–63.

[5]Citations from Spenser are taken from *The Works of Edmund Spenser: A Variorum Edition,* ed. Edwin Greenlaw, C. G. Osgood, and F. M. Padelford (Baltimore: Johns Hopkins Press, 1932). References will be given in the text. I also cite in the text

That molten starres do drop like weeping eyes;
And *Phoebus* flying so most shamefull sight,
His blushing face in foggy cloud implyes,
And hides for shame.

(1.6.6)

The fauns and satyrs who rescue her lead her to old Sylvanus, whose response is an awed memory of the goddesses Venus and Diana:

The God himselfe vewing that mirrhour rare,
Stood long amazd, and burnt in his intent;

. . . . .

And old *Syluanus* selfe bethinkes not, what
To thinke of wight so faire, but gazing stood,
In doubt to deeme her borne of earthly brood;
Sometimes Dame *Venus* selfe he seemes to see,
But *Venus* neuer had so sober mood;
Sometimes *Diana* he her takes to bee,
But misseth bow, and shaftes, and buskins to her knee.

(1.6.15–16)

This masculine response of awed contemplation is considerably more generous than the feminine response of the nymphs and naiads, who envy Una and flee for fear of being disgraced through comparison with her.

This episode is about the social decorums and indecorums of vision, and the issues that it raises appear throughout Spenser's work. The questions that can be asked of it are questions that this book addresses in relation to all of Spenser's work. Sansloy wishes to "feed his fyrie lustfull eye": What is the relationship between desire and sight? How does vision evoke desire? Are there kinds of desire besides lust which are aroused through vision? Phoebus blushes and hides for shame: What are the effects on an observer beholding intimacies or events not meant for outsiders' eyes? Why do privacies observed make the observer blush? How are social scenes complicated by the presence of an observer? Why is Phoebus an appropriate mythic figure for shame and blushes? Sylvanus

---

A. C. Hamilton's fine commentary from his edition of *The Faerie Queene* (New York: Longman, 1977).

gazes admiringly on Una, and muses reminiscently on Venus and Diana: Why does Spenser's heroine evoke such diverse responses from Sansloy, Sylvanus, the fauns and satyrs, and the nymphs? How does gender affect vision? Why does Spenser choose Venus and Diana as resembling Una, among all the goddesses? Why does a crowd of these lascivious mythic creatures adore Una and rejoice, rather than attack her, as she first expects? In short, what kinds of social relations exist between Una and her viewers, and how is her radiance interpreted not only by the viewers within the narrative but also by readers who recognize its iconographic significance? These are matters of social and aesthetic decorums simultaneously; such decorums are challenges to the interpretive capacities of the viewer and the reader, and to the representational capacities of the artist.

This is an elegant story and, the danger of Sansloy's "fyrie lust-full eye" notwithstanding, a relatively gentle one. The threat is to Una's chastity, but the chief act of violence is the snatching of her veil from her face. This is shameful enough as an act of raw violence against Una's choice of reticence, and wicked enough as an act of impiety against the Truth that she signifies. But the narrative remains decorous about her bodily life and the threat to it, and Sansloy beats a hasty retreat when he sees the fauns and satyrs approaching. The horned god's gaze is mild and not at all an aggression against Una. Sylvanus is repeatedly called old; he dozes in a "shady arber" while Una shrieks in the hands of her attacker; his contemplation of her enkindles in him a gentle and sociable memory of his acquaintances Venus and Diana, and a passing memory of the boy he loved long ago, Cyparissus, to whom he compares Una. The vigorous, potentially dangerous sexual energy of fauns and satyrs emerges benignly in the form of exuberant dancing and a loyal, persistent adoration of Una.

The passage's indebtedness to Ovid is limited to a general Ovidian sense of life in these mythic woods and to a single stanza's reference to Sylvanus's love for Cyparissus, derived from *Metamorphoses* 10.106–42, via the mythographic work of Boccaccio and Natalis Comes. Acts of vision in the episode range from Sansloy's lustful burning, to the nymphs' envious glances, to the fauns' and satyrs' mistaken adoration, to Sylvanus's natural, pagan approximation of Neoplatonic wonder. Elsewhere in Book 1, human responses to Una's beauty are a richer blend of wonder before the beloved woman, derived in part from lyric and Neoplatonic traditions, and recognition of eternal Truth (most notably at 1.12.21–41). Elsewhere in the epic, feminine beauty and unexpected marvels are beheld with a similar range of responses, in episodes in which imitations of Ovid, and of Vergil as well, become richer and more detailed. The last of these in the work as we have it concerns that other horned god, Faunus, whom Horace calls "*nympharum fugientum amator*" (*Odes* 3.18), a phrase that happily identifies a great interest shared by Ovid and Spenser: reticent nymphs who cherish the solitude and secrecy of the woods but who are regularly exposed by observers with fiery lustful eyes.

In one of several scenes of absorbed feminine life scattered throughout Spenser's work, Diana and her nymphs end their day's hunt with a bathe in her favorite spring on Arlo Hill, a place chosen for its solitude and its sensory pleasures:

> In her [Molanna's] sweet streames, *Diana* vsed oft
> (After her sweatie chace and toilesome play)
> To bathe her selfe; and after, on the soft
> And downy grasse, her dainty limbes to lay
> In couert shade, where none behold her may:
> For, much she hated sight of liuing eye.
>
> (7.6.42)

Faunus, with a much greedier, cruder, and more lurid imagination than Sylvanus shows, craves the sight of Diana's nakedness—more exactly, her nakedness "mongst her Nymphes in priuity," a specification that nicely shows the particular tastes of this voyeur (7.6.42). To this end he bribes and corrupts Diana's nymph Molanna, and wins a choice seat at the show that he has made of Diana's easy openness with her nymphs (contrast the accidental revelation that gives such pleasure to Sylvanus):

> There *Faunus* saw that pleased much his eye,
> And made his hart to tickle in his brest,
> That for great ioy of some-what he did spy,
> He could him not containe in silent rest;
> But breaking forth in laughter, loud profest
> His foolish thought. A foolish *Faune* indeed,
> That couldst not hold thy selfe so hidden blest,

But wouldest needs thine owne conceit areed.
Babblers vnworthy been of so diuine a meed.

$$(7.6.46)$$

This famous peeping and the consequent laugh justifiably earn Faunus the wrath of Diana and her nymphs.[6] But their angry revenge on him is an unexpected turn in the epic, for throughout Spenser's work, characters spied on or exposed who discover their exposure invariably respond with embarrassment, shame, increased vulnerability and awkwardness, a desire to hide. Diana and her crew show unexpected assertiveness here, and though Diana ultimately quits Arlo Hill (the most serious single consequence of vision in the epic), she does so not in flight or panic but apparently in a choice: it is not that she wants to hide, but that she is disgusted with Faunus's behavior.

How does Spenser evaluate the voyeur? What motives and desires fuel the character who wishes to be privy to feminine life? Why is this episode so dense an imitative amalgam of several Ovidian tales (Diana and Actaeon, *Met.* 3.155–252; Diana and Callisto, *Met.* 2.401–65 and *Fasti* 2.153–92; Alpheus and Arethusa, *Met.* 5.572–641; Faunus, Hercules, and Omphale, *Fasti* 2.303–58)? Why is it reminiscent of other episodes in Spenser's own epic (e.g., Belphoebe and Braggadochio, 2.3.21–46; Venus and Diana, 3.6.16–20)? Why does Spenser condemn not Faunus's looking per se but his crudity as a beholder? Why do the nymphs, of all creatures, attack?

The terms with which to consider these episodes and others like them in Spenser's work I hope to provide in the following chapters. Here I have used as an example the culturally rich *topos* of a numinous woman beheld; although there will be other objects beheld both in Spenser's work and in the following pages, that *topos* needs to be traced back to Vergil and Ovid. They are the two great sources and transmitters of this most frequent epic, lyric, and chivalric romance marvel in European literatures, and the wellheads of Spenser's explo-

---

[6]My brief description of the Faunus episode should be supplemented with studies by Richard N. Ringler, "The Faunus Episode," *Modern Philology* 63 (1966), 12–19; Anthony E. Friedmann, "The Diana-Acteon Episode in Ovid's *Metamorphoses* and the *Faerie Queene*," *Comparative Literature* 18 (1966), 289–99; Michael N. Holahan, " '*Iamque opus exegi*': Ovid's Changes and Spenser's Brief Epic of Mutability," *English Literary Renaissance* 6 (1976), 244–70; William P. Cumming, "The Influence of Ovid's *Metamorphoses* on Spenser's 'Mutabilitie Cantos,' " *Studies in Philology* 28 (1931), 241–56.

rations into the motions of vision, desire, secrecy, and vulnerability.[7] We may of course adduce many general reasons for Spenser's prolifically inventive imitations of Vergil and Ovid: their status as cultural resources; their ubiquity in the medieval and Renaissance genres that Spenser made his own; their thematic affinities with each other and with Spenser; their contrasting narrative techniques, which Spenser adapts and interweaves; their iconographic and story motifs. Most important for my purposes are two facts. First, Vergil and Ovid are the great ancient narrative poets of human vulnerability. Second, both poets make the social and physiological dynamics of vision central to their understanding of desire and of human relations to the world.

But why are Spenser's episodes of vision and hiddenness so consistently imitative in the first place? It might be possible to suppose descriptions of characters regarding divine and naked beautiful women to be intrinsically and simply erotic. But Spenser regularly builds such scenes on multiple subtexts, largely from Vergil's *Aeneid* and Ovid's *Metamorphoses*, as if to acknowledge that the mediation of language precludes an eroticism appealing directly and only to the natural instincts of the reader. Spenser's imitative depictions assume that there is no such thing as an innocent eye, pure vision and affect prior to interpretation. This is true whether the represented visual field centers on a figure freighted with traditional significance or on more quotidian, less allusive objects: there is no "Adamic vision."[8] Semiotic theorists of our century can plausibly argue that there is no such thing as a pure, transcendent view of an object in itself. Spenser might say instead that *for mortals* there is no such hope of Adamic vision, although certain gazes do greater justice than others to the alterity of the object viewed.

To depict a numinous woman beheld as an avatar of Venus, Diana, or sylvan nymph is already to acknowledge the visual field as a network of familiar signs, interpretable precisely because there is no innocent eye. In Norman Bryson's terms, *recognition* is more adequate

---

[7]Any study of Spenser's relationship to Vergil must begin with Merritt Hughes's *Virgil and Spenser* (Berkeley and Los Angeles: University of California Press, 1929), a work in which Spenser seems a remarkably disappointing heir to Vergil. But see also Angus Fletcher, *The Prophetic Moment: An Essay on Spenser* (Chicago: University of Chicago Press, 1971), 76–90. On Spenser's relationship to Ovid, see especially *Prophetic Moment*, 90–106, and Holahan, " '*Iamque opus exegi.*' "

[8]Norman Bryson, *Vision and Painting: The Logic of the Gaze* (New Haven: Yale University Press, 1983), 61.

than *perception* as a term for what happens when a viewer regards an image: "Neither the account of denotation as pure perception, nor the description of viewing in terms of perception rather than recognition, can be accepted."[9] Recognition makes possible *denotation*—Sylvanus can deduce that Una's radiant form is not Diana because she lacks the inconographic, public, recognizable accoutrements of bow and buskins—while recognition merges into the viewer's and reader's work of understanding *connotation*: the Neoplatonic implications of the narrator's calling Una "that mirrhour rare," for instance, or Sylvanus's own subsequent action of reviving his "ancient loue" for Cyparissus (1.6.17). Sylvanus's awed but comfortable reminiscence of Venus and Diana is an indication that the iconographic *is* the social—and in his case, also the sociable. Indeed, it is just because the iconographic is the social in Sylvanus's originary world of myth that it makes sense not to rest with recognition of iconic denotation, but to go on to the narrative surplus surrounding the image.

To recognize iconographic signs in Spenser's work is to recognize its generic sweep as well. For instance, characters stand appropriately amazed, feeding the hunger of the eye, before romance and allegorical marvels: the Dragon killed by Redcrosse, Lucifera's palace, Busyrane's tapestry, the enchantments of the Bower of Bliss. These romance marvels viewed occur at a high level of frequency throughout the poem.[10] They also merge into more quotidian visual encounters from

[9]Ibid. On the functions of denotation and connotation, see especially pp. 61–65. The possibility of perception's perfect transparency to the object is a common point of discussion in the philosophy and psychology of perception. See, e.g., Hans-Georg Gadamer, *Truth and Method* (New York: Sheed and Ward, 1975; rpt. ed., New York: Crossroad, 1988), 81–82: "Even perception conceived as an adequate response to a stimulus would never be a mere mirroring of what is there.... Pure seeing and pure hearing are dogmatic abstractions which artificially reduce phenomena. Perception always includes meaning."

The issue of the relational status of beholder and beheld and the related problem of interpreting the visual image are central to recent work in the visual arts. Among many others, I have learned from Stanley Cavell, notably *The World Viewed: Reflections on the Ontology of Film*, enlarged ed. (Cambridge: Harvard University Press, 1979); Michael Fried, *Absorption and Theatricality: Painting and Beholder in the Age of Diderot* (Berkeley and Los Angeles: University of California Press, 1980); Edward Snow, *A Study of Vermeer* (Berkeley and Los Angeles: University of California Press, 1979).

[10]Such episodes have always evoked readers' testimony to the appeal of the vivid, pictorial quality of Spenser's work, one of the most engaging aspects of Spenser criticism. Although that vividness is not one of my concerns in this book, it is a handy indicator of the hungers and gratifications of the eye in the poem. Rudolf B. Gottfried

the romance tradition, the social dynamics of which Spenser emphasizes: the frequent sighting of an anonymous and putatively hostile
knight in armor at a distance, who turns out to be a friend; Arthur
and Timias misinterpreting their view of the assistance given by the
Salvage Man to Serena when her horse's gear needs adjustment; Calidore's long and connoisseur-like scrutiny of Tristram, whose royal
and romance history emerges only through the most sophisticated
social decorums in their encounter. These frequent visual encounters
contribute to Spenser's allegorical fusion of romance and romance-
epic.

Or again, in episodes of the numinous woman observed, we see
beautiful generic fusions, from ancient mythological narrative and
epic, of an encounter between a hero and a patron goddess (Aeneas
with Venus, Odysseus with Athene) with certain strands of European
love-lyric and the figure of the *donna angelicata*. These fusions would
have appealed to Spenser's eclectic creative processes for many reasons, not least because the lady's Neoplatonic radiance could impart
new kinds of dignity and sacrality to the mythic meetings of ancient
epic, while the momentum of mythic stories could contribute narrative
drive and narrative functions to the lyric figure of the numinous
woman. *The Faerie Queene* develops a very large group of episodes
about a numinous woman observed, narratives that provoke issues
not addressed in Spenser's earliest work: social and gender relations
between beholder and beheld, the possibility of consciousness in the
observed character, the granting and depiction of the alterity of the
observed woman, the nature of desires aroused by vision, the problem
of agency or will in vision, the desire for hiddenness and its conflict
with the drive to see. These are issues that appear in episodes discussed
throughout this book.

As the stories of Una and Diana suggest, and as Hazlitt perceives,
Spenser is interested in the pudencies of sight and in the implication
that unimpeded sight might have something indecent about it; he is
interested in that part of the story of vision which acknowledges the
conflict or tension of seeing hidden things. It is a popular notion, if
not a rigorously accurate one, that "Spenser's heroes and heroines,

---

surveys the history of remarks on Spenser's visual force in "The Pictorial Element in
Spenser's Poetry," *English Literary History* 19 (1952), 203–13, rpt. in *That Soueraine
Light*, ed. William R. Mueller and D. C. Allen (Baltimore: Johns Hopkins Press,
1952), 123–33. See also John B. Bender, *Spenser and Literary Pictorialism* (Princeton:
Princeton University Press, 1972).

good and evil [*sic*] alike, never seem to gaze or stare—they peep and espy, as if looking itself were wicked."[11] Such an impression needs refining, and this book refines it. What remains true is that peeping is a morally laden issue, not a silly one, in Spenser's work; the activities of peeping and spying may not necessarily imply wickedness, but they do imply that the objects viewed have an active will and resistance to being seen. That is, they have volition at least, sometimes consciousness, and part of the narrative problem that Spenser faces is that of representing consciousness in beheld characters. Hiddenness in the secrecy of secluded places accompanies, or more precisely precedes, acts of vision in Spenser's work, as he tries to articulate and to depict both a profound human wish to see and an equally profound wish to remain in a condition of invisibility, to remain a subject to oneself rather than to become an object to another. How to show hiddenness without violating it and turning it into display becomes a matter of some importance to Spenser, as an ethical issue and as a representational problem. This is partly because both the desire to see and the desire to honor privacy are conceived as profoundly erotic desires; that Spenser frames depictions of lovers and numinous women as secrecies or mysteries to which a spectator is privy is one reason for the sexual power of the passages, and one reason that Spenser has a reputation as a literary voyeur.

Moreover, because persons within the poem and readers of the poem are often imagined as "Ideal Spectators," in Joseph Dallett's useful phrase, characters become loci of observable and observed events in their inner lives, events manifest in their bodily form or appearance.[12] Sight and hiddenness are linked not only through the tension between those who seek solitude and those who wish to see the solitary, but also through the notion of inwardness as a place within the person. The frequency with which Spenser uses the words *secret, private,* and their etymological relations focuses attention on the inner life, the life of affect in the process of becoming aware of itself as it becomes external and social, subject to observation.

Anne Ferry's study of the "inward" language developed in Renaissance sonnets suggests precise limits on the denotations of words like *secret* and *private* in the Renaissance; but Spenser pushes against

[11] J. W. Saunders, "The Façade of Morality," *English Literary History* 19 (1952), 81–114 at 108.

[12] Joseph Dallett, "Ideas of Sight in *The Faerie Queene*," *English Literary History* 27 (1960), 87–121 at 89.

these limits.[13] He expands such concepts to embrace not only affective life but also a notion of individuality set within and yet distinct from social life. Thus *private* can mean, simply, solitary or personal, distinct from the public: King Lear is said to give up his public responsibilities and lead "a priuate life" "in Albania with Gonorill" (2.10.29). Privacy can be withdrawal from society, or a state of concealment, as when Paridell woos Hellenore and observes her attraction to him: "Which he perceiuing, euer priuily / In speaking, many false belgardes at her let fly" (3.9.52). "Privitee" can also refer to an event within the heart. Redcrosse and Sansjoy both take spices before their battle "to kindle heat of corage priuily" (1.5.4), and Radegund's maid Clarinda

> turn'd the trust, which was in her affyde,
> To feeding of her priuate fire, which boyld
> Her inward brest.
>
> (5.5.53)

—this last a usage that conflates the sense of secrecy or concealment with the sense of the heart's interiority, and perhaps with the notion of self-interest. "Privitee" can refer not only to the place of the heart, but to its contents: Arthur and Amoret travel together but "neither shewed to other their hearts priuity" (4.9.19).

Throughout Spenser's mature work there are secret sights, all kinds of objects and scenes not meant for others' eyes. The most familiar of these are the pairs of lovers who are intruded upon in Book 6. Their unguardedness appears in other contexts throughout the epic, among characters, especially but not solely female, who assume the privileges of their solitude or privacy. There are interestingly complicated episodes in which an ostensibly private exchange is staged for an observer, who is made to feel like a voyeur of others' intimacies: Redcrosse watching the bogus Una making love with her demon-lover in Book 1; Phedon, whom Guyon meets in Book 2, betrayed by his friend and the maid of his betrothed posing as lovers. These in turn

---

[13]Anne Ferry, *The "Inward" Language: Sonnets of Wyatt, Sidney, Shakespeare, Donne* (Chicago: University of Chicago Press, 1983). For interesting work on privacy in other areas of English Renaissance culture, see David Starkey, "Representation through Intimacy: A Study in the Symbolism of Monarchy and Court Office in Early-Modern England," in *Symbols and Sentiments: Cross-Cultural Studies in Symbolism*, ed. Ioan Lewis (London: Academic Press, 1977), 187–214, and Patricia Fumerton, "'Secret' Arts: Elizabethan Miniatures and Sonnets," *Representations* 15 (Summer 1986), 59–97.

merge into episodes of true voyeurism: Cymochles with his nymphs in the Bower of Bliss (Book 2), for example. (There are far fewer instances of this most insidious hunger of the eye than one might guess, however.)

These are the kinds of episodes that I consider in the chapters that follow. They show how Spenser inflects the dynamics of desire and will in vision in Vergil's *Aeneid* and in Ovid's *Metamorphoses* (and occasionally in other Ovidian pieces), and suggest that he generally opposes the ethos of vision in Vergil's work to that in Ovid's. From these works he evolves powerful notions of how to depict objects, characters, and especially compelling female characters who assume their own solitude, so as to protect that solitude and their innocence before watchers. From them also he develops a model of the body as an eloquent, vulnerable surface and a creative, hallowed interior space. These are my emphases in discussions of Books 1, 2, and 3 of *The Faerie Queene*.

Ultimately, literary, social, and political experience leads Spenser to dismay at the necessity of display or spectacle and its use by characters who represent the good. In the works published in 1595 and 1596, he articulates several problems with intentional display and its failure of candor in court life. One of these problems involves the presentation of self in the conscious deployment of demeanor and countenance by courtiers—a problem that he depicts as the divorce between attractive external appearance and corrupt internal reality in *Mother Hubberds Tale* and in *Colin Clouts Come Home Againe*. It is by this same interest in demeanor, though, that Spenser overcomes the impasse of his unease with theatricality and display, and he does this in two ways. First, he sketches countenance not only as the intentional and ethically suspect control of the visible but also, elsewhere, as the unintended and beautiful revelation of interior secrets. Second, the disturbing tendency of representatives of government to control demeanor and display is modified, chiefly in Book 6, to an ideal capacity to study characters encountered with a decorous and generous tact that seeks not to control others but to enable their inward *virtù* and the substance of their interior treasury—one of Spenser's frequent images—to emerge like a flower unfolding to the air and the sun.

These issues do not emerge clearly until the time of *The Faerie Queene*. In the earliest works, the translations of *A Theatre for Worldlings* and the related *Complaints* of 1591, solitude and privacy are not imagined at all, and vision is largely a matter of poetic and visionary inspiration. The speaker or poet contemplates a granted vision of mutability or "the worlds vanitie"; his response is to welcome, "embrace," and suffer the grandeur and the pity of the vision:

> Vnto my eyes strange showes presented were,
> Picturing that, which I in minde embraced,
> That yet those sights empassion me full nere.
>   ("Visions of the worlds vanitie" 10–12)

The body of the viewer in these works is an impediment left behind in order that the pageant may unfold; it will become more present to objects viewed in the mature work.

The pieces in *A Theatre for Worldlings* and the *Complaints* are thus peripheral to the main concerns of this book. The same is true of *The Shepheardes Calender* (1579), in which the questions that Spenser later raises about sight simply do not occur. The important exception is the "Aprill" eclogue, which provides the first of many instances in Spenser's work of a beloved woman at the center of a ring. It is a crucial shift: from emblematic or other-worldly spectacles to hierarchic vision of a woman, ideal but of this world, viewed by other corporeal creatures. To this eclogue I will return presently.

The chapters that follow argue changes and some development, in Spenser's career, of the decorums of vision and mastery of the representational problems that vision raises. But our knowledge of pertinent chronology is rough at best, especially in regard to the composition of *The Faerie Queene*, and I have not felt constrained to produce a book-by-book analysis of the work. Anyone who has lived with Spenser's work for a long time has unverifiable hunches about bits that seem to have been composed, say, very early in the career and then incorporated into work of a later period; organizing this study by strict sequence only increased the temptation to construct a career and an epic for him with a far firmer and clearer teleological shape than our knowledge can justify. Instead I have built chapters on a sequence of related issues and topics which will honor our limited historical knowledge while making an argument about Spenser's development. Nor do I discuss authors whose works are intermediaries between the ancient writers and Spenser—Ariosto and Tasso, for instance, among writers of epic, or Boccaccio and Natalis Comes, among mythographers. I am less interested in transmission and me-

diation of sources than in one kind of intertextuality, and so I focus
on a limited number of allusions and passages from Vergil's and
Ovid's works. This focus has the advantage of limiting the book to
a size that can fit between two covers; in any case, the exhaustive
citations provided in the splendid annotated editions would make
superfluous any more extensive development of Spenser's imitative
practice, relative to my subject of vision, than those I offer in the
following chapters.

Chapter One is devoted to matters of vision and desire in Vergil's
Aeneid and Ovid's *Metamorphoses*. Books 1 to 6 of the *Aeneid*, the
Odyssean *Aeneid*, form for Spenser a foundation plot of wandering,
yearning, and wonder. More precisely, the Odyssean *Aeneid* carries
into later European literatures the capacity of the Homeric romance
hero for marvel before wonders beheld. "As I looked...my heart
admired long," says Odysseus repeatedly; for Vergil's Aeneas, a less
confident and boisterous hero in a less vigorous and trustworthy
world, wonder is a thing *borne*, a suffering of sight and the hopeless
responses that it evokes of desire for love and stability. In Ovid's
Metamorphoses, especially in the many tales of nymphs seen, desired,
taken, and transformed by gods, it is not the beholder but the beheld
who suffers the gaze of others, others who are always more powerful
and violent. As a result, hiddenness becomes the object of a poignant
wish in the *Metamorphoses*; characters seek the woods and groves
in a futile hope of escaping the desirous gaze of an aggressor. These
two anatomies of vision and desire, the subject of Chapter One, draw
into Spenser's work not only the themes of vision-as-sufferance and
the wish for hiddenness, but also character structures: the vulnerable
nymph; the responsive, marveling hero; the aggressive god.

Chapter Two turns to Book 2 of *The Faerie Queene*; it is the one
place in which I give a reading of a single book. It is in Book 2 that
we first see large-scale set piece imitations of both the *Aeneid* and the
Metamorphoses, notably in the luxurious blazon of Belphoebe and
her meeting with Braggadochio and Trompart. The blazon itself is
heavily Vergilian, and the meeting a tissue of Ovidian comic motifs;
put together, they form a generic tension in modes of beholding a
numinous woman. Genre is the center of this chapter, its argument
that Spenser's creation of a moral and allegorical epic, a miniature
Aeneid, is pressured not only by the comic Ovid but also by certain
features in the praise of Queen Elizabeth, and by her literary affiliations with visual wonder in the *Aeneid*. She is both a reader of the

book and an object of vision within it; the presence of Elizabeth and the presence of Ovidian nymphs, who appear as well-developed characters on whom the narrative relies heavily for the first time in the epic, destabilize and enrich the genre of allegorical epic, and push it toward the epic-romance form of the central books.

Chapter Three considers the human body as the form most often beheld in Spenser's work. Perhaps because of his social and Ovidian sense of the body as both viewed and seeking protection from view, the body's structure in *The Faerie Queene* is conceived as a hallowed inner space and a vulnerable surface. (Or it may be the other way round—that apprehending the body as precious interior and vulnerable surface provokes a sharp awareness of the world's gaze.) This hallowed inner space, its pristine beauty and integrity, and the ubiquitous threat of invasion of the vulnerable surface of the body—these qualities of bodily existence regularly accompany awareness of the world's gaze in *The Faerie Queene*.[14] The argument of this chapter is pointed toward issues of gender differentiation, partly because in Spenser's work as in his literary tradition female characters are more often made objects of vision than are men, and partly because of the curious fact that Spenser's work takes the female body as the normative human condition of greatest interest. It is in this chapter too that I articulate most fully Spenser's manifold attempts to imagine and represent the ways in which men and women can be present to each other: he experiments in depicting an encyclopedic range of the ways that men and women desire, accept, or reject each other's presence, and in depicting ideal gratifications of the wish for candid mutual presence.

Chapter Four brings to the surface a current that runs through the whole book: defensiveness as a response of the hidden to unexpected and undesired visibility. Being seen, in Ovid's work and thence in Spenser's, is one fundamental intrusion on the vulnerable self from which other violations follow; to wish to be hidden is to wish for freedom from predatory eyes and to wish for a condition of candor, of being happily without any need for defenses against the gaze of another.[15] The experience of defensiveness takes a variety of forms throughout Spenser's work, especially in Book 3 of the epic and in

[14]Mary Douglas discusses this threat as pollution in *Purity and Danger: An Analysis of Concepts of Pollution and Taboo* (New York: Praeger, 1966), 122 and passim.

[15]For the notion of candor I am indebted to Stanley Cavell's *The World Viewed*, 111 and passim.

most of the work published in 1595 and 1596. Chapter Four shows how characters within the poem respond to the threat of exposure, predominantly in the third book of the epic. Chapter Five shifts to discuss a concept linked to exposure, the problem of purposive display in the work published in 1595–96.

A moment ago I mentioned the "Aprill" eclogue as an early instance of the vision of an elevated, revered woman who evokes love and awe. One reason that the depiction of Elisa in "Aprill" is worth particular attention is its anticipation, in lyric form, of many of Spenser's later narrative interests, interests I will be addressing in this book. First, the blazon is a form that occurs in Spenser's work frequently, and opulently. But he eventually criticizes its fundamental act of display, a notion that comes to trouble him a good deal. Second, the passing anecdote of Pan and Syrinx anticipates work published later in its mythic pattern of pursuing god and fleeing nymph. Here, however, their significance is emblematic and allegorical (E.K. says that Pan is Henry VIII); Spenser does not yet pursue the relationship of vision to violence which will open up for him when he reconsiders Ovid in later work. Third, we find mythic narrative, but only briefly deployed. Phoebus thrusts out his head to gaze on Elisa, but her brilliance so abashes him that he blushes and hastily withdraws; the narrator hesitates to pitch Elisa against the brilliance of Cynthia, for fear of evoking the same kind of petrifaction that overtook Niobe when she boasted of her superiority to Latona. These brief myth-making forays are light notes only, anecdotes that suggest but do not confront the dangers of exposure and shame or the petrifaction that can be a Petrarchan consequence of the male contemplation of woman. Finally there is the motto "*O dea certe!*", an elegant and graceful allusive compliment to Elizabeth—but one that develops none of the tones or themes in Vergil's story of the weary hero meeting his mother disguised as a young huntress. This blazon raises none of the questions about social decorums or the consciousness of beholder and beheld which I have already suggested are important to Spenser later. Vision is not a matter of agency; it is only, simply and beautifully, a matter of unquestioned presence. This simplicity of tableau will give way before the drive to narrative in *The Faerie Queene* and in some of the later short works. To the narrative drive of the *Aeneid* and the energy of the *Metamorphoses*, to apprehensions of feminine life in Vergil's and Ovid's largest works, and to the encompassing notion of vision as a mode of address to the world, I now turn.

Chapter One

Vergil and Ovid:
The Sufferance of Vision

The great passages that Spenser imitates repeatedly from Vergil's *Aeneid* and Ovid's *Metamorphoses* give primacy to the act of beholding a numinous woman: Aeneas's meeting with his mother, Venus, disguised as a huntress, her subsequent epiphany, and Dido's aura of queenly beauty in the *Aeneid*; the gods' abrupt perceptions of reticent nymphs, and Actaeon's accidental transgression on Diana, in the *Metamorphoses*. In spite of crucial differences between Vergil's work and Ovid's, the mythic motif of beholding the numinous feminine creates certain conceptual affinities between the two Augustan writers, and these affinities extend to other acts of vision as well. Vision, for the ancients, is physiologically both a cause of desire and an expression of it; vision's dynamics include an experience of sufferance, for either the viewer or the object; vision is always an experience of engrossment or absorption for the viewer. These aspects of vision are consistent throughout the *Aeneid* and the *Metamorphoses*. The two works may be said to mirror each other, in their analyses of vision and in their narrative embeddings of it.

Contrasts between Vergil and Ovid have long pervaded thinking about them. During the nineteenth- and twentieth-century eclipse of Ovid's reputation, Vergil represented Roman grandeur, *gravitas*, and *labor* while Ovid represented the new fashioning of old Alexandrian decadence, frippery, and irresponsibility. The gradual recuperation of the Ovidian imagination, aided in part by Hermann Fränkel's influential if ambivalent study, was interestingly complicated by Brooks Otis's paired books on Vergil and Ovid. Otis inclined to pose for Vergil Arnoldian literary values of high seriousness, values against which Ovid seemed to come up wanting.[1] But the last twenty years of discussion have created a climate in which both Vergil and Ovid are no longer valued chiefly, in the one case, for being the poet of grown-ups, and, in the other, for a slick and trivial handling of neoteric interests. But the critical attitude that sees Ovid as a serious poet who engages in an energetic dialogue with the Roman epic of his master clears ground for more fruitful explorations of that charged relationship.[2] The *Metamorphoses* clearly honors its predecessor both in its elegantly designed similarities and in its divergences from the *Aeneid*, Ovid assuming and transforming certain of Vergil's themes: the violence and capriciousness of the natural and political worlds, the pressures of eros on public and private life, the inscrutability of the gods, the necessary but baffling ubiquity of power and of injustice, the human urge to create protected spaces. These are subjects structured by acts of looking in both poems.

In this chapter I examine paradigmatic acts of looking in the two Roman works, as well as some Homeric passages that Vergil imitiates. In the *Aeneid*, these are Aeneas's meetings with Venus and Dido; his retrospective description of meeting with the shades of Creusa and Hector (I defer discussion of the important meeting with the shade of Anchises in the underworld until Chapter Two) and his retrospective description of the fall of the palace at Troy; Dido's experiences of falling in love and abandonment. In the *Metamorphoses*, I turn to the groups of tales of sylvan nymphs seen, desired, and pursued by gods; to the groups of tales about spies; to the groups of tales about exposure—all in the early books of the poem.

---

[1] Hermann Fränkel's *Ovid: A Poet between Two Worlds* (Berkeley and Los Angeles: University of California Press, 1945) is a book that itself stands poised between admiration and puzzlement over its subject, and shows occasional contempt for Ovid's poetry and sensibilities. See also Brooks Otis, *Virgil: A Study in Civilized Poetry* (Oxford: Clarendon Press, 1963), and *Ovid as an Epic Poet* (Cambridge: Cambridge University Press, 1966).

[2] For the modes of imitation and allusion open to Roman poets, see Gian Biagio Conte, *The Rhetoric of Imitation: Genre and Poetic Memory in Virgil and Other Latin Poets,* trans. and ed. Charles Paul Segal (Ithaca: Cornell University Press, 1986); Richard Thomas, "Virgil's Georgics and the Art of Reference," *Harvard Studies in Classical Philology* 90 (1986), 171–98.

Meeting and Acknowledgment

Our entry into Vergil's meditations on sight is Aeneas's meeting with Venus (*Aen.* 1.320–410) outside Carthage, a text that was to haunt major writers later and become a paradigm for Spenser.[3]

> "nulla tuarum audita mihi neque visa sororum,
> o quam te memorem, virgo? namque haud tibi vultus
> mortalis, nec vox hominem sonat; o, dea certe
> (an Phoebi soror? an Nympharum sanguinis una?),
> sis felix nostrumque leves, quaecumque, laborem
> et quo sub caelo tandem, quibus orbis in oris
> iactemur doceas: ignari hominumque locorumque
> erramus vento huc vastis et fluctibus acti.
> multa tibi ante aras nostra cadet hostia dextra."[4]
>
> (*Aen.* 1.326–34)

["None of your sisters have I heard or seen, oh—what shall I call you, maiden? For there is no trace of mortal in your face, nor does your voice sound like a human being's. O goddess surely! Phoebus's sister? a nymph? Be favorable to us, whoever you are, and lighten our labor, and tell us beneath what sky, in what region of the globe we may finally be thrown; ignorant of men and the region we wander, driven here by wind and vast waves; many victims will fall for you before the altar by our hands."]

A good many of Aeneas's qualities emerge in this response to the maiden, even before her full epiphany as goddess and mother. Aeneas takes for granted that numinous beings can enter the human world, but, as we shall see, there is none of the sense of easy familiarity with

[3]Among works on Vergil which have been most instructive for my purposes, I might cite not only Fränkel and Otis but Viktor Pöschl, *The Art of Virgil: Image and Symbol in the "Aeneid,"* trans. Gerda Seligson (Ann Arbor: University of Michigan Press, 1962); W. R. Johnson, *Darkness Visible: A Study of Virgil's "Aeneid"* (Berkeley and Los Angeles: University of California Press, 1976); Elizabeth Block, *The Effects of Divine Manifestations on the Reader's Perspective in Virgil's "Aeneid,"* rev. ed., ed. W. R. Connor (Salem, N.H.: Ayer, 1981); Barbara Bono, *Literary Transvaluation: From Vergilian Epic to Shakespearean Tragicomedy* (Berkeley and Los Angeles: University of California Press, 1984); Gordon Williams, *Technique and Ideas in the "Aeneid"* (New Haven: Yale University Press, 1983).

[4]The text is that of R. A. B. Mynors (Oxford: Oxford University Press, 1969); the translations are mine.

which Odysseus in the *Odyssey* had greeted Athene, in the meeting that was the Homeric model for Vergil's passage. Rather, there is a sense of awe compounded with need and with uncertainty: "leves, quaecumque, laborem." It is this fusion of wonder with yearning that typifies acts of sight in the *Aeneid*, as we can see in Aeneas's response to Venus's epiphany:

> Dixit et avertens rosea cervice refulsit,
> ambrosiaeque comae divinum vertice odorem
> spiravere; pedes vestis defluxit ad imos,
> et vera incessu patuit dea. ille ubi matrem
> agnovit tali fugientem est voce secutus:
> "quid natum totiens, crudelis tu quoque, falsis
> ludis imaginibus? cur dextrae iungere dextram
> non datur ac veras audire et reddere voces?"
> talibus incusat gressumque ad moenia tendit.
>
> (*Aen.* 1.402–10)

[She spoke, and on turning away her rosy neck shone bright, and her ambrosial hair breathed out a divine fragrance; her gown flowed down to her feet, and her pace revealed a true goddess. When he recognized his mother, he followed her as she moved away, with these words: "Why do you too, cruel one, delude your son so often with false images? Why may we not join hand in hand, and hear and exchange truthful words?" Thus he accused her, and directed his step toward the city walls.]

The sudden and unexpected beauty, expressed first in terms of radiant color and the fine movement of her human form, is no sooner revealed than it is snatched away; Vergil emphasizes the simultaneity of acts of recognition and loss with participial forms: "*avertens* refulsit... Aeneas secutus est *fugientem*" (emphases mine). Bonds are affirmed only to slip out of reach. The act of sight elicits an impulse to direct action—the extensive movement outward from son to mother, from mortal to goddess—at the same time that it thwarts such action and enforces on the viewer responses that must remain frustrated and passive. Aeneas loses not only Venus's numinous beauty but also the potential stability of motherhood with which she is, for him, invested. And the strength and subtlety of Aeneas's *perceptions* contribute much to our sense of him as an admirable hero, suffused with warmth in spite of the painful and sometimes brutal *actions* that he must perform. These aureate lines condense and link issues that preoccupy both

Vergil and his hero: the force of powerful sights in this epic; the observer's ability to recognize and respond to such sights and to the presence of persons within them; the radical unreliability of vision's promise; the cost to the observer who evinces the internal resources for the sufferance of vision.

The longing for full meeting and full mutual acknowledgment between persons which pervades this episode can hardly be overstated. Aeneas yearns for the complete presence of his goddess-mother, and for his full presence to her, but the capriciousness of her behavior, offering yet withholding the means of stability, paradoxically makes him experience her divine presence as an absence, or rather an absenting. Meeting and the presence of persons one to another, in full acknowledgment and recognition of each other, are ideals that carry an almost insupportable valence in this poem, because such meeting is so rarely sustainable. Presence continually turns into absence, the plenitude promised by the meeting of an other into an experience of deprivation.

On this matter of deprivation within encounters, it is helpful to follow the venerable habit of commentaries that proceed by making comparisons between Homeric and Vergilian passages, for two reasons. First, the *Odyssey* contributes to Vergil's epic an element of wonder before marvels beheld, and it is largely by looking at the sources of Vergil's imitations that we can perceive Vergil's inflections on Odyssean visual wonder. Second, acts of sight in the *Odyssey*, while plentiful enough, are not epistemologically problematic, as they most often are in the *Aeneid*, and examining Homeric passages alongside Vergil's imitations of them underscores the relative clarity and trustworthiness of the grounds of perception and knowledge in the *Odyssey*, and the murkiness and unreliability of those grounds in the *Aeneid*. Specifically, the lines in which Vergil describes Venus's meeting with her son tell us something about Vergil's understanding of Homer in the way that they conjoin a Homeric radiance of object and a Homeric awe within the viewer with a Vergilian nostalgia for a now all but impossible ease and lucidity of relation between viewer and object. The first of the passages that Vergil drew upon for this meeting depicts the great reunion of Athene and Odysseus in Book 13 of the *Odyssey* :

> The goddess, gray-eyed Athene, smiled on him, and stroked
> him with her hand, and took on the shape of a woman both

beautiful and tall, and well versed in glorious handiworks, and
spoke aloud to him and addressed him in winged words, saying:
"It would be a sharp one, and a stealthy one, who would ever get
      past you
in any contriving; even if it were a god against you.
You wretch, so devious, never weary of tricks, then you would not
even in your own country give over your ways of deceiving
and your thievish tales. They are near to you in your very nature.
But come, let us talk no more of this, for you and I both know
sharp practice, since you are far the best of all mortal
men for counsel and stories, and I among all the divinities
am famous for wit and sharpness; and yet you never recognized
Pallas Athene, daughter of Zeus, the one who is always
standing beside you and guarding you in every endeavor."[5]

(*Od.* 13.287–301)

This confirmation of homecoming and the celebration of Odysseus's
inner resources allow a gaiety of tone from which Vergil obviously
departs in Aeneas's meeting with Venus, the form of which reflects
the instability and anxiety of his uncertain journey. Athene takes the
initiative in touching Odysseus's hand, while Aeneas's very mother
eludes his effort to touch her; Athene is both tangible and tactile as
Venus is not. It is in knowing himself that Odysseus knows Athene,
and vice versa; her patronage of him is not simply a cause or a result
of his own sagacity, but an expression of it as well. Such fusion of
function and identity between goddess and hero cannot obtain in the
relationship between Venus and Aeneas; her role as the goddess of
love reflects in no intrinsic way upon Aeneas's character, and there
is no implicit unity between them. Homer's Athene, on the other hand,
presides over the sagacious not only because she has specific powers
in that line, as Vergil's Venus does in matters of passion, but because
she is in an essential way sagacity itself.

[5]Translations from the *Odyssey* are those of Richmond Lattimore (New York:
Harper and Row, 1965). On the value of Homeric comparisons, see K. W. Gransden,
Virgil's Iliad: An Essay on Epic Narrative (Cambridge: Cambridge University Press,
1984), 1–2, 4–5.
    Points like those I am about to make about Vergil's development of his sources
could equally be made about his adaptation of Anchises' first meeting with Aphrodite,
just before Aeneas is conceived, in the Homeric *Hymn to Aphrodite*: " 'Lady, welcome
to this house, whoever of the blessed ones you are: / whether you are Artemis, or
Leto, or golden Aphrodite, /.../ I shall make you an altar and offer you fair sacrifices
/ In all seasons' " (92–102). Cited from the translation by Apostolos N. Athanassakis
(Baltimore: Johns Hopkins University Press, 1976).

Athene and Odysseus meet each other as goddess and protegé, but also as old comrades who know each other's wily ways, and as female and male linked in mutual admiration. Odysseus accuses her of having abandoned him, but we know otherwise: the fact that Book 1 opens with Athene's intercession for him places his suffering in a context that already promises a triumphant ending. And Odysseus's charge of abandonment, with this kind of goddess, is as much as to say that he himself had been acting the fool in his earlier adventures. Homer depicts no painful act of vision, no pathos of loss, resentment, or interior pain in this reunion, but a fine comic meeting of persons, each of whom acknowledges the other.

A similar clarity obtains when Odysseus first responds to the sight of Nausikaa, and asks for her help, in the second Homeric passage that Vergil imitates. Here the act of vision itself is important in a way that it is not in the meeting with Athene. Nausikaa's unflappable gaze at the alarming, naked, salt-encrusted stranger; Odysseus's relief, caution, and articulate wonder at the sight of the young princess; the comedy and delicacy of the social decorums of vision—all of these are important elements in Homer's passage:

> Then in the division of his heart this way seemed best to him,
> to stand well off and supplicate in words of blandishment,
> for fear that, if he clasped her at the knees, the girl might be angry.
> So blandishingly and full of craft he began to address her:
> "I am at your knees, O queen. But are you mortal or goddess?
>
> · · · · ·
>
> I have never with these eyes seen anything like you,
> neither man nor woman. Wonder takes me as I look on you.
> Yet in Delos once I saw such a thing, by Apollo's altar.
> I saw the stalk of a young palm shooting up. I had gone there
> once, and with a following of a great many people,
> on that journey which was to mean hard suffering for me.
> And as, when I looked upon that tree, my heart admired it
> long, since such a tree had never yet sprung from the earth, so
> now, lady, I admire you and wonder."
>
> (*Od.* 6.145–49, 160–68)

Odysseus gives voice to what is probably his truly felt awe at Nausikaa's girlish beauty—he is likely to feel this after his ordeal at sea. But in fact the question of veracity hardly arises; Homer concentrates on the need for blandishing speech here, and Odysseus's verbal resourcefulness in producing it. What Odysseus does is characterize himself as a looker and an appreciator, and more precisely a pilgrim admiring a tree of Delos. The indirection of the compliment, eliding delicate suggestions of religious awe and masculine appreciation of her palmlike slenderness, refines the frank and happy visual pleasure that he takes in her, a pleasure he offers as a gift to her: "I have never with these eyes seen anything like you, / neither man nor woman. Wonder takes me as I look on you."

The poise and subtlety in the delivery of this compliment are the more remarkable, and the more comic, for the facts of Odysseus's nakedness and his observer's youthful innocence. It is comic, and typical of Odysseus, that he can reverse their relative positions as witnesses of each other: the status of the vulnerable, exhausted suppliant exposed to the view of a princess secure and confident with the strength of her city and her family is turned, in his compliment and in his comic transcendence of his own exposure, to the status of a suave, alluring older man with an exotic past, himself witnessing Nausikaa's youth and freshness. To be the witness rather than the exposed is a strength, and this strength he also allows to Nausikaa, first by giving her the privilege of witnessing a remarkable man, and second by granting her the dignity of his compliment. He transforms the awkward moment into a moment of two noble creatures contemplating each other with wonder, pleasure, and exhilaration.

In the *Odyssey*, characters regard one another and present themselves to one another with an abundant rhetoric describing their situation and needs. This is true even when Odysseus makes up stories about himself: they issue from the recognition that such explanations and presentations are expected from strangers, and in any case they usually contain a good deal of truth about Odysseus. So when Odysseus leaves Phaiakia and takes his leave of Nausikaa, there is full acknowledgment on both sides of the respect, attraction, and energy that has existed between them; the memory becomes a real possession for Odysseus, a hard-won guarantor of order in his tempest-tost universe:

> Then Nausikaa, with the gods' loveliness on her,
> stood beside the pillar that supported the roof with its joinery,
> and gazed upon Odysseus with all her eyes and admired him,
> and spoke to him aloud and addressed him in winged words, saying:
> "Goodbye, stranger, and think of me sometimes when you are

back at home, how I was the first you owed your life to."
   Then resourceful Odysseus spoke in turn and answered her:
"Nausikaa, daughter of great-hearted Alkinoös,
even so may Zeus, high-thundering husband of Hera,
grant me to reach my house and see my day of homecoming.
So even when I am there I will pray to you, as to a goddess,
all the days of my life. For, maiden, my life was your gift."
                                                    (*Od.* 8.457–68)

Observers of persons throughout the *Odyssey* are alert, careful, and
socially sophisticated watchers. This is true not only in the cautious
meetings between Odysseus and the members of his household in the
second half of the epic, but in meetings between any characters of
intelligence. Helen immediately recognizes Telemachos as the son of
his father; she, Menalaos, and Nestor apprehend the qualities of his
character that launch him on his quest for his father; the sharp-eyed
Alkinoös perceives Odysseus's tears at the song of the bard and can
make shrewd guesses about their source. (A similar finely tuned ability
to apprehend the meanings of countenance and demeanor will later
characterize Spenser's Calidore.) Intelligent watching apprehends true
knowledge of social and natural realms alike. And, as we have seen,
observers of marvels in the *Odyssey* tend to respond with awe, wonder, zest. In the *Aeneid,* the grounds and reliability of perceptual
knowledge are more treacherous, and Vergil infuses visual wonder
with a pervasive nostalgia—sometimes for the stability that eludes the
wanderers; sometimes for a repletion and peace of being, the image
of which can only baffle Aeneas, as when he meets Venus; sometimes
for the very ability, largely lost to them, to take direct meetings between persons happily for granted. (The failure of sensibility which
will later make such nostalgia inaccessible to Spenser's Braggadochio,
as he gazes on Belphoebe in a passage that imitates this scene from
Vergil, is what makes him both gross and comic.) Vergil's imitations
of Homer are thus heuristic, in Thomas Greene's sense. They admit
and embrace—and lament—the historical distance between Greek and
Roman poet; they abide the transitive function of poetry.[6]

---

[6]Here is Greene on heuristic imitation: "Heuristic imitations come to us advertising
their derivation from the subtexts they carry with them, but having done that, they
proceed to *distance themselves* from the subtexts and force us to recognize the poetic
distance traversed.... Each imitation embodies and dramatizes a passage of history,
builds it into the poetic experience as a constitutive element." From *The Light in*

Vergil's depictions of Dido and Aeneas similarly evince both the characters' and the narrator's awe at their Homeric grandeur, freshness, and plenitude of being, and a more purely Vergilian sadness about the real discrepancies and ambiguities in Dido's and Aeneas's understandings of their affair. Vergil is reticent in the extreme about the precise qualities of their meeting, and offers only hints about Aeneas's emotions and behavior.

The first moments of Dido's falling in love are, not surprisingly, moments of gazing; Greek and Roman traditions had long conceived of eros aroused through the eyes.[7] The narrator's tone is typically elegant and pitying; the pity arises from his capacity to presage the catastrophic future in imagery, and from the transforming feats he performs with traditional notions of erotic vision:

> mirantur dona Aeneae, mirantur Iulum,
> flagrantisque dei vultus simulataque verba
> pallamque et pictum croceo velamen acantho.
> praecipue infelix, pesti devota futurae,
> expleri mentem nequit ardescitque tuendo
> Phoenissa, et pariter puero donisque movetur.
> ille ubi complexu Aeneae colloque pependit
> et magnum falsi implevit genitoris amorem,
> reginam petit. haec oculis, haec pectore toto
> haeret et interdum gremio fovet inscia Dido
> insidat quantus miserae deus. at memor ille
> matris Acidaliae paulatim abolere Sychaeum
> incipit et vivo temptat praevertere amore
> iam pridem resides animos desuetaque corda.
>
> (*Aen.* 1.709–22)

[They marvel at Aeneas's gifts, marvel at Iulus and the glowing looks of the god and his dissembled words, and the robe and veil embellished with the yellow acanthus. Especially the unhappy Phoenician, condemned to ruin, cannot be satisfied in mind and burns with beholding;

Troy: Imitation and Discovery in Renaissance Poetry (New Haven: Yale University Press, 1982), 40–41.

[7] A convention whose backgrounds are traced in Ruth Cline, "Heart and Eyes," *Romance Philology* 25 (1971–72), 263–97; A. C. Pearson, "Phrixus and Demodice: A Note on Pindar, *Pyth.* IV 162f.," *Classical Review* 23 (1909), 255–57; Lance K. Donaldson-Evans, *Love's Fatal Glance: A Study of Eye Imagery in the Poets of the Ecole Lyonnaise* (University, Miss.: Romance Monographs, 1980), 9–49.

she is moved equally by the boy and by the gifts. When he has hung on the embrace of Aeneas, and has satisfied the great affection of his false father, he advances to the queen. With her eyes, with her whole heart Dido, unknowning, fixes on him and sometimes fondles him in her lap, ignorant how great a god settles there, oh unhappy woman! But he, remembering his Acidalian mother, begins by degrees to abolish Sychaeus and tries to preoccupy with a living love her mind, long since unmoved, and her unaccustomed heart.]

This passage, which will modulate to that final sympathy and pain for Dido, begins with the Homeric awe and admiration of the Tyrian crowd, set in the context of a Homeric feast honoring the Trojan strangers; both feast and mode of vision recall Odysseus's wonder before the opulent handiworks of the Phaiakians, and the delicate mutual awareness of his meetings with individual Phaiakians. But in Vergil's passage Dido emerges from the crowd by virtue of her hungrier and less reliable mode of vision; her intense gaze bespeaks the Eros born of poverty. Both sight and emotion become species of touch ("haec oculis, haec pectore toto / haeret"); more important, this clinging is directed not at Aeneas but at the child, ostensibly Iulus but in fact Cupid. The irony of her embracing her poisoner is clear enough. But it is curious also that the child should be a surrogate for the father; the mutual gazes that usually mingle between adult male and female are modified to Dido's solitary gaze on the boy. Moreover, Vergil evades clarity in favor of an intentional opaqueness about Aeneas's role and feelings, and he darkly suggests Dido's imminent tragedy. The only reference to Aeneas is purposefully vague, and tells us merely that the child is a mediator, rousing first Aeneas and then the queen. There is clearly some kind of causal relation between these two acts, and between Cupid's movements and Dido's arousal; but Vergil states only a temporal relation between them: "ille ubi complexu Aeneae colloque pependit / et magnum falsi implevit genitoris amorem, / reginam petit."

Both literal obscurity and affective obscurity increase the pain of the meeting between Dido and Aeneas in the underworld:

> inter quas Phoenissa recens a vulnere Dido
> errabat silva in magna; quam Troius heros
> ut primum iuxta stetit agnovitque per umbras
> obscuram, qualem primo qui surgere mense

aut videt aut vidisse putat per nubila lunam,
demisit lacrimas dulcique adfatas amore est.

(Aen. 6.450–55)

[Among them Phoenician Dido, with her fresh wound, wandered in the
great forest. When the Trojan hero stood near and knew her, an obscure
figure in the shadows, as at the first of the month one either sees or
thinks he sees the moon rise through the clouds, he shed tears and spoke
to her with sweet love.]

The obscuring elements of vision in this episode—Dido's dim form
surrounded by shadows, the simile of cloud-covered moon, the observer who perhaps *thinks* he sees—figure the obscurities of their
relationship. Dido and Aeneas are depicted as swerving away from
the direct, mutual gazes that attend meetings in the Homeric world,
away from the gaze that signifies each one's full acknowledgment of
the other. He suffers the sight of her presence, perceives the bodily
marks of his effect on her, and grants her suffering fully, as he could
not do when he left her. But she refuses to look in return, refuses to
change her countenance in acknowledgment of his presence. This
refusal to accede in mutual regard, to make a meeting of persons,
leaves both Aeneas and the poem shadowed by Dido's catastrophe.

These qualities attendant upon stricken, shocked, intensely responsive yet helpless sight are particularly Vergilian: they have no place,
for example, in Homer's Odyssean descent to the underworld. Among
many others, Odysseus sees Ajax, with whom he has quarreled, and
tries to speak to him. But there is no simile creating an atmosphere
of uncertainty and darkness, no speech reflecting anguish on Odysseus's part, no haunting insubstantiality of the dead. In fact, the dead
are relatively lively and vivid, and Odysseus is as urbane as ever and
above all curious to see more. So the moment of tension between
himself and Ajax passes. Ajax is still brooding as when last alive, but
his silence does not represent the refusal of acknowledgment that
Dido's silence and averted gaze do.

Much of what Aeneas sees in the first books can be characterized,
then, as a violent absenting of beloved persons and things whose
presence had sustained him. This creating of voids where there had
been substance and fullness reverses the narrative line of the *Odyssey*,
in which persons and things gradually accrue to the hero as he crafts
order and demarcations in his world. Aeneas's roles in the first half
of his epic, his narration of Troy's fall and of his wanderings, and

his responses to events, often mark him less as an agent than as patient in his own story. One means by which Vergil explores the necessity and tragic implications of suffering actions rather than performing them is by mapping kinds of sight—which the characters not so much experience as undergo. Sight is synecdochic for the paradoxical qualities of actions in the *Aeneid*: characters are often passive, helpless, or severely constricted by their perceptions of the situations in which they find themselves, yet responses and actions are demanded of them.

Vergil's development of sight as a synecdoche for relations between human consciousness and world was made possible by the usual ways of thinking about how sight operated. Physiological optics, like other studies of perception, was a field pursued with some vigor, and theories of vision debated notions of rays or images moving actively into (intromissive theories) or emerging from (extramissive theories) the eye.[8] The value of such proposals for Vergil, and for Ovid after him, lies in the theories' terms and premises. Sight is literally a species of touch; all theorists use the notion of direct contact of some kind (through rays from the eyes, or films from the object of sight, or external air mixed with fire from the eye) as a mediation between eye and object. All theories also implicitly raise the issue of the activity or passivity of the eye. The eye is thought to emit radiation, or to receive radiation from the object viewed, or to mingle its extended substance with the mediating air. The viewer may be understood as aggressor, thief, or violator, if the eye emits rays; or the viewer may be understood purely as recipient, if the eye is a receptor. The object seen may be the passive object of radiation before the viewer's eye, or may function as an active agent by emitting radiation to another's view. All of these possibilities raise complicated issues of active or passive participation in acts of sight.

The passivity of sight, and the violence of frustration that this

[8]For full discussions of optics in the ancient world, see David A. Lindberg, *Theories of Vision from al-Kindi to Kepler* (Chicago: University of Chicago Press, 1976), 1–17; Edward N. Lee, "The Sense of an Object: Epicurus on Seeing and Hearing," in *Studies in Perception: Interrelations in the History of Philosophy and Science*, ed. Peter Machamer and Robert G. Turnbull (Columbus: Ohio State University Press, 1978), 27–59; David E. Hahm, "Early Hellenistic Theories of Vision and the Perception of Color," ibid., 60–95; Bernard Saint-Pierre, "La Physique de la vision dans l'antiquité: contribution à l'établissement des sources anciennes de l'optique médiévale" (diss., University of Montreal, 1972); Willem van Hoorn, *As Images Unwind: Ancient and Modern Theories of Visual Perception* (Amsterdam: University Press of Amsterdam, 1972).

passivity can inflict on the observer, are especially clear in Book 2 of Vergil's poem, in Aeneas's descriptions of the fall of Troy. The description of the serpents' strangulation of Laocoön and his sons (*Aen.* 2.199–229) is a presage of the violence shortly to be inflicted on vulnerable Troy; more, the spectators' helpless horror as they watch the grotesque struggle presages Aeneas's own enforced passivity as he watches first from the roof of Anchises's house and then from the roof of Priam's. From this second vantage point he sees the heart of destruction: the rapelike penetration of the palace, the exposure of the halls and spaces of the home, the fall of the bedchambers that have guaranteed the generation of the city, and the exposure of the altar at the center of the city's life:[9]

> "ipse inter primos correpta dura bipenni
> limina perrumpit postisque a cardine vellit
> aeratos; iamque excisa trabe firma cavavit
> robora et ingentem lato dedit ore fenestram.
> apparet domus intus et atria longa patescunt;
> apparent Priami et veterum penetralia regum,
> armatosque vident stantis in limine primo."
>
> (*Aen.* 2.479–85)

[Pyrrhus among the first, seizing a battle-axe, breaks through the hard doors and tears the bronze doorposts from their hinges; already, after cutting out a timber, he has pierced through the stout oak, and made a huge, wide-mouthed breach. The house within appears and the long halls are open to view; the recesses of Priam and of ancient kings appear, and they see armed men standing on the edge of the threshold.]

The nightmarish quality of this scene and the tone of horror at exposure are consequences of the scene being described by a narrator victimized by his own powerlessness, figured by the passivity of sight:

> "vidi ipse furentem
> caede Neoptolemum geminosque in limine Atridas,
> vidi Hecubam centumque nurus Priamumque per aras
> sanguine foedantem quos ipse sacraverat ignis."
>
> (*Aen.* 2.499–502)

[9]See Bradford Lewis, "The Rape of Troy: Infantile Perspective in Book 2 of the *Aeneid*," *Arethusa* 7 (1974), 103–14, for a detailed discussion of these episodes.

["I myself saw Neoptolemus on the threshold, furious with slaughter, and the sons of Atreus; I saw Hecuba and her hundred daughters, and Priam amid the altars, polluting with his blood the fires he himself had hallowed."

The sight of horror is imposed upon Aeneas; his narration emphasizes his own thwarted participation in battle and, more, the pain of passively endured sight.

This shocked helplessness extends to other characters. What shocks Priam is not only the fact of his own death but the fact that Pyrrhus has degraded him by forcing on him the sight of his own son's death:

> "at tibi pro scelere," exclamat, "pro talibus ausis
> di, si qua est caelo pietas quae talia curet,
> persolvant grates dignas et praemia reddant
> debita, qui nati coram me cernere letum
> fecisti et patrios foedasti funere vultus."
>
> (*Aen.* 2.535–39)

["For your crimes," he exclaims, "for such outrageous enterprises, may the gods—if there is any pity in heaven which troubles about such things—pay you appropriate thanks and render just recompense to you, who have made me openly see the death of my son, and have defiled a father's countenance with a corpse."]

Priam echoes not only Aeneas's pain in his description of the rape of the household, but also Aeneas's astonished disbelief that he should be seeing such things: "vidi ipse."

There are few acts of sight in Book 2 which are not sights of beloved objects lost. Aeneas's vision of Hector, though it predicts the foundation of another city, occurs immediately before the havoc of Troy's destruction, and we see Hector only torn and mutilated, without his Homeric grandeur. Hector's words are a prophecy of a productive future, but Aeneas responds with woe and a sense of loss at the sight of Hector ("quibus Hector ab oris / exspectate venis?"; "From what shores do you come, oh Hector much longed for?," *Aen.* 2.282–83). The ghost of Creusa, rising up as Aeneas searches for his wife, speaks briskly to him, overriding his sobs, and advises that he give up mourning to get on with the business at hand. But her promise of "res laetae regnumque et regia coniunx" ("prosperity, a kingdom, and a royal wife," *Aen.* 2.783) is small consolation at this moment; here he can only know a bereft response to the sight of her, in his pathos-filled attempt to embrace her. She has advised him to transcend his need for her tangible presence, but it is just this capacity to fix on the potency of another's identity, to respond with a full regard to the presence of others, that makes his consciousness tragic.

The Prospect: Distance and Its Ironies

Ironies and paradoxes in the experience of sight, ironies revolving around the simultaneous pressures toward action and inaction, crystallize in moments of vision from a height, moments in which characters see with a long view. In Book 1, after the storm that has tossed the Trojans onto the shore near Carthage, Aeneas ascends a hill in order to gain perspective on the damage done to the fleet. In particular he searches, with failing hope, for his men lost at sea:

> Aeneas scopulum interea conscendit, et omnem
> prospectum late pelago petit, Anthea si quem
> iactatum vento videat Phrygiasque biremis
> aut Capyn aut celsis in puppibus arma Caici.
> navem in conspectu nullam, tris litore cervos
> prospicit errantis; hos tota armenta sequuntur
> a tergo et longum per vallis pascitur agmen.
>
> (*Aen.* 1.180–86)

[Aeneas meanwhile climbs a promontory and searches extensively the whole prospect of the sea, that he may see anything of Antheus, tossed by the wind, and the Phrygian galleys, or Capys, or the arms of Caicus on the high stern. No ship lies in sight, but three stags he sees wandering on the shore; a whole herd follows behind and in a long column they feed through the valley.]

The pathos of the brief catalogue individualizing the men reinforces the insistence on loss and futile action, although this insistence is immediately qualified by the discovery of the stags. The tone of the feast that follows is appropriately subdued, and the talk reflects not simply loss but the desolating uncertainty of loss. The salient contrast is with the Homeric model, Odysseus's killing of the stag after the Greeks' own shipwreck:

"[I] went up quickly from beside the ship to find a lookout
place, to look for some trace of people, listen for some sound.
I climbed to a rocky point of observation and stood there. . . .

.   .   .   .   .

. . . On my way [back to the ship] . . .
some god, because I was all alone, took pity upon me,
and sent a great stag with towering antlers right in my very
path. . . .

.   .   .   .   .

I hit him in the middle of the back. . . .

.   .   .   .   .

I set my foot on him and drew the bronze spear out of
the wound it had made and rested it on the ground, while I
pulled growing twigs and willow withes and, braiding them into
a rope, about six feet in length, and looping them over
the feet of this great monster on both sides, lashed them together. . . .

.   .   .   .   .

But after [the men] had looked at him and their eyes had enjoyed
him, they washed their hands and set to preparing a communal high
feast. So for the whole length of the day until the sun's
setting we sat there feasting on unlimited meat and sweet wine."
             (*Od.* 10.146–48, 156–59, 161–68, 181–84)

In this Homeric passage the act of vision is unproblematic; it is simply
one of a number of relations between human consciousness and physical world, relations that exemplify both the plenitude of that world's
resources and the confidence of the human mind in its own resources.
Odysseus's ascent in order to achieve perspective is the least important
aspect of this scene, and his scouting is uninformed by the grief that
Aeneas shows. The stag, a gift from a god, crosses his path, and as
usual Odysseus turns to advantage the materials at hand. He does so
not with Aeneas's lamentation for the lost which characterizes
Aeneas's acts of leadership, but with the typically bravura narrative
swagger of placing himself and his skill at the center of the story. The
subsequent feast links Odysseus's craft and braggadochio, the admiring gaze of the men, with the abundance that allows the possibility
of zestful encounter with the world. Aeneas's own search, by contrast,
centers on the pathos of both landscape and viewer; the prospect fails
his desire. We might clarify the relation of sight to an answering

abundance in the Homeric world, and of sight to absence in the Vergilian, by saying that Odysseus is characteristically a surveyor, Aeneas characteristically a seeker.

The conjunction of hopeless seeking, narrative clouding of the emotional dynamics of erotic vision, and the implicit certainty of loss bears down with force at the end of Aeneas and Dido's affair, when Dido regards from her palace heights the preparations of the fleet after Aeneas abandons her:

> . . . opere omnis semita fervet.
> quis tibi tum, Dido, cernenti talia sensus,
> quosve dabas gemitus, cum litora fervere late
> prospiceres arce ex summa, totumque videres
> misceri ante oculos tantis clamoribus aequor!
> improbe Amor, quid non mortalia pectora cogis!
>
> (*Aen.* 4.407–12)

[. . . the whole path seethed with the work. What did you feel then, Dido, beholding such things? What groans did you utter, when from the height of the tower you saw, far off, the shores stir, and saw before your eyes the whole sea confused by such a clamor? O cruel Love, to what do you not drive mortal hearts!]

The sight that Dido endures in agony here is the sight of her life receding; the distance of her view is psychic as well as physical. The vacancy not only from loved object but from oneself which descends on the victim of abandonment is suggested by the vigorous, crowded bustle and noise of Aeneas's preparation and the concomitant suppression—explicitly by the narrator, implicitly by Dido as she focuses only on Aeneas—of reference to the great building over which she had presided earlier. Her abdication of active supervision of this worldly and civilizing labor is obliquely recalled by her passive misery in the view of Aeneas's activity, through an angle of vision that underscores distance.

If vision is generally problematic or shadowed by the narrator's knowledge of imminent trouble, in the *Aeneid* it is not always as painful as it is to Dido when Aeneas leaves her. We have already seen, in the meeting of Aeneas and Venus, that Vergil imagines states of wonder and deep receptivity to the numinous and the marvelous, and that he imagines potential states of human felicity and harmony with objects of desire. Wonder, though, is double-edged, as we have seen:

Aeneas's capacity for wonder is central to his greatness of heart, but wonder can cause the pain of unfillable longing. Further, in a poem in which the characters move darkly through a cosmos presided over by arbitrary, often malevolent, and inscrutable forces, human wonder is often vested in deceptive objects. Aeneas's first view of Carthage in Book 1, followed immediately by his view of the temple, together instantiate both his capacity for awe and the ironies created by his ignorance of Juno's wrathful capriciousness.

The prospect from the height, as always in the *Aeneid*, seems to offer a true and reliable sight, certainly a moving one:

> iamque ascendebant collem, qui plurimus urbi
> imminet adversasque aspectat desuper arces.
> miratur molem Aeneas, magalia quondam,
> miratur portas strepitumque et strata viarum.
> instant ardentes Tyrii: pars ducere muros
> molirique arcem et manibus subvolvere saxa,
> pars optare locum tecto et concludere sulco;
> iura magistratusque legunt sanctumque senatum.
> hic portus alii effodiunt; hic alta theatris
> fundamenta locant alii, immanisque columnas
> rupibus excidunt, scaenis decora apta futuris.
>
> (*Aen.* 1.419–29)

[And now they ascend the hill that looms large over the city and faces the opposed towers from above. Aeneas marvels at the massive structures, cottages once; he admires the gates and the noise and the pavements of the streets. The Tyrians press on ardently, some to extend the walls and to erect a tower and to roll up stones with their hands; others to select a place for a dwelling and to enclose it with a furrow. They choose their laws and magistrates and a sacred senate; here some excavate a harbor, there others set deep foundations for theaters, and cut huge columns from rocks, fit decorations for future stages.]

Aeneas perceives a field of activity and brings to bear on this sight a historical consciousness. He sees not only what is, but what was, and he imagines what will be. His mode of vision is characterized by breadth of spatial detail and by depth in time. This image of the city resonates with his deep love for the institutions and communal life of Troy. Signs of such institutions and community at Carthage are the more valuable, and evoke a stronger sense of admiration in him, because of his own losses. These not only have made him a more responsive observer, but have made desire implicit in the act of sight: "'o fortunati, quorum iam moenia surgunt!' / Aeneas ait et fastigia suspicit urbis" ("'Oh happy you whose walls are rising already!' cries Aeneas, surveying the heights of the city," *Aen.* 1.437–38).

Wonder in this poem is thus compounded of a multiplicity of affects: yearning, the appetite of the eye, consciousness of loss, pleasure, generosity toward others' achievements. Given so complex a human quality, it is unsurprising that the wonder felt by Aeneas in observing Carthage from a height blurs into the more difficult and less reliable viewing of the friezes on the temple. The syntax suggests that the two acts glide imperceptibly into each other, and perhaps that there is no easy distinguishing among objects of wonder:

> namque sub ingenti lustrat dum singula templo
> reginam opperiens, dum quae fortuna sit urbi
> artificumque manus inter se operumque laborem
> miratur, videt Iliacas ex ordine pugnas
> bellaque iam fama totum vulgata per orbem,
> Atridas Priamumque et saevum ambobus Achillem.
>
> (*Aen.* 1.453–58)

[For while awaiting the queen in the huge temple he examines each object, while he marvels at the city's fortune, and the hands of the artists and the labor of their works, he sees the Trojan battles set in order, and the wars now spread by report throughout the whole world, the sons of Atreus and Priam, and Achilles, cruel to both.]

The ironies of this scene are very dense, not so much because appearances are deceptive as because they are partial. Aeneas is, first of all, struck with wonder at a temple dedicated to Juno, whose unappeasable *ira* fuels the disasters that befall the Trojans. The scenes depicted are taken from the war that was a triumph for Juno and a catastrophe for the Trojans—but Aeneas cannot know how she presides over this temple as she presides over his suffering. For all the depth, historicity, and generosity that typify his field of vision throughout the poem, he is necessarily blind to the malice that pursues him.

Second, his own response suggests a welter of affects that are brilliantly suggested but left intentionally obscure.[10] There is the relatively simple and direct Homeric appreciation of "artificumque manus... operumque laborem." But there is also the different *labor* of the Trojans at war (1.460). Aeneas certainly feels grief, perhaps a new liberation from his past through seeing it as an object on these walls, and an exaltation that leads him to feast on the very source of his pain:

> constitit et lacrimans "quis iam locus," inquit, "Achate,
> quae regio in terris nostri non plena laboris?
> en Priamus. sunt hic etiam sua praemia laudi,
> sunt lacrimae rerum et mentem mortalia tangunt.
> solve metus; feret haec aliquam tibi fama salutem."
> sic ait atque animum pictura pascit inani
> multa gemens, largoque umectat flumine vultum.
>
> (*Aen.* 1.459–65)

[He stood, and weeping cried, "What place now, Achates, what region of earth is not full of our distress? Behold Priam! Even here there is praise for his worthiness; there are tears for misfortune and mortal affairs touch the heart. Do not fear; this fame will bring to you some salvation." So he spoke, and fed his spirit on an empty picture, lamenting greatly, and his face was wet with abundant tears.]

In the passage from the *Odyssey* in which Odysseus gazes in wonder at the city of Alkinoös and which Vergil has in mind in his passage, Homer is up to things other than such Vergilian ironies and ambiguities:

> But Odysseus now admired their balanced ships and their harbors,
> the meeting places of the heroes themselves and the long lofty
> walls that were joined with palisades, a wonder to look at.
>   ... the heart pondered
> much in him as he stood before coming to the bronze threshold.
> For as from the sun the light goes or from the moon, such was

---

[10]See the discussion of this passage and of Adam Parry's commentary on it in Johnson's *Darkness Visible*, 99–100, 104–5. Parry's remarks can be found in "The Two Voices of Vergil's *Aeneid*," *Arion* 2 (1963), 66–80. See also Lee W. Patterson, " 'Rapt with Pleasaunce': Vision and Narration in the Epic," *English Literary History* 48 (Fall 1981), 455–75.

the glory on the high-roofed house of great-hearted Alkinoös.
And there long-suffering great Odysseus stopped still and admired it.
But when his mind was done with all admiration, lightly
he stepped over the threshold.

(*Od.* 7.43–45, 82–85, 133–34)

Odysseus gazes in admiration, but we would not say that he is the focus of the poet's attention in the long passage from which these lines are taken. Homer brings us information about the habits and skills of the Phaiakians, but this knowledge is not brought to bear by Odysseus himself; instead, the listener is encouraged to enter into the pleasure of appreciative vision and the knowledge that it brings. There are implicit comparisons between this society, that of the Cyclopes, and that of Ithaka, but Odysseus does not make them; instead, the listener is encouraged to understand the significance of vision within the whole architecture of the poem. Odysseus moves from city to palace, as Aeneas moves from city to temple, and like Aeneas he moves in a protective mist provided by an affectionate goddess. But Odysseus's sense of wonder contains no sense of loss. Indeed, the opposite is true: both city and observer exude a sense of life's fullness and the joyfulness of human making. Nor is there duplicity in the object of sight: it is what it appears to be, without situational ironies in which the hero is perforce enmeshed. The achievement of the city is valued because it is an instance of the fusion of human mind and natural materials in communal mastery. And this mastery is itself an instance of the resourcefulness and confidence that always pervade Odysseus's acts of beholding.

We began with Aeneas's meeting with Venus; we can close by returning to Aeneas's first view, from a distance, of Dido. That view has been carefully prepared by Vergil in the earlier meeting of Aeneas with Venus, where the latter's appearance as a Diana-like huntress before her full epiphany as goddess of love and as his mother has aroused Aeneas's susceptibilities to Dido. The impact of Venus's divine and maternal identity, the failure of rapprochement between mother and son, the particular form her disguised beauty takes, and his aroused interest in beholding—all these things are brought together in the radiant description of Aeneas's first perception of Dido:

Haec dum Dardanio Aeneae miranda videntur,
dum stupet obtutuque haeret defixus in uno,
regina ad templum, forma pulcherrima Dido,

incessit magna iuvenum stipante caterva.
qualis in Eurotae ripis aut per iuga Cynthi
exercet Diana choros, quam mille secutae
hinc atque hinc glomerantur Oreades; illa pharetram
fert umero gradiensque deas supereminet omnis
(Latonae tacitum pertemptant gaudia pectus):
talis erat Dido, talem se laeta ferebat
per medios instans operi regnisque futuris.

(Aen. 1.494–504)

[While these wonderful things appeared to Dardan Aeneas, while in his stupefaction he stood suspended in a single gaze, Dido the queen advanced to the temple, most beautiful in appearance, attended by a great throng of youths. As on the banks of Eurotas or the heights of Cynthus, Diana trains her troop of dancers, followed by a thousand Oreads gathered on this side and that; she bears her quiver on her shoulder and walks, surpassing all goddesses; joy courses through the silent breast of Latona. Such was Dido, so she carried herself joyful among them, urging the work and the future kingdom.]

Aeneas brings to his first prospect of Dido the sympathies, strengths, and vulnerabilities that he has learnt from his past. The loss of his homeland gives him a nostalgia-laden appreciation of her strength as ruler of a flourishing city; his more recent meeting with his mother and his response to her Artemisian beauty give him an intensified response to Dido's Diana-like grandeur. Hence the mythic simile, which properly belongs to the narrator, aptly describes not only Dido's appearance but also the amplitude of Aeneas's perception. As usual, he takes in a large field of vision. For him the salient details include the jubilant and youthful throng, Dido's luminous presence, her stately joyousness, and the urgency of her labor in the institution of the city. The splendor, dignity, and mythic resonance of this description modulate into a conversational hospitality that is ceremonious, formal, and warmly admiring.[11] Aeneas's first speech to her, for example, illustrates his own *pietas* as he imagines her links with past and future:

[11]See also the parallel to this mythic effulgence of Dido in *Aen.* 4.136–50, in which the queen-huntress meets Aeneas figured as Apollo. See Bono, *Literary Transvaluation,*15–29, for eloquent comments on the early meetings of Dido and Aeneas. Francis Cairns discusses Vergil's imitation, in *Aen.* 1.494–504, of Homer's *Odyssey* 6.102–9, in *Virgil's Augustan Epic* (Cambridge: Cambridge University Press, 1989), 129–35.

"quae te tam laeta tulerunt
saecula? qui tanti talem genuere parentes?
in freta dum fluvii current, dum montibus umbrae
lustrabunt convexa, polus dum sidera pascet,
semper honos nomenque tuum laudesque manebunt,
quae me cumque vocant terrae."

(*Aen.* 1.605–10)

["What fortunate ages have borne you? What worthy parents have be-
gotten you? While rivers run into the seas, while shadows move round
the slopes of the mountains, while the Pole feeds the stars, always your
honor, your name, and your praises shall continue, whatever lands call
me."]

Thomas Greene notes that Aeneas "is forever open to a capacity
in earthly things for assuming divinity";[12] he is also open to the
fullness of identity, either the simple dearness or the numinous splendor of another. This capacity is one of the most attractive things
about him. It is what makes his meeting with Dido so profound and
his abandonment of her so painful to contemplate; but it is also what
mitigates the otherwise harsh judgment that it is possible to make
against him. Vergil puts enough pressure on this attractive quality,
this responsiveness to presence, to guarantee that we understand its
costliness by the end of Book 4, as Aeneas sails from Carthage. But
here in Book 1, the tone is that of historically aware and communally
sanctioned awe at the spectacle that reveals the beheld presence.

Ovid: Hiddenness and the Invasive Eye

W. R. Johnson speaks of shadows and depths in the *Aeneid;* Joseph
Loewenstein remarks that Ovid, in his *Metamorphoses*, is a poet not
of textures but of patina.[13] Their metaphors suggest one of the key
means by which Ovid answers Vergil in the *Metamorphoses*: he flat-
tens atmosphere, character, and the relationships among interior human world, physical world, and the heavens—spatial and causal

---

[12]Thomas Greene, *Descent from Heaven: A Study in Epic Continuity* (New Haven:
Yale University Press, 1963), 87.
[13]Johnson, *Darkness Visible*, chap. 3; Joseph Loewenstein, *Responsive Readings:
Versions of Echo in Pastoral, Epic, and the Jonsonian Masque* (New Haven: Yale
University Press, 1984), 36.

relationships that in the *Aeneid* demonstrate the inscrutability of taut networks of emotion and causation. Ovid is unconcerned with the Vergilian narrative drive, in the *Aeneid*, to plumb the depths and motivations of individual characters or events, and the Vergilian preoccupation with obscurity and complexity of affect. He *is* interested precisely in the superficial, *facies* and *superficies*; this is true of his style as well as of his subjects in the *Metamorphoses*. The enfant terrible of the early poems, playing with stances of sophistication and aligned with the neoteric poets in situating himself outside the Stoic ethos of *gravitas* and *pietas*, challenges Vergil, the literary shaper of this ethos in its tragic form, in the great comic poem of his maturity.

With the suavity of a powerful self-awareness he flouts Vergilian tragic causality and eschews the shadows of human motivation. Vergil develops these in a narrative of few characters, each with an elaborate history providing dimensionality in time and complexity of interior life, characters linked to each other in a tightly knit plot. Ovid chooses rather to exploit the fluent redundancies of the myths at his disposal in his encyclopedic anatomy of human suffering. His predecessors (in lyric, epic, and tragedy alike) find incentive to elaborate and develop the sketchiness of character development so tantalizingly conspicuous in myths. This thinness of character Ovid not only retains, but turns to his advantage, a witty choice made with the confidence of the virtuoso. He takes pains to display the skeletal structures of myths by working hard the abundant iterations of story elements. Hence the multiplication of versions of gods pursuing and raping nymphs; hence the replications of transgressions leading to punishment; hence also the ease with which paragraphs in studies of Ovid become catalogues, themselves examples of the *copia* that he orders with such energetic finesse.

Ovid exploits but also wittily resists the drift of his narrative toward anthology or catalogue form—a drift that would feed later centuries' hunger for compendia and handbooks of mythology.[14] One of the

---

[14]See Don Cameron Allen's *Mysteriously Meant: The Rediscovery of Pagan Symbolism and Allegorical Interpretation in the Renaissance* (Baltimore: Johns Hopkins Press, 1970), 163–99, for editions and commentary on Ovid. Later handbooks and encyclopedias that draw heavily on Ovid, or are based on his poem, become un-Ovidian to the degree that they remove or ignore the witty arbitrariness, the audacious assertion of pattern and meaning in links between stories, which Ovid takes pains to display. Golding perceives and admires in Ovid precisely this high-wire balance between encyclopedic inclusiveness and significant form: "For whatsoever hath bene writ of auncient tyme in greeke / By sundry men dispersedly, and in the latin eeke, /

excitements of reading the *Metamorphoses,* as it was one of the excitements of composing it against the trend toward the brief forms of Hellenistic and neoteric poets, is that built-in tension between the *carmen perpetuum* and the flattened, discrete units that can be broken up and moved around, forming diverse recombinations of family resemblances among the stories—an authorial and readerly feat of dexterity alien to Vergil's mode of invention. Ovid's is a bravura performance in which the singer draws attention simultaneously to the fashioned strength and to the tenuous arbitrariness of links between tales.

Ovid thus turns superficiality from a potential defect into a virtue; I use the word here to mean his interest in the psychology of *facies* (form, shape, countenance, outward appearance) and *superficies* (surface), and his stylistic use of them as a consciously chosen response to Vergilian depth. The pressure toward inclusiveness, toward structures allied to catalogue and encyclopedia, characteristic of Ovid's entire career, issues in a poem with a multitude of characters, few of whom appear for more than an episode or two, and few of whom have an elaborated personal history. Nor are the characters, by and large, deeply implicated in *communitas* and its values, as they are in the works of Vergil and the Greek tragedians, with whom Ovid enters into such various dialogues. The obvious figure of comparison in the *Aeneid* is Aeneas, whose every impulse and action is a product of the loss of homeland, his yearning for a new community, and his commitment to his displaced comrades—in short, of his history and geography. The same is true of Dido, whose tragedy, larger than herself, lies not only in her torment when abandoned by Aeneas but in the decline of her city when abandoned by its queen. No character in the *Metamorphoses* has any such history, no such social identity, except,

---

Of this same dark Philosophie of turned shapes, the same / Hath Ovid into one whole masse in this booke brought in frame." Epistle to Leicester, II.5–8, in *Shakespeare's Ovid: Arthur Golding's Translation of the Metamorphoses,* ed. W. H. D. Rouse (New York: W. W. Norton, 1961), 1.

Debate about the issues of unity and balance in the design of the *Metamorphoses* is of long standing in Ovid commentary. For helpful treatments of this century, see Otis, *Ovid as an Epic Poet,* 74–90; Fränkel, *Ovid,* 77–78; G. Karl Galinsky, *Ovid's "Metamorphoses": An Introduction to the Basic Aspects* (Oxford: Blackwell, 1975), 79–109; Gordon Williams, *Change and Decline: Roman Literature in the Early Empire* (Berkeley and Los Angeles: University of California Press, 1978), 91–101, 246–53; Grundy Steiner, "Ovid's *Carmen Perpetuum,*" *Transactions and Proceedings of the American Philological Association* 89 (1958), 218–36.

significantly, Aeneas himself in Ovid's conflation of Homeric and Vergilian narratives of their wanderers' adventures. Ovid's characters are aggressively one-dimensional; we are not to probe for the depth of their suffering, or the consequences of an event for diverse aspects of their lives, not in the ways that we are invited to meditate on the social and political consequences of Dido's private love for Aeneas.

Instead, elements of stories are disposed with diagrammatic elegance and clarity. Moreover, this elegance gains toughness and often a wicked comic edge through its tense relation with the chaotic violence of emotion and action dominating long sequences of episodes. An Ovidian narrative forces the reader to look to the surface of the tale, and deliberately suppresses those versions, with which his readers were familiar, which pursue social and ethical implications veering away from the specific, stylized patterns that Ovid wishes to create. Thus he ignores altogether the Aeschylean handling of Io's story in *Prometheus Bound*, with its revolutions around matters of justice and implacable vengeance, the reflection that Io casts on Prometheus and vice versa, the elaboration of Io's torment, her description of Zeus's terrifying courtship, the effect created by the Chorus of giving Io's pain a social context. Aeschylus remains conspicuous by his absence in the *Metamorphoses'* Io episode; Ovid's narrative remains concentrated on the farce of the squabble between Juno and Jove as it contrasts with the pathos of Io—a pathos described without the expansiveness of dramatic lyric and dramatic plot contexts. The lyric suffering of Io, spun out in Aeschylus's play to form a deep reflection on and parallel with the equally detailed suffering of Prometheus, is grounded in the later poem rather by its multiple links with other relatively brief stories, treating not primarily of justice and injustice but of diverse pairings of beauty and violence. Its obvious affinities are with the tales of nymphs pursued by voracious gods; it also binds itself to the other stories of bestial-transformation-as-punishment in the poem, and to Jove's own metamorphosis into a bull in the Europa story.

Ovid's attention to narrative surfaces and to diagrammatic clarity of story motifs bears its own ethos and its own premises about character, relationship, and causality; we can most fruitfully consider his interest in surfaces by considering episodes in the poem's early books which depict acts of vision and the vulnerability of visible creatures in the *Metamorphoses*. Ovid's interest in the visibility of surfaces and their penetrability by the eye is one of the qualities by which we can understand his indebtedness to and his distinctness from Vergil. If Vergil creates, as I have suggested, fields of vision with depth and breadth, Ovid instead plots rays of vision, kinds of sight that are less multidimensional than Vergil's depiction of the burdens of sight, and more liable to invade and act on other characters. Ovid's poem reveals the variety of relations between suffering and powerlessness, on the one hand, and power and aggression, on the other. It is because of Ovid's conception of desire that observers do not take in fields of relations so much as single, specific objects.

Desire is simpler, though not less forceful, in the *Metamorphoses* than in the *Aeneid*. It is not compounded of multiple and elusive affects. It is not the complex yearning of Vergil's characters for intimate communion or for daily bonds; it is not a product of a character's history, nor an implication of the character's experience of loss, of love, or of citizenship. It is not a wish to know another or to find a stability that can be trusted—all elements of desire in Vergil. Desire in the *Metamorphoses* is most often a drive to possess the other, and this is effectively equivalent to destruction or transformation of the other's identity. (The exceptions to this assertion stand out by virtue of their rarity: the faithful married lovers Procris and Cephalus, Ceyx and Alcyone, the happy lovers Mercury and Herse.) The phenomenon of sight is correspondingly flattened into anatomies of powerful, simple, uncontrollable, and disastrous impulses: curiosity, greed, aggressive desire to possess, and accidental transgression of spatial and bodily boundaries. Sight is compelling because it arouses strong and simple appetites. Ovid conspicuously ignores the Vergilian character's capacity for awe and the Vergilian character's profound recognition of the alterity of other characters.

It is not sight of which a reader can first become aware in reading the *Metamorphoses*, but hiddenness. This quality is not, as in Vergil's works, a function of the impenetrability or the deceptiveness of appearances. Rather, hiddenness is a condition urgently sought but difficult to attain, as Ovid's nymphs discover. It is the protectiveness of being unseen which is wished for, not the isolation. Leo C. Curran argues, in an essay about what happens to identity in an Ovidian metamorphosis, that "much of the poem deals with people kept apart from each other; it is so much a world of 'Don't touch me,' so much a world of trying to maintain boundaries, so much a world in pursuit of loneliness."[15] But creatures of Ovid's world are not generally in pursuit of loneliness. There are in fact all sorts of groups of characters: married couples, siblings (usually sisters), family units of all types; there are crows and ravens exchanging news, sacred serpents mating, gods visiting mortals, spies observing whatever they can. Ovid's is a world highly sociable, gossipy, and bustling, and dangerous in the very density and frequency of its meetings. What Ovid does depict is characters in pursuit of solitude, a privacy that could guarantee the intactness or integrity of the self, the maintenance of profoundly cherished boundaries of selfhood. The appetite for this hidden solitude is tantamount to a wish to preserve selfhood and to taste it in liberty, unpressured by the predations of others. This is most evident in the case of Ovid's chaste nymphs, for example Daphne, who rejoices "silvarum latebris," "in the sylvan hiding places." The present participle in Ovid's sentence reinforces the intimate relation of pressure between Apollo's pursuit of her and her love of *silva latebra*:

> protinus alter amat, fugit altera nomen amantis
> silvarum latebris captivarumque ferarum
> exuviis *gaudens* innuptaeque aemula Phoebes.
>   (*Met.* 1.474–76; emphasis mine)[16]

[At once he loves, whereas she flees the name of lover, rejoicing in the hiding places of the woods and the spoils of beasts taken in hunting, vying with the maiden Phoebe.]

---

[15]Leo C. Curran, "Transformation and Anti-Augustanism in Ovid's *Metamorphoses,"Arethusa* 5 (1972), 71–92. Curran is not the only critic whose premises seem to imply an affable insensitivity to Ovid's elucidations of the pursued nymphs' wish for solitude. See, e.g., Fränkel, *Ovid*, 78, on Daphne: "Thus the young woman, who by her beauty was bound to inspire tender emotions, was incapable of sharing them . . . ; she was like a fine but frigid plant, one might say." And Otis, *Ovid as an Epic Poet*, 105–7, on Io: "[Jove] is no god to put up with a virgin's notions. . . . The effect of the cow on the woman is highly comic." Comic in a mordant way perhaps, but Otis apparently doesn't mean that. Ovid's tone reveals a good deal more sympathy with the nymphs' suffering, and the pathos of Ovidian nymphs is often found in Renaissance depictions of them. In his 1567 translation of the *Metamorphoses*, for instance, Arthur Golding interpolates an expression of sympathy after Jove's rape of Io: "Poore foole," he calls her (*Shakespeare's Ovid*, p. 35; Book 1, line 744). See William Keach, *Elizabethan Erotic Narratives: Irony and Pathos in the Ovidian Poetry of Shakespeare, Marlowe, and Their Contemporaries* (New Brunswick, N.J.: Rutgers University Press, 1976).

[16]Texts of Ovid are from the Loeb editions: *Metamorphoses*, text of G. P. Goold, 3d ed. (Cambridge: Harvard University Press, 1921 [vol. 1, 2d ed.], 1916 [vol. 2]).

The silvan landscapes of the poem may often be, as Charles Paul Segal argues, images of freed libidinal desire, an expansion of "the pastoral dreamworld."[17] But they are perhaps more often the vulnerable site of wishes for solitude and the ease of chaste selfhood. To be unseen in grove or wood is to protect the boundaries of space as boundaries of the self, to protect them from the pollution of invasion.[18]

The *Metamorphoses'* depicted urge to solitude and its attendant anxieties concern both the preserver of a precarious quotidian stability, most often a nymph, and the aggressor against individual integrity. The poem's early grouping of attempted rapes by gods makes this clear. The gods have the advantage of geographically superior sight; the combination of their invisibility to mortals and their ability to scan the earth beneath them becomes a formidable power to invade.[19] In the tale of Io, for example, Ovid emphasizes the contrast between the motivation of the nymph's urge for the hiddenness of wilderness and the motivations of Jove's drive to hiddenness, in this case his desire for Io and a relish of the opportunity to put one over on his consort:

> Viderat a patrio redeuntem Iuppiter illam [Io]
> flumine et "o virgo Iove digna tuoque beatum
> nescio quem factura toro, pete" dixerat "umbras
> altorum nemorum" (et nemorum monstraverat umbras)
> "dum calet, et medio sol est altissimus orbe!
> quodsi sola times latebras intrare ferarum,
> praeside tuta deo nemorum secreta subibis."
>
> (*Met.* 1.588–94)

[Jupiter had seen her returning from her father's river. "O maiden worthy of Jove, and likely to make I know not whom happy in bed, make for

---

Fasti, ed. James G. Frazier (Cambridge: Harvard University Press, 1931). Translations are my own. I can mention here my indebtedness not only to Fränkel's and Otis's studies of Ovid, already cited, but also to W. R. Johnson, "The Problem of the Counter-Classical Sensibility and Its Critics," *California Studies in Classical Antiquity* 3 (1970), 123–50; Gordon Williams, *Change and Decline*, 52–101; Clark Hulse, *Metamorphic Verse: The Elizabethan Minor Epic* (Princeton: Princeton University Press, 1981).

[17]Charles Paul Segal, *Landscape in Ovid's "Metamorphoses": A Study in the Transformations of a Literary Symbol* (Wiesbaden: Franz Steiner Verlag GMBH, 1969), 12.

[18]The threats to Ovid's vulnerable nymphs exemplify Mary Douglas's first kind of social pollution, "danger pressing on external boundaries." See *Purity and Danger: An Analysis of Concepts of Pollution and Taboo* (New York: Praeger, 1966), 122.

[19]On ancient writers who use the notion of the gods' superior sight, see Waldemar Deonna, *Le Symbolisme de l'oeil* (Berne: Francke, 1965), 96–108.

the shaded places of the deep woods," he had said (and he had pointed to the shady woods) "while it is hot and the sun is at its zenith! But if you fear entering the beasts' abode alone, you may steal into the hidden woods safely, protected by a god."]

Both Jove and the narrator underline the urgency of the desire for hiddenness. Ovid ends two consecutive lines with *umbras,* and Jove moves from *umbras* to the stronger emphasis of *secreta.* These lines are of course broadly comic at Jove's expense, in the transparence of the tactic he uses on Io and in our knowledge that its obviousness makes it bound to fail with any female, much less one of Ovid's reserved nymphs. But the lines are also taut with the tension between this broad comedy and the ominous reverberations that underlie it. Tension lies in the force about which Jove has no compunctions and which Ovid passes over with a callous brevity suited to the aggressor:

> iam pascua Lernae
> consitaque arboribus Lyrcea reliquerat arva,
> cum deus inducta latas caligine terras
> occuluit tenuitque fugam rapuitque pudorem.
>
> (*Met.* 1.597–600)

[Now she had left behind the pastures of Lerna and the Lyrcean region thickset with trees, when the god concealed the wide earth with a darkness spread over it; he restrained her flight and he ravished her.]

Tension lies in Jove's power to create his own hiddenness with the thick, obscuring cloud, a power that throws into relief Io's own powerlessness to remain hidden. Most of all it lies in the suspicions of Juno, arriving with power to disperse Jove's cloud and trailing her own clouds of malice and wrath from the *Aeneid.* The tensions that inform this tale thus reveal Ovid's perceptions of power and powerlessness, as well as the clarity with which these are focused through the desire for hiddenness.

That Ovid broods on the privacy of the self and its relation to being unseen is clear from his two treatments of Callisto's story, in *Metamorphoses* 2.401–530 and *Fasti* 2.153–92, cousin to the tales of Io and Actaeon. The shame of exposure dominates both narratives. In the *Metamorphoses,* Callisto enters a virginal forest where she entrusts herself to the earth:

Ulterius medio spatium sol altus habebat,
cum subit illa nemus, quod nulla ceciderat aetas;
exuit hic umero pharetram lentosque retendit
arcus inque solo, quod texerat herba, iacebat
et pictam posita pharetram cervice premebat.

(Met. 2.417–21)

[The sun was beyond its zenith when she entered a grove which no age had cut. Here she took her quiver off her shoulder, unbent her supple bow, lay upon the ground which the grass had covered, and placed her neck upon her painted quiver.]

But Jove sees her *fessam* and *vacantem*, "weary and unprotected," and rapes her; afterward, "huic odio nemus est et conscia silva," "her aversion is the grove and the cognizant wood" that she had loved and trusted (*Met.* 2.438). It is Diana's sexual ignorance that saves Callisto during part of her pregnancy, a comical ignorance the obverse of that virginal intactness of identity usually valued by Ovid, and an ignorance underscored by the probability that Diana's own band of nymphs is more knowing than she. In the *Metamorphoses*, Callisto's plight is the occasion for a tone of trivial and salacious gossip, and for malice when the nymphs finally force her to comply with Diana's wishes by disrobing. To hide is her only defense in a life of permanent defensiveness.

The *Fasti* version suppresses the violence of Jove; it concentrates instead on the relationship of trust between Diana and Callisto, and the breaking of that relationship; it breaks up chronological sequence, and fills in the plot by means of brief, elliptical, and oblique flashback. What Ovid presents here is not the pathos of Callisto's powerless hidden moment in the forest with Jove, but the isolation of Callisto from her intimates, an isolation that is the result of her being seen pregnant by Diana:

"hic" ait "in silva, virgo Tegeaea, lavemur!"
    erubuit falso virginis illa sono.
dixerat et nymphis: nymphae velamina ponunt,
    hanc pudet et tardae dat mala signa morae.
exuerat tunicas; uteri manifesta tumore

proditur indicio ponderis ipsa suo.
cui dea "virgineos, periura Lycaoni, coetus
    desere nec castas pollue" dixit "aquas."

(*Fasti* 2.167–74)

["Here," (Diana) said, "let us bathe in the woods, Tegaean maiden";
she blushed at the false sound of the word maiden. Diana had spoken
also to the nymphs; they disrobed; Callisto was ashamed and gave weak
signs of lingering delay. She had taken off her tunic; self-detected, she
was betrayed by her belly's swelling, proof of the weight she bore. The
goddess spoke: "The company of maidens forswear, perjured daughter
of Lycaon; nor pollute the pure waters."]

The bond between Diana and Callisto has been one not only of votaress to goddess but of privileged intimacy: Diana had rewarded
Callisto's vow of virginity by making her "comitum princeps...
mihi," "the foremost of [her] company" (*Fasti* 2.160). The chief narrative mark of such intimacy with Diana is the privilege of bathing
with her. This privilege is really two, as it will be in Spenser: first the
luxury of full relaxation of self, in privacy, after strenuous exertion,
and second the intimacy of being fully seen and mutually seen. Such
a privilege carries with it the charge and the delight of exclusiveness;
it is explicitly a sexual privilege in that it is the result of a sexual
pledge made to the goddess; Diana reacts to Callisto's pregnancy as
one betrayed. The seclusion from outsiders' eyes that characterizes
and even defines the intimacy between Callisto and Diana balances
the exposure to each other which has been a mark of love and ease
between them, but which now marks the degree of Callisto's defenselessness before the virgin goddess. Jove hardly enters the narration of
the *Fasti* at all, but both of Callisto's sufferings (rape by the god,
rejection by the goddess) are measured by hiddenness and exposure.

It is the diagrammatic disposition of such motifs, rather than the
depth of characterization, which tells us about Ovid's preoccupations,
and about Io and Callisto. The pathos of their victimization in a harsh
world emerges from the tension between the urbanity of narrative
tone (e.g., in that glib, rapid, and brutal passing over of the rape itself)
and the violence so smoothly depicted in this balanced and precise
mode of narration.

A salient quality of mortal beings in the *Metamorphoses*, of course,
is that their suffering leads in diverse ways to shape-changing; char-

acters become other than they are and yet, often, become, or remain, the same as they were. Identity is changed via transformation into an alien form (Callisto and bear, two natures in one), or via fusion (Salmacis and Hermaphroditus). In either case Ovid conceives of a selfhood defined by boundaries and surfaces, which are unpredictably fluid or penetrable. When Dryope turns into a tree (*Met.* 9.327–93), the process consists, first, of the body's surface being covered by bark and then of the bodily surface itself becoming the form of a tree:

> subcrescit ab imo,
> totaque paulatim lentus premit inguina cortex.
> ut vidit, conata manu laniare capillos,
> fronde manum implevit: frondes caput omne tenebant.
> at puer Amphissos, (namque hoc avus Eurytus illi
> addiderat nomen,) materna rigescere sentit
> ubera; nec sequitur ducentem lacteus umor.
>
> (*Met.* 9.352–58)

[It grew up from below, and little by little a clinging bark covered all of her groin. When she saw this and tried to tear her hair with her hands, she filled her hand instead with foliage: leaves held fast all her head. But the boy Amphissos (for his grandfather Eurytus had so named him) felt the breast of his mother grow stiff, nor did the milky fluid follow his drawing.]

Premit, "covered," exerts its full pressure and even intimacy here; it pushes on with some urgency to *rigescere,* "to harden."[20] Dryope's half-sister Iole, the narrator of the tale and observer of the transformation, yearns for contact, perhaps union, with the spirit of her sister; this compassionate yearning leads to her desire to participate in the

---

[20]The world of the *Metamorphoses* is one characterized by pressures and weights, one object leaning with some force upon or against another: in aggression, in love, or in the simple tendency of things to impinge on and press on each other. The visceral force of *premere*—to exert a force against, to hem in, to surround, to overwhelm, to cover, hide, squeeze, confine, press with the body—pervades the poem. Often it expresses a Vergilian sense of the weight involved in tending the earth: 3.104, 7.211, 11.31, 14.629. For the pressure of violence, see, e.g., 3.91, 4.719, 8.425, 9.45–78, 12.140–41. For the human body pressing against the earth's body, see 5.135, 6.347, 7.608, 9.651, 15.694, 15.698. For the pressing force of the elements, see 1.30, 1.48, 1.70, 1.268, 1.290, 7.529, 11.521, 11.558. For the urgency of erotic contact between fellow creatures, see, e.g., 4.369, 10.258.

action of *premere* by entering the boundary that defines the tree and to hide there:[21]

> ...quantumque valebam,
> crescentem truncum ramosque amplexa morabar,
> et, fateor, volui sub eodem cortice condi.
>
> (*Met.* 9.360–62)

[...and as long as I could, I delayed the growing trunk and branches with an embrace, and, I confess, I wished to be covered beneath the same bark.]

Dryope's ontological status is blurred by virtue of her doubleness: she both becomes the tree and becomes hidden by the covering form of the tree. Ovid plays on this doubleness: " 'viximus innocuae. si mentior, arida perdam / quas habeo frondes, et caesa securibus urar' " (" 'I lived innocent. If I lie, dry may I lose the leaves that I have, and cut with hatchets may I be burnt,' " *Met.* 9.373–74). More often than being malleable, as Dryope's surface is here, the boundaries of the self are permeable or penetrable, not only in the sexual sense, but also in the larger sense that the surface of the self is vulnerable to transformation under any pressures of the world. All of these pursuits are invasions: invasions of privacy, as we now say; invasions of that integrity of the boundaries of selfhood which is both cherished and vulnerable in these characters. The initial means of invasion and of the multiple kinds of *raptus* which Ovid sketches is sight, an act of vision often used as a weapon or as an assertion of personal power.

We can turn once again for clarification to the possible modes of vision which physiological optics suggested. If, as for Plato and the Stoics, the mediating air interacts with substances from the eyes, then the air becomes an extension of the self. If there is such a thing as visual radiation or extramission, then sight is active and extensive, but also involuntary; and the choice of object can be either voluntary or not. On the other hand, if corpuscular simulacra stream into the eye, as atomist theory suggested, then being seen is simultaneously a

---

[21]Anderson's commentary draws the pertinent contrast: "The grotesque action of Iole is merely ridiculous, as she tries to slow down the metamorphosis by embracing Dryope. Yet she has the same desire as Anna in *Aen.* 4.672ff.: to share her sister's fate—but how different and unepic a fate!" *Ovid's Metamorphoses Books 6–10*, ed. William S. Anderson (Norman: University of Oklahoma Press, 1972), 443.

passive act and an active (though unwilled) extension of the self. Ovid thoroughly exploits this balanced paradoxy in his poem, in which acts of vision are exertions of power but also passive accidents. Moreover, if sight is a mode of touch, then it can be invasive, as touch can be. And if we take an interest in surfaces, which constantly emit simulacra retaining the exact shape of the surfaces, as a constant in all of these theories, then the activity of seeing becomes implicated with problems of boundary definition: Where does the object's surface or boundary begin and end? If the object gives off images of itself, in what way can the image be said to be part of the object, or distinct from it? Such questions provoked philosophers of physiological and geometric optics, and they provoked Ovid, as well, in his handling of the kinds and the consequences of contact between observer and object. The sheer number of tales in the *Metamorphoses* treating of inflamed vision, *raptus*, spying, visual transgressions, and metamorphoses that expose the shame or the interior identity of the changed creature suggests that Ovid conceives of a world in which merely to exist as a visible body is risky business.

Hence the nightmare of total visibility, the poem's antithesis of and balance to its dream of protective hiddenness. The shame of Io helpless in her bovine form is exacerbated not only by being made a prisoner, but by being constantly exposed to Argus's hundred eyes. The anguish and shame of her transformation, itself a consequence of both Jove's and Juno's superior vision, are compounded by the punishment of constant exposure, through another's eyes, to her own loss of identity.

Tending or guarding, the *labor* of watching, turns out to be a dangerous occupation, not only for Argus but for the several spies dominating the second half of Book 2 of the *Metamorphoses*. Sight and sound pair off, for these spies, in matters of concealment and exposure, especially erotic matters. Sight and sound are linked as phenomena that mark and violate boundaries, as the most promiscuous of sensory phenomena. Hearing was in ancient theory as much a species of touch as sight was; the motion of the air begun by sounding objects travels to and touches the 'internal air' enclosed in the ear, and so produces sound.[22] The attempt to conceal, another form of the thrust toward privacy, arouses an irresistible and generally malicious urge to see the secret, and then to announce the exposure

[22]Alistair C. Crombie, "Early Concepts of the Sense and the Mind," *Scientific American* 210 (May 1964), 108–16.

in the hopes of self-aggrandizement. There is, for instance, Battus, the old shepherd who observes Mercury's theft of Sol's cattle and is bought off by the god, only to betray him to himself, Mercury, who returns in disguise to test the shepherd. The comedy of the scene takes the sting out of the punishment to follow: it is a tale of one rascal meeting another, of their mutual shrewdness, and of one's defeat by the superior resources of the other. Still, Battus is punished for his feeble attempt to exercise power through sight, though he is hardly more immoral than the gods who never question their own rights to use sight actively against mortals.

The diagram of spying in the *Metamorphoses* begins lightly, with a silly crow warning a sillier raven not to expose the sexual secret that the raven has discovered (the unchastity of the nymph Coronis), a lesson earlier learned by the crow when she herself revealed illicit sexual secrets. The mention of those secrets leads to the crow's narration of the two stories of Aglauros, which lay down the lines of relation among spying, malice, *cupiditas*, powerful secrets, verbal and visual exposure. The crow tells the first story of Aglauros, one of three sisters whom Minerva has set to guard a chest with strict orders "not to look upon her secret." The crow spies on the sisters, as if she grasps that a command not to look will evoke a desire to do just that: " 'abdita fronde levi densa speculabar ab ulmo,/quid facerent.' " (" 'Hidden in the light leaves, from a thick elm I spied out what they were doing,' " *Met.* 2.557–58). Aglauros's opening of the chest leads to the discovery of the infant Erichthonius; the crow reveals this crime of exposure to Minerva, and is punished by her for the disclosure.

The details of this version of the story are worth examining. First, Ovid teases by all but suppressing the tale of the infant's birth; we are told only that he is a child without a mother, "prolem sine matre creatam" (2.553). In fact he is the son of Vulcan, who failed in his attempted rape of Minerva but whose seed fell upon her leg or, sometimes, simply upon the ground; when she wiped it off in disgust and threw it to the ground, the child was formed. Ovid subordinates this narrative, and lays all the weight of the narrative instead on the giving of the command to secrecy and the motif of spying. Second, Ovid's creation of one shameless and two trustworthy sisters revises those versions of the tale in which two of the sisters, Aglauros and Herse, violate the secret; this is Aglauros's compulsion alone, as is the violation of the next story. Third, Aglauros escapes punishment altogether: not only are she and her sister not driven mad by the sight, as elsewhere, but the transgressor is left alone while the crow is punished as a surrogate for her.[23] Finally, it is not Aglauros's visual transgression that is punished but the crow's oral one. (It is worth noticing that Actaeon, too, is punished not purely for seeing the forbidden but in order to prevent his reporting what he has seen.)

Aglauros's punishment is deferred until her second episode (*Met.* 2.737–832). As sister to Herse and guardian to the secret of Mercury's love for Herse, she cannot bear either to observe the lovers' happiness or to carry the burden of the secret. She successfully blackmails Mercury, whose initial acquiescence ominously belies his strength while it fills out the comedy of petty intrigue and the sketch of Mercury as spruce young lover. As a result of the blackmail, however, Aglauros incurs Minerva's wrath. The indirection in Aglauros's punishment is a departure for Ovid, and it never occurs again in the poem. Minerva's anger is ostensibly sparked by Aglauros's shabby treatment of the lovers, whom Aglauros's has been asked to protect and conceal; this treatment recalls to Minerva Aglauros's earlier spying, which had gone unremarked in the interim. Causality is thus more tightly woven than is usual in Ovid's work: first by this redounding impact of a character's own history on her present role, second by the convoluted chain of causes which jogs Minerva's memory, third by the tight link between this act of greedy eyes and the earlier act, now seen by the goddess to have its roots in Aglauros's malice and greed, and not only in curiosity. Meaning emerges from her history, and this meaning is the revelation of the causes at work in Aglauros's psyche. The punishment itself—Aglauros's infection by the ghastly Invidia—is both an act of divine vengeance and an inevitable outcome of Aglauros's own nature.

As usual, what Ovid can afford not to reveal in his deployment of myth tells us a good deal about his precise interests. The story not told here is the happiness of Mercury and Herse; they appear only obliquely, in Aglauros's tormented imagination:

[23]For other treatments of Aglauros, her sisters, and Erichthonius, see Euripides, *Ion* 20–24 and 260–74; Apollodorus, *The Library* 3.14.2, 3.14.6; Pausanius, *Description of Greece* 1.18.2–3.

germanam ante oculos fortunatumque sororis
coniugium pulchraque deum sub imagine ponit
cunctaque magna facit.

(*Met.* 2.803–805)

[(Envy) places before her eyes her sister, her sister's fortunate marriage, and the god with a beautiful appearance, and magnifies it all.]

Ovid, we might say, respects the lovers' seclusion a good deal more than Aglauros does: not only does she seek to prevent it, or perhaps to muscle in on it, but once infected she cannot stop visualizing it imaginatively. All she knows how to do, in both of her tales, is violate secrets, and this mode of existence becomes a torment to her when she can no longer close her eyes to the objects before her. From invading the hidden visually, she has come to be invaded by the imagined sight of the hidden, and she has no defense with which to exclude this vision from the bounds of her own identity:

saepe mori voluit, ne quicquam tale videret,
saepe velut crimen rigido narrare parenti;
denique in adverso venientem limine sedit
exclusura deum. cui blandimenta precesque
verbaque iactanti mitissima "desine!" dixit,
"hinc ego me non sum nisi te motura repulso."

(*Met.* 2.812–17)

[Often she wished to die, in order not to see such a thing; often to tell it, as if it were a crime, to her stern father. Finally she sat down on the forepart of the threshold, to exclude the god when he came. He threw out blandishments and prayers and the most gentle words to her, to which she declared, "Cease! I will not move from here until I have thwarted you."]

Aglauros's hope for relief from the burden of vision lies in three desperate expedients: to be freed by death from seeing at all; to be freed from the solitariness of seeing this maddeningly joyful secret by telling; to prevent the lovers altogether. It is her lack of clarity about her own desires that Ovid echoes in his refusal to discuss them in his usual precise terms; it is the nature of Aglauros's envy that she cannot be sure whether she actually wants the lovers' happiness for herself or wants Mercury or wants to profit from the situation, or wants simply to stop the lovers' happiness. This purposeful ambiguity about affect, like the complex network of causation and history in Aglauros's tales, and the use of the Vergilian figure Invidia, is also atypical of Ovid's procedure in the *Metamorphoses*.

Aglauros's desires circulate around the desire of the have-not to be on the inside: first, she wants to know the secret of Minerva; next, she wants money. But this desire, given its role in a story of Envy, seems to be a displacement of her third and real desire, for Mercury and for the happiness her sister knows. That this is a desire too great to be borne Ovid demonstrates with a story of substitutions and deferrals: money instead of Mercury, crow instead of Aglauros punished for spying, Aglauros finally punished less for a specific crime than for the character that allows such crimes. The envious have-not is the victim of her own evilly disposed eye; the envier is painfully, if not always accurately, aware of standing outside an excluding boundary, outside an enclosed circle that she takes to be a source and a concentration of desired happiness. This fascination with the picture of an envied happiness will be developed by Spenser, who links the tormented regard of a vision of happiness in others' lives with an envious destructiveness.

Aglauros's stories, framed by the story of the crow narrator, are further contextualized by being grouped with other stories of spies, most of them either more comic or more slight than the tale of this nasty girl pursued by an inflated Vergilian allegorical figure like Invidia. These include Battus; the raven who finally does report Coronis to Apollo, to whom she has been unfaithful; Sol, who self-righteously exposes Venus's affair with Vulcan. Venus's revenge on Sol is to make him love Leucothoe, who is in turn exposed by the jealous and pathetic Clytie. This sequence of solar tales in Book 4 acts as a bridge from the compulsive and malicious spying of Aglauros to the stronger compulsions of erotic hunger fed through the eyes. Again, meanings created by precise disposition of elements balance the chaos and destructiveness depicted in the tales. And the psychological precision of Ovid's paradoxy and dramatic ironies balances by opposition the flatness of characters, whose only dimension is their role as desired or desiring sufferers.

The overarching balance of the tales of Sol in Book 4 relies on the witty fusion, inherited by Ovid from Hellenistic poets, of god-as-character and god-as-natural-phenomenon. When Sol the anthropomorphic god loves Leucothoe (*Met.* 4.190–233), Sol the sun, the eye of the world, gazes on her obsessively, and this naturally creates difficulties for the earth, whose time sequences and climates are thus threatened. This is a comic twist on the vision of erotic desire and on the lovesick wooer of elegy. But the picture that balances this comic one is the pathetic image of Clytie-as-heliotrope (both human and plant in her sensibilities; in the world of mortals, this fusion fails to amuse), turning and turning to face the sun:

> tabuit ex illo dementer amoribus usa;
> nympharum inpatiens et sub Iove nocte dieque
> sedit humo nuda nudis incompta capillis,
> perque novem luces expers undaeque cibique
> rore mero lacrimisque suis ieiunia pavit
> nec se movit humo; tantum spectabat euntis
> ora dei vultusque suos flectebat ad illum
>
> . . . . .
>
> illa suum, quamvis radice tenetur,
> vertitur ad Solem mutataque servat amorem.
>
> (*Met.* 4.259–70)

[She wasted away from that time, maddened by passion, impatient of the other nymphs, and beneath the open sky night and day she sat on the bare ground, her head bare and unkempt, and for nine days, destitute of water and food, fed her fast with pure dew and tears. Nor did she move from the ground; she only looked on the face of the god as he went, and turned her gaze toward him.... She, although she is held fast by a root, is turned toward Sol and, herself changed, preserves her love.]

Now it is not the fusion but the disjunction of beloved god (Sol) and natural object (sun) that is painfully apparent, a disjunction that emphasizes the pathos of Clytie's alienated distance from him. If nearly everyone else in the erotic tales of the *Metamorphoses* is driven to seek hiddenness, Clytie is conspicuously driven by the double nature of her loved object to expose herself to the elements. This exposure is itself double, because it is identical with her emotional exposure. Her revelation of the secret of Sol's love for Leucothoe rebounds on herself, and prevents both her own private intimacy with Sol and the interior secret of her love for him.

Ovid and the Sufferance of Exposure

Clytie's exposure *is* her metamorphosis, and the secret love borne within her is exposed, too. Metamorphosis in Ovid's poem is often an exposure of inner consciousness, sometimes a grotesquely literal reification of it, as in the case of Clytie or Niobe. The pathos of metamorphosis lies not only in the alteration or diminishment of human form, but in the shame of human consciousness retained; shame is a frequent quality of bodily metamorphosis and of psychic change in the *Metamorphoses*. A key image in Ovid's recurrent treatments of shame is the blush, and this is so not only for the obvious reason that the blush is the most visible and frequent somatic sign of shame, but also because the blush is a tiny, passing bodily metamorphosis. There are important blushes, bearing the weight of imitations from Homer, Sappho, and Vergil, to be found throughout Ovid's works; here I want to look at only one, leaving others until Chapter Four, when I will adduce Ovidian blushes in relation to Spenser.

To observe the rising blood in the face, in Ovid's amorous social world, is to observe the most deeply internal being made external and visible against the will; as an opening up of interior identity, the blush functions as a proffer of intimacy, even against the consent of the blusher. This is the case in the blush of Hermaphroditus, male counterpart to the young virginal nymphs of Ovid's poem, which inflames Salmacis's already roused desire (*Met.* 4.285–388).[24] Salmacis has addressed to the youth a fine speech, modelled on Odysseus's speech to Nausikaa; but she ends her speech with a bold plea for marriage, and with an unsolicited embrace. Hermaphroditus sends her away, fiercely; she goes, but only as far as a thicket from which she may watch him undetected. Ovid then depicts the extensiveness and delight of the self in privacy, as we can tell by Hermaphroditus's real happiness of the senses, a happiness always linked with solitude in the *Metamorphoses*:

> tum quoque respiciens, fruticumque recondita silva
> delituit flexuque genu submisit; at ille,
> scilicet ut vacuis et inobservatus in herbis,

---

[24]I treat this tale more fully in "Sappho's Apples: The Allusiveness of Blushes in Ovid and Beaumont," *Comparative Literature Studies* 25 (March 1988), 1–22.

huc it et hinc illuc et in adludentibus undis
summa pedum taloque tenus vestigia tinguit;
nec mora, temperie blandarum captus aquarum
mollia de tenero velamina corpore ponit.

(*Met.* 4.339–45)

[Then looking back, concealed in a thicket, she hid herself and crouched
on bent knees. But he, as if alone and unseen, went here and there on
the gentle grass, and dipped his toe and then his ankle in the lapping
waters. Without delay, taken with the temper of the pleasing waters, he
took his soft garments from his tender body.]

This ease of Hermaphroditus's self-possession within nature is almost
immediately threatened by the pressure of Salmacis's watching; Ovid
keeps a tight focus on the single relation between Salmacis and Hermaphroditus, figured in the line of sight from her eyes to his
nakedness:

tum vero placuit, nudaeque cupidine formae
Salmacis exarsit; flagrant quoque lumina nymphae,
non aliter quam cum puro nitidissimus orbe
opposita speculi referitur imagine Phoebus.

(*Met.* 4.346–49)

[Then truly he pleased her, and Salmacis took fire with desire for his
naked form. Her eyes blazed too, just as when Phoebus's brightest orb
is reflected from the opposed image of a mirror.]

The simile of the glass is an image of erotic intensification that looks
toward other reflective images in the poem, and toward the under-
current of the Narcissus myth, another tale in which the dazzle of
polished surfaces intersects with the redness of interior life exposed.
Here, the consequence of Salmacis's kindling is a frantic, funny, and
ghoulish drive toward the triumph of possession, as the bodily boundaries of each merge into those of the other. That large metamorphosis
is anticipated, though, by the transient metamorphosis of Hermaphroditus's blush:

... sed et erubuisse decebat:
hic color aprica pendentibus arbore pomis

aut ebori tincto est aut sub candore rubenti,
cum frustra resonant aera auxiliaria, lunae.

(*Met.* 4.330–33)

[But it became him to have blushed. This color have apples hanging on
a tree in the sunlight, or dyed ivory or the moon, red under white, when
bronze vessels ring in vain to assist it.]

Hermaphroditus's blush is one of innocence embarrassed and made
awkward, innocence the more poignant for being on the verge of the
loss that is sexual experience in Ovid's work. The blush and its ultimate consequence—indeed, all the movements and exposures of
Hermaphroditus's body in the tale—argue Ovid's sense of a bodily
self comprised of organic spaces enclosed within a surface vulnerable
to invasions of the world.

Ovid's evident interest in the destructive capacities of vision and
in the power of the observer makes the more curious his insistent
refusal to attribute to Actaeon any urge to see, or even any pleasure
when he does see, illicit sights, while the narrator himself goes to
some lengths to depict the spectacle of the goddess bathing. Brooks
Otis has commented on the comedy of Diana's Roman-matron toilette
and its trivialization of divine power.[25] But the description of this
toilette also has the more serious effect of making the reader, already
within the sacred grove, privy to the leisurely and exquisite bath
preparations. These invite the same aesthetic-erotic responses that
Hermaphroditus's bathing does, but Ovid raises the possibility of
Actaeon's sexual relish only to step around it:

quo postquam subiit, nympharum tradidit uni
armigerae iaculum pharetramque arcusque retentos,
altera depositae subiecit bracchia pallae,
vincla duae pedibus demunt; nam doctior illis
Ismenis Crocale sparsos per colla capillos
colligit in nodum, quamvis erat ipsa solutis.
excipiunt laticem Nepheleque Hyaleque Rhanisque
et Psecas et Phiale funduntque capacibus urnis.
dumque ibi perluitur solita Titania lympha,
ecce nepos Cadmi dilata parte laborum

[25]Otis, *Ovid as an Epic Poet,* 134–35.

per nemus ignotum non certis passibus errans
pervenit in lucum: sic illum fata ferebant.

(*Met.* 3.165–76)

[After she entered the cave, she handed to one of her nymphs, her armor-bearer, her javelin and quiver and slack bow; another placed on her arm the robe that Diana had laid aside; two others removed the sandals from her feet. For, more skilled than they, Ismenean Crocale gathered into a knot the hair that lay scattered on Diana's neck, her own hair falling free. Nephele and Hyale and Rhanis and Psecas and Phiale bring the water and pour it out from wide jars. And while Titania is washed there in her customary spring, behold the grandson of Cadmus, part of his labor put off, wandering with uncertain steps through the unknown grove, came into the sacred grove: thus fate directed him.]

Ovid here draws on the cultural force of ritual prohibitions against seeing divinity, and of myths that punish visual and sexual transgressions,[26] but his interests in the episode lie chiefly in the dynamics of the meeting between goddess and involuntary transgressor:

qui simul intravit rorantia fontibus antra,
sicut erant, nudae viso sua pectora nymphae
percussere viro subitisque ululatibus omne
inplevere nemus circumfusaeque Dianam
corporibus texere suis; tamen altior illis
ipsa dea est colloque tenus supereminet omnis.
qui color infectis adversi solis ab ictu
nubibus esse solet aut purpureae Aurorae,
is fuit in vultu visae sine veste Dianae.

(*Met.* 3.177–85)

[As soon as he entered the cave bedewed with springs, the nymphs, naked as they were, beat their breasts and filled all the grove with sudden cries on seeing the man. They gathered round Diana and covered her

---

[26]For examples of rituals prohibiting sight of the sacred, see Pausanius 7.23.9, 7.24.3. For a list of lesser-known myths and events in which blindness is the punishment for a sexual transgression, see G. Devereux, "The Self-Blinding of Oidipous in Sophokles: *Oidipous Tyrannos,*" *Journal of Hellenic Studies* 93 (1973), 36–49 at 40.

There is a version of the Actaeon myth, perhaps as old as the sixth century B.C., in which Actaeon is punished for wooing his maternal aunt, Semele. For various redactions, see Callimachus, Hymn V, "On the Bath of Pallas"; Apollodorus, *The Library* 3.4.4; Pausanius, *Description of Greece* 9.2.3; Nonnus, *Dionysiaca* 5.287–551.

body with theirs; but the goddess is a head taller than they are and stands above them all. The color with which the clouds are tinged when the sun sets opposite them, or the color of rosy Aurora—this was the color of the face of Diana, seen without her robe.]

The maids' giddy howling certainly contributes to Roman-socialite satire, as Otis says, but Diana's numinous potency emerges sublimely from her little flock. That this numinosity is compromised, in Ovid's treatment of the story, is signalled by her blush, the sexual blush that exposes vulnerability and undermines the perfect self-possession that characterizes her generally. It is the loss of that contained poise, rather than a matronly primness (as Otis suggests), that seems to me to account for her response.

Nor is the response itself quite the rising to a huffy dignity which Otis proposes:

> quae, quamquam comitum turba est stipata suarum,
> in latus obliquum tamen adstitit oraque retro
> flexit et, ut vellet promptas habuisse sagittas,
> quas habuit sic hausit aquas vultumque virilem
> perfudit spargensque comas ultricibus undis
> addidit haec cladis praenuntia verba futurae:
> "nunc tibi me posito visam velamine narres,
> sit poteris narrare, licet!"
>
> > (*Met.* 3.186–93)

[Although her crowd of attendants was closed round, she stood sidelong and turned back. How she wished that she had her arrows at hand— but what she had she took up: she flung water in the man's face, and, sprinkling his hair with avenging drops, she added words that presaged his approaching disaster: "Now you may tell that you saw me here without my robes, if you are able to!"]

What Diana does reveal is a good deal of embarrassment, defensiveness, and fear that she may be made a fool through Actaeon's anticipated gossip—not an unrealistic worry in this poem. She lashes out with a gesture that in a flustered and angry mortal would be inconsequential, even childish; though it is catastrophic here, Ovid suggests some sympathy for it. She has notable affinities with the nymphs of the beginning of the poem, votaresses of hers, after all, who are attacked by gods: she craves the security of protected and hidden places, and she is easily undone by unexpected intrusions. The valence that protected enclosures possess for her is a measure of her anxiety when their boundaries are threatened. Geographical boundaries are continuous with personal boundaries, and the transgression of the grove continuous with transgression of her selfhood—hence the blush, itself an unwilled exhibition of vulnerability.

That Ovid can grant this much sympathy to Diana, by his structuring the scene so as to justify her psychic responses, is worth some attention because the sympathy is balanced by so strong a disapproval of her violence against Actaeon. Much more space is given to the nightmare of his transformation than to the little contretemps leading to it; and the gossipy society of the poem debates the punishment rigorously—in a handling of ethics which is unusually explicit for Ovid. We are back to the prevailing themes of power and powerlessness, and the perilousness of sight, which obtained in the early tales of the nymphs. But in this episode of the nymphs' goddess, the points are reversed. Seeing, not being seen, is the real danger; the male, not the female, is threatened with loss of identity: Actaeon's view of Diana guarantees him (at least to Diana's mind) a measure of power over her which cannot be tolerated.

Leonard Barkan makes a good case for the notion that sight in the tale becomes the power of forbidden knowledge,[27] and we can see the degree to which this is true: Actaeon's "holy voyeurism" will be picked up in most later treatments, as it exists in earlier versions of the tale. The trouble is that Ovid remains noticeably silent on this point. A sight in the *Metamorphoses* may indeed become forbidden knowledge, but it does not become insight. The numinous object of vision, even if it is seen clearly (as Cadmus has a clear view of the serpent that he gazes on earlier in Book 3), sets the viewer apart from other humans, but its significance remains opaque. The act of vision is crucial but remains meaningless, random, and violent to human observers. That is, its only meaning for mortal is its imponderable secrecy.

Vergil, I said at the start of this chapter, traditionally represents the gravity and greatness, the epoch-making significance, of Augustan

[27]Leonard Barkan, "Diana and Actaeon: The Myth as Synthesis," *English Literary Renaissance* 10 (Autumn 1980), 317–59 at 318–22.

Rome; the values of *pietas* and *labor* in the building of the city made the *Aeneid* crucial to the developing national literatures of Europe. And Ovid's work bears the burden of its reputation as licentious, culpably erotic, and decadent. It is no accident that Edmund Spenser has generally presented to his readers two faces: the sage and serious moralist, exalted singer of Troynovant, on the one hand; and the voluptuous, erotic decadent, on the other. For it is partly Vergilian and Ovidian imitations and impulses in Spenser's work which evoke these perceptions. In the next two chapters I turn respectively to a markedly Vergilian work, Book 2 of *The Faerie Queene*, to see what happens to the genre of Vergilian moral epic as it moves away from and then back toward romance; and to Books 3, 4, and 6 of Spenser's epic, to consider Ovidian conceptions of bodily life.

Chapter Two

Streams Entering through the Eyes: Vision and Genre in Book 2 of *The Faerie Queene*

Book 2 of *The Faerie Queene* is a work which the twentieth century has found especially slippery to interpret, a book notoriously full of visual pleasures "not of the purest kind," a book whose major episodes William Hazlitt thought some of the finest things in Spenser.[1] (It is not accidental, given Hazlitt's perceptions about Spenser, that the episodes he singles out all exemplify the dynamics of desire and vision: the epiphany of Belphoebe, the House of Mammon, and the Bower of Bliss.) It is a book full of puzzles and surprises with which critics have wrestled as strenuously as Guyon does with his enemies. To make Guyon a classical hero, valuing classical ideals of self-sufficiency and fortitude, but to deprive him of the glamor of heroic furor and the glory of self-assertion, qualities that the Italian romance-epics relied on, is a surprise. To have Belphoebe burst into canto 3, bearing so little apparent relation to Guyon's fictive world that Harry Berger could invent the perennially useful notion of conspicuous ir-

---

[1]"The finest things in Spenser are, the character of Una, in the first book; the House of Pride; the Cave of Mammon, and the Cave of Despair; the account of Memory . . . ; the description of Belphoebe; the story of Florimel and the Witch's son; the Gardens of Adonis, and the Bower of Bliss; the Mask of Cupid; and Colin Clout's vision, in the last book." From "On Chaucer and Spenser," in *Lectures on the English Poets,* in *The Complete Works of William Hazlitt,* centenary ed., ed. P. P. Howe (London: J. M. Dent, 1930), 5.19–44 at 38.

relevance to account for her, is a surprise.[2] To punctuate the efforts of the earnest hero as he struggles with angry or hostile allegorical figures with the broad miles gloriosus comedy of Braggadochio and Trompart, and then to confront these characters with Belphoebe, is a surprise. To give to female characters like Phaedria and the nymphs of the fountain in the Bower of Bliss senses of humor that range from giggling silliness to ironic mockery of Guyon's solemnity—this is another surprise. To open with a Proem on the delights, the trustworthiness, and even the amorousness of outward ventures, then to close with a heroic allegorical journey over treacherous and destructive moral seas, the successful navigation of which requires recoil from the world into the constancy of the self—this is a surprise and a puzzle.

My aim in what follows is to look at some of the surprises of Book 2, and to consider them first as generic, hence tonal, choices and only then as ethical choices. Specifically, I want to look at them as Spenser's struggle with ways of reading Vergil—that is, with modes of imitation. The book is so slippery because it veers among diverse strains from Vergil's epic and from the Vergilian interpretive tradition; it is so interesting because of the ways that these strains work against each other and the ways that they are intersected by the occasional influences of Ovid and Queen Elizabeth.

Genre, Imitation, and Epideictic: The Spectacle of Belphoebe

The Faerie Queene is a romance, the données of the whole poem those of medieval chivalric romance: story elements of knights errant, the customs of castles, damsels who need aid, adventures and quests with spiritual significance, dragons and other monsters; values of spiritual and chivalric idealism, fealty to the sovereign, and the elevation of women; structural features like interlacing. Within this large chivalric romance are other species of the genus, like the Ariostan romance of Book 3 and the pastoral romance inset of Book 6. These are truisms of Spenser criticism; I adduce them here as a context for my arguments about the genre affiliations of Book 2 and the role of Book 2 in the movements of the whole epic. *The Faerie Queene* opens

[2]This chapter, like any work on *The Faerie Queene* 2 since 1957, must acknowledge a large and happy debt to Harry Berger's *The Allegorical Temper: Vision and Reality in Book 2 of Spenser's "Faerie Queene"* (New Haven: Yale University Press, 1957). For "conspicuous irrelevance," see 120–60.

with the legend of the Redcrosse Knight, a Spenserian form of medieval romance in which Una, not only socially and psychologically elevated as elsewhere in medieval romance but also metaphysically elevated as a bearer of the numinous, enriches and complicates her genre and paves the way for the role of women in the allegorical romance-epic genre of the middle books. Book 2, notwithstanding its retention of certain forms of chivalric romance, represents a complex withdrawal from that mode's representations of eros. What it offers instead is a bifold imitation of ancient epic, notably the *Odyssey* and the *Aeneid*.

The career of Spenser's hero in Book 2 is modelled on the careers of Homer's and Vergil's heroes as they were understood in the moral-allegorical interpretive tradition.[3] Guyon struggles to purge vices, to overcome the passions, to resist a spurious ambition, and to achieve a temperance that will free him from reliance on and attachment to any earthy resource but his interior self-possession. Like the careers of Ulysses and Aeneas in the allegorical commentaries, Guyon's career is arduous, the world harsh, threatening, and full of alluring deceptions. In Guyon's world as in the commentary, sensory perception is unreliable and even illusory; the virtues required to resist its imperious claims are vigilance, fortitude, skepticism, renunciation. The ethos of moralized epic is a stern and ascetic one; the hero must lose or turn from any external object in which he mistakenly vests value. Among the most important of these external objects are desirable and desired women characters, who may represent for the hero libidinal passion, sensual vice, capitulation to the world of sensory appearances, pleasure as opposed to virtue and responsible duty. Moral-allegorical commentary, for example, underscores the threat to Aeneas of the faintly decadent, Eastern opulence of Dido's world, while it underplays the Euripidean tragedy and the pathos of Vergil's heroine. Later allegorical romance-epic responds powerfully to this threatening female character type and draws on the *Odyssey's* Circe and Sirens as

---

[3]This tradition has been meticulously documented by Don Cameron Allen, *Mysteriously Meant: The Rediscovery of Pagan Symbolism and Allegorical Interpretation in the Renaissance* (Baltimore: Johns Hopkins Press, 1970), 83–106 and 135–62; Michael Murrin, *The Allegorical Epic: Essays in Its Rise and Decline* (Chicago: University of Chicago Press, 1980); Robert Lamberton, *Homer the Theologian: Neoplatonist Allegorical Reading and the Growth of the Epic Tradition* (Berkeley and Los Angeles: University of California Press, 1986). See also James Nohrnberg, *The Analogy of "The Faerie Queene"* (Princeton: Princeton University Press, 1976), 23–34, especially 29–30, on the educational intentions attributed to epic.

well as on the *Aeneid*'s queen for its fatal temptresses. Boiardo's *Orlando Innamorato*, says Michael Murrin, followed the precedent of the *Odyssey* in its multiplication of enchantresses, and the precedent of the *Aeneid* in making them mostly evil.[4] Hence Trissino's Acratia; Boiardo's Falerina, Dragontina, and Morgana; Ariosto's Alcina; and Tasso's Armida, from whom the heroes escape in passages imitative of Aeneas's departure from Dido. Hence also Guyon's great adversary Acrasia, and her servant Phaedria.

But for Spenser, this Vergilian moral arduousness, this skepticism about perception, this threat of passionate temptresses who destroy heroic manhood—these features of moralized epic are not the whole story. In the last chapter I described not only the darkness of Aeneas's struggle but also his awed responses to the grandeur of Venus and Dido, and Vergil's adaptions of Odyssean wonder before objects viewed. Spenser carries into *The Faerie Queene* 2 imitations of these passages. In doing so he follows Vergil's actual practice more than he does allegorical commentary on the *Aeneid*, while he transforms the Vergilian unreliability of vision's promise into vision's benign nourishment of human hungers. On the one hand there is Guyon's moralized epic career, with its dark and dangerous temptresses Acrasia and Phaedria, who descend ultimately from the *Odyssey* and the *Aeneid*, in a world where it is both mistaken and fatal to attempt fulfillment of the desires aroused by vision. On the other hand, in passages that lie outside Guyon's ken, Book 2 offers as spectacle certain bearers of numinous glory, notably Belphoebe, the Angel, and Queen Elizabeth as addressed in the Proem. In these passages Spenser encourages the reader not to resist perception like the hero but to give herself or himself to an expansive and exalted activity of vision. Moreover, these episodes elevate moralized epic's dangerous stimuli of woman, eros, and visual perception to the potentially healthy and admirable roles that they will play in the epic's middle books. The values of such episodes pull the moralized epic of Guyon's career back toward romance—that is, toward the romance-epic genre of Books 3 and 4.

This movement from moralized epic to Spenserian romance-epic, ultimately depending on the imitation of two strains in the *Aeneid*, happens partly because of the roles that Queen Elizabeth plays in *The Faerie Queene*. She provides the occasion of Spenserian inflections on

[4]Murrin, *Allegorical Epic*, 53, 126–27.

both Vergilian and Ovidian imitations. In the blazon of Belphoebe, for example, modelled with such explicit allusiveness on Venus's appearance before Aeneas, Elizabeth replaces the goddess as the person underlying the nymph's disguise. Yet the goddess herself remains as the ground of the imitative passage, bestowing lustre on both the fictive Belphoebe and the historical Elizabeth. Both of these, in turn, are images of the fuller, eikastic image of Gloriana. This complex glorification of woman is atypical of medieval romance and contrary to moralized epic with its predatory temptresses—on both counts unexpected, therefore, in Book 2, and worth some attention. Or again, Belphoebe's origins lie not only in the *Aeneid* but also in the *Metamorphoses*: she is an Ovidian nymph, and she and her sisters throughout *The Faerie Queene* owe their Spenserian developments partly to the facts that Belphoebe figures Elizabeth and that nymph-like chastity provides an especially decorous way to address the charged matter of Elizabeth's virginity. Both Spenser's genre interests and Elizabeth's roles as woman and ruler occasion the complex genre movements and imitations of Book 2, a book that gives us not only the harsh necessity of Guyon's suppression of responsiveness to perceptions but also Homero-Vergilian awe before objects viewed; not only the succubae sisters of Dido but also the Vergilian and Ovidian apprehension of the numinous woman.

The act of drawing Elizabeth into the poem as reader, patron, and inspiration, and the act of drawing on the domains of myth, lyric, and allegorical romance rhetoric that suffused epideictic art forms about her, import into Book 2 a functioning defense of imaginative activity which sits uneasily with the moral journey of Guyon as he battles the world and the flesh. One of the ways that Gloriana functions in the poem is to sanction an expansive, potentially exalted, and Aeneas-like imaginative "reading," to use Spenser's favorite umbrella term for interpretive engagement with objects in the world, whether in books or in visual perception. In episodes in which manifestations of the numinous enter Book 2, this imaginative reading or interpretive engagement is an act that characterizes both observer-characters, like Trompart beholding Belphoebe, and any literal readers of the poem, its audience. Trompart's words to Belphoebe are a parody of Aeneas's response to Venus but also a sincere echo of it; this kind of responsive engagement Spenser admires, as we can tell from the clear superiority of Trompart's words to Braggadochio's response. The crucial text for this argument about the value of interpretive engagement with objects of perception is the blazon of Belphoebe; to its tonal elements and their implications for imitation we now turn.

The description of Belphoebe and her contretemps with Bragga-dochio and Trompart (2.3) is famously indebted to Vergilian and Ovidian episodes, the powerful fusions of which have attracted elegant critical perceptions.[5] We have already looked in some detail at the salient passages in works of both ancient writers: Vergil weights the early books of his epic with the splendor of Venus and Dido, and with intimations of Diana; Ovid imagines a desired privacy of the self and its destructive, comic invasions by visual predators. As for Spenser's imitation—a key episode of a woman beheld which engages diversely with Vergil and Ovid, looking both to old books and to modern social realities—its polyvalence characterizes much of what I wish to argue for Spenser.

> Her yellow lockes crisped, like golden wyre,
>   About her shoulders weren loosely shed,
>   And when the winde emongst them did inspyre,
>   They waued like a penon wide dispred,
>   And low behinde her backe were scattered:
>   And whether art it were, or heedlesse hap,
>   As through the flouring forrest rash she fled,
>   In her rude haires sweet flowres themselues did lap,
> And flourishing fresh leaues and blossomes did enwrap.

> Such as *Diana* by the sandie shore
>   Of swift *Eurotas*, or on Cynthus greene,
>   Where all the Nymphes haue her vnwares forlore,
>   Wandreth alone with bow and arrowes keene,
>   To seeke her game: Or as that famous Queene
>   Of *Amazons*, whom *Pyrrhus* did destroy,

[5]See, for example, Edgar Wind, *Pagan Mysteries in the Renaissance*, rev. and enlarged ed. (New York: Norton, 1958), 76–80; Berger, *Allegorical Temper*, 120–60; Barbara Bono, *Literary Transvaluation: From Vergilian Epic to Shakespearean Tragicomedy* (Berkeley and Los Angeles: University of California Press, 1984), 70–75. Berger argues a different relationship between Belphoebe and Guyon than I do, one both intimate and allegorical: "And here lies the significance of Belphoebe: Guyon's turning away from the facts of mortality is embodied in her special and withdrawn excellence. Together, Belphoeban Honor and Shamefastnesse dramatize, or allegorize, the hero's sophrosyne" (195–202 at 199).

> The day that first of *Priame* she was seene,
>   Did shew her selfe in great triumphant ioy,
> To succour the weake state of sad afflicted *Troy*.
>
>   (2.3.30–31)

One of Spenser's possible, even likely, choices of tone in this passage could be Vergilian nostalgia at this manifestation of the numinous, since Belphoebe appears as an avatar of Vergil's Venus/Diana figures and of Ovid's chaste nymphs. But although Belphoebe repeats the radiance of Venus in *Aeneid* 1, elusiveness is not a marked feature in the description of Spenser's nymph. Within the simile, Diana is unaware of her own potential pathos in being "forlore"; her keen engagement with her rightful occupation keeps her from the problematic consciousness that Venus has of awakening desire in a viewer. Diana's concentration on the hunt is a mark and a guarantor of her self-containment and inner solitude, and a liberation for the reader from the intense regard of yearning between Vergil's Venus-within-a-Diana and her son. Belphoebe bolts finally, for reasons with which one can only sympathize, but she is not meant to tantalize and torment the observer with intimations of a splendor or intimacy denied. Rather, her appearance gratifies the viewer's hunger for an affluence of being guaranteed by Spenser's providential cosmos. This hunger is not freighted with Vergilian need, or with the narrator's awareness of the hopelessness of such need. With phrases like "pourtraict of bright Angels hew" (2.3.22), "when she presented was to sight" (2.3.26), "gazers sense with double pleasure fed" (2.3.22), Spenser urges the reader to trust the rectified sensory pleasure of Belphoebe's presence, to have the courage of the wishes she both arouses and feeds, and to gaze on her frankly. The language of the stanza, while acknowledging her attractiveness, imagines and addresses more precisely a deep, even infantile and non-gendered wish simply for proximity to her presence, experienced as gazing on her:

> Her face so faire as flesh it seemed not,
>   But heauenly pourtraict of bright Angels hew,
> Cleare as the skie, withouten blame or blot,
>   Through goodly mixture of complexions dew;
>   And in her cheekes the vermeill red did shew
>   Like roses in a bed of lillies shed,
>   The which ambrosiall odours from them threw,

And gazers sense with double pleasure fed,
Hable to heale the sicke, and to reuiue the ded.

(2.3.22)

Certain assumptions of this stanza make its readers into observers, along with the observers in the poem. The insistence on gratification of the senses is quite generous; the therapeutic powers of Belphoebe's presence match, in their active giving forth, the presumably deep desires of her viewers, and the hunger of all the senses is acknowledged. Her kindling of felicity is of such potency as to bear thaumaturgic powers to those who gaze at her. The observer characters, it is important to note, are comic characters; Spenser need not pity them, nor anticipate their catastrophes with proleptic nostalgia, as Vergil does. He is instead liberated from pathos to hail the providential arrangements of a universe that can grant such manifestations. Belphoebe's presence is saluted, admired, even fed upon—in an important trope drawn from Renaissance medical understandings of anatomy—without the Vergilian tensions created by need in an intractable world.

Physical distance between observer and observed in the *Aeneid* is often a sign of loss or of the inability to sustain the contact promised by initial vision; witness the space that marks Dido's distance from Aeneas as he prepares the fleet for departure. In that episode, the crowding of fruitful activity into space perceived at a distance serves to mark Dido's unwanted and unwonted estrangement from Aeneas. Spenser's happier sense in *The Faerie Queene* that space and distance may preserve the integrity, the solitude, and the alterity of the observed character comes rather from Ovid's *Metamorphoses*; the two poets share a palpable apprehension of sylvan space as potential sanctuary (though Ovid's characters are more regularly disappointed of this wish, and in nastier ways, than Spenser's characters).

The reader's point of observation is initially with Trompart, standing to one side while Belphoebe enters grandly ("step[s] forth") into a demarcated central space. The narrator provides a temporal and spatial scope in which to evaluate her social standing through the telling details of her surface:

But *Trompart* stoutly stayd to taken heed,
Of what might hap. Eftsoone there stepped forth
A goodly Ladie clad in hunters weed,

> That seemd to be a woman of great worth,
> And by her stately portance, borne of heauenly birth.
>
> (2.3.21)

In the *Aeneid*, as we have seen, the description of the huntress-goddess is pressed hard for its effects of pathos by the immediate burden of Aeneas's nine-line speech expressing yearning as well as awe: "o dea certe!...leves, quaecumque, laborem" (*Aen.* 1.328–30); Venus literally creates distance between herself and her son by moving away from him at the very moment of her epiphany. But Spenser's Belphoebe stands still, as it were, for our benefit, and Spenser suspends the response of his characters, bestowing instead the dilation of ten more descriptive stanzas. Those stanzas are preceded by Braggadochio's dive into the bushes, and followed by the comic mutation of "o dea certe!" into Trompart's quivering "O Goddesse, (for such I thee take to bee)" (2.3.33). In the figurative spaciousness of those ten descriptive stanzas, the watcher's distance (which the reader shares) thus metamorphoses from Vergil's pathos to the blessing of a distance that enables awed contemplation, a distance bestowed by the narrator's tone; he reverses the anxiety that is a necessary response to reality in Vergil's world. Belphoebe's is a presence *granted* to us and to Trompart, as Venus's presence never is allowed Aeneas.

This inflection of Vergil's episode occurs in an ideal portrait of Elizabeth, whose presence in early parts of the book complicates and enriches the generic norms of the moralized epic, as I have suggested. Belphoebe figures the Queen in her fusion of the erotic and the majestic, the Queen who is the focus of Spenser's desire for acknowledgment by a woman in whom authority and love unite. Spenser's intricate, tentative relationship with the Queen becomes a salient emphasis of the imitation—the Queen whom he both addresses and depicts (questions of tact thus arise), who is potential patron as well as Muse (raising questions of the practical colliding with the ideal), and who is the beneficiary of the narrator's epideictic rhetoric. Elizabeth, as we know, challenged the imaginative capacities of her courtiers to find new and provoking ways of acknowledging her power in forms of love, and of acknowledging love itself. For a poet the challenge was multilayered. Spenser's work tries to establish with Elizabeth a traditional poet-patron relationship, which in the 1590s was still predominantly a male-to-male bond and traditionally a public one. But it also establishes her as the poet's Muse, a relationship that is traditionally male-to-female, and traditionally private and imaginative. Elizabeth's persona fuses but does not blend these roles, and both consequently become more volatile, more charged with hope and with anxiety. The presiding of Elizabeth destabilizes literary conventions, but it energizes them, too.

Belphoebe's comic and wonderful eruption into the poem is a salute to Elizabeth's presence. For a moment, the norms of allegorical epic, and the traditional moral-allegorical depiction of the temptress-woman, no longer apply; nor does the traditional epistemological mistrust of objects viewed. Elizabeth's presence both within and outside the blazon, and the concomitant glorification of woman, stand outside the moralized epic; hence the decorous tonal qualities of Spenser's pleasurable and sustained depiction of Belphoebe. His admiration is also intimate and affectionate; hence the ease with which he can convey not only her grandeur but also her girlishness. With this warmly admiring distance, Spenser is free, for instance, to admire and convey Belphoebe's nascent sexuality:

> And in her hand a sharpe bore-speare she held,
>   And at her backe a bow and quiuer gay,
>   Stuft with steele-headed darts, wherewith she queld
>   The saluage beastes in her victorious play,
>   Knit with a golden bauldricke, which forelay
>   Athwart her snowy brest, and did diuide
>   Her daintie paps; which like young fruit in May
>   Now little gan to swell, and being tide,
> Through her thin weed their places only signifide.
>
> (2.3.29)

Imitation plays a role also in the relation of the blazon to its entire episode, as the larger Ovidian context of the episode impinges on Vergilian vision. Belphoebe's meeting with Braggadochio and Trompart counterpoints two Roman voices—as Vergil confronts Ovid, epic elevation meets comic deflation in a mongrel form always congenial to Spenser. The consequences are both generic and social. I have already argued that Ovid depicts the desire to trust the protectiveness of invisibility; the comic and violent world of the *Metamorphoses* relies partly on the ways hiddenness, spying, and exposure create piquant plot dispositions of power and helplessness. Spenser raises related issues of sight and power, through a parodic Ovidian plot, with manifold effects. One is to distinguish between power as aggression (Braggadochio's) and power as majesty (Belphoebe's), and thus to define Gloriana's "dear dred" as benignly as possible—an ethical distinction that allows Spenser a tactful gesture toward the Queen.

Another effect is to distinguish different kinds of visual regard. Voyeurism, distinguished from other forms of covert watching, may be wicked and destructive, as Spenser proposes elsewhere in his poem; but in this episode Spenser clearly has no objection to Trompart's prolonged, marvelling contemplation of Belphoebe, nor to the reader-viewer's total immersion in the beautiful dilations of her description. How and why is this kind of viewing sanctioned? Why is the reader invited to be a gazer upon Belphoebe's resplendence? Why are we encouraged to pause for so many stanzas over her solitary absorption, and how does Spenser differentiate such a readerly action from spying or voyeurism?

One answer lies in a simple plot detail. Trompart and Braggadochio are surprised by Belphoebe's appearance in their world, and so are the readers: our literary parallel to their social surprise stems from the unexpectedness and incongruity of Belphoebe's presence in Guyon's book, an incongruity so pronounced and so remarked by readers that Harry Berger accounted for it with the wonderful notion of conspicuous irrelevance. The unexpectedness of Belphoebe's entrance and of her glamor and the accidental nature of her revelation are characteristic of other characters in the poem, most notably Britomart, and this kind of entrance regularly evokes a benign and legitimate gaze from bystanders in *The Faerie Queene*. Moreover—to suggest a second answer—this benign responsive gaze is often depicted as an imitation of Aeneas's response to Venus in *Aeneid* 1; so Trompart echoes Aeneas with the opening of his reply to Belphoebe's business-like query about the deer that she has been hunting: "O Goddesse, (for such I thee take to bee) / For neither doth thy face terrestriall shew, / Nor voyce sound mortall" (2.3.33). And it is Spenser's imitations of *Aeneid* 1 in the blazon which encourage the reader toward an Aeneas-like, sanctioned, wondering gaze.

Third, once we have granted this Aeneas-like predisposition in the reader-viewer, it is also the case that the reader's lingering absorption in the heavily visual description is made possible just *because* of Belphoebe's assumption of solitude. The integrity of her interior solitude is manifest in this episode through the charm of her Ovidian candor, her perfect openness and presence only to herself and her pursuits. This openness, this engagement with the hunt, and this utter absorp-

tion in her own life occur "independently of . . . any audience," in
Stanley Cavell's words.[6] Insofar as Belphoebe's self-possession is constituted regardless of a possible watcher, the reader-viewer may legitimately and actively enjoy the extended vision that Spenser offers.
Her self-possession is on one level a simple matter of being unaware
that Trompart and Braggadocchio quake nearby. But it is also a matter
of her being completely un-self-conscious and at ease, because no one
has yet broken into her inner solitude. The awareness of the subjectivity of another will happen, in a limited way, when she encounters
Timias in Book 3; here she is immersed fully and innocently in a
resplendence both natural and spiritual.

In Belphoebe's meeting with Braggadochio, it is the failure of the
braggart knight's vision which is at issue, or the failure of his sensibility to register the glory borne by the body he sees. Belphoebe is an
Ovidian chaste huntress-nymph, suffused with Vergilian splendor but
Ovidian in her natural affinity for hidden and private places and in
the emphasis on the intactness of her identity. Braggadochio is a
debased cousin of the predatory and comic Jove who hides from Juno
in a cloud. And the Ovidian Jove's precarious purchase on his own
godly dignity becomes Braggadochio's marvelous complacence. But
by an intricate set of comic inversions, this Ovidian aggressor first
leaps into the bushes only for the purpose of protecting himself; hiding
is an act not of power but of cowardice for him, and exposure, far
from the humiliation that it brings to Ovid's Jove, becomes a way of
restoring his false sense of self-esteem:

> As fearefull fowle, that long in secret caue
>   For dread of soaring hauke her selfe hath hid,
>   Not caring how, her silly life to saue,
>   She her gay painted plumes disorderid,
>   Seeing at last her selfe from daunger rid,
>   Peepes foorth, and soone renewes her natiue pride;
>   She gins her feathers foule disfigured
>   Proudly to prune, and set on euery side,
> So shakes off shame, ne thinks how erst she did her hide.
>
> (2.3.36)

Even the talk between Belphoebe and Braggadochio carries on a comic
version of Ovidian characters' concern with privacy and hiddenness.

---

[6]Stanley Cavell, *The World Viewed: Reflections on the Ontology of Film*, enlarged
ed. (Cambridge: Harvard University Press, 1979), 111.

The hiddenness to which Ovid's characters entrust their secrets or intimacies is continually being exposed to the prying eyes of a garrulous and gossipy social world, the very world Braggadochio recommends to Belphoebe. (It is also the world of the court, the values of which are placed in the mouth of a fool.) But his vulgar valuation of display she scorns as promiscuous and contemptible. Display, so powerful a value generally in Renaissance culture, is here a dark inversion of the Vergilian *revelation* that Belphoebe simply carries as part of her identity.

The lack of subtlety in Braggadochio's attempt on Belphoebe can be so brightly comic because after the reader's Vergilian witness in the blazon it is clear to all observers but himself that Braggadocchio is no match for her majesty. Nor is he a match for the sensibility of the reader; Spenser has openly made use of our easy superiority to his philistinism. As a courtier he lacks all the necessary perceptual skills, and his rapid and automatic progression from sight to violent desire characterizes him as a crude Ovidian observer. The contrast between Vergilian and Ovidian watchers is strengthened by Trompart, who functions here as a liminal figure. He is affiliated with Braggadochio, but his sturdy refusal to join him in the bushes aligns Trompart with the reader and narrator instead. He is foolish but also imaginative, and this allows him to carry into the poem Aeneas's response to Venus, "O dea certe!"

This comedy of Braggadochio's response further helps to circumvent a Vergilian tone of pathos in an episode of beholding a numinous woman, while Trompart's parodic but moving Vergilian response deflects the Ovidian aggressiveness of his companion. These mutual controls that Vergilian and Ovidian imitations exert on each other have a couple of effects. First, Belphoebe's innocence will survive; Spenser thus bows to the chastity of her regal British analogue. The survival of her chastity also makes possible a longer and richer narrative life for Belphoebe than any of Ovid's nymphs can have. Second, we are offered the Vergilian grandeur of Venus and Dido and the freshness of Ovidian nymphs, but without the consciousness of imminent loss present in Vergil's and Ovid's tales; instead, the positive qualities of Vergil's and Ovid's female characters are offered as a sustaining vision, on which readers may feed their hungry gazer's sense. Elizabeth's presence sanctions, and perhaps partially makes possible, these inflections in this episode of Belphoebe observed. Such inflections move toward a glorification of woman and toward a notion of visual perception as reliable and exalted knowledge, both of which Spenser has used earlier in his poetry, but which are uncharacteristic of moralized epic and of Guyon's career.

So we may try to supplement Thomas Greene's observations about Spenser's imitative practice, and especially to account for the fact that Spenser cannot be one of the heroes of Greene's book because he is so untroubled by historic "rupture" between himself and older poets. Spenser's practice in the blazon is eclectic rather than heuristic or dialectical, and allows him the flexibility to maneuver in his typically elusive and idiosyncratic way.[7] He uses imitation to reflect not chiefly on his relation to a past father poet and not at all on his relation to a lost past, but on his relation to a present feminine figure of order and harmony, and to allow the exfoliation of favored subjects and ethical questions through the encounter of one ancient text with another.

This notion of perception appears not only in Belphoebe's appearance but also in the Proem, the book's most explicit acknowledgment of the Queen's presence and a request for her sanctioning gaze on Spenser's fictive "mirrhour" of "Faerie lond." The rhetorical courtesy of the stanzas tactfully assumes her understanding regard and addresses the bulk of Spenser's advice to a hypothesized "he," whose skepticism and hostility must be disarmed before the story begins. As in the blazon, the Queen's presence licenses what we might call an epistemological optimism, quite at odds with the necessary mistrust of Guyon's *Aeneid*-based career of sacrifice and self-containment.

> But let that man with better sence aduize,
>   That of the world least part to vs is red:
>   And dayly how through hardy enterprize,
>   Many great Regions are discouered,

[7]Greene's important passing comments on Spenser, while true enough by the categories of his book, provoke some attempt to articulate how Spenser does approach imitation. These passages are from *The Light in Troy: Imitation and Discovery in Renaissance Poetry* (New Haven: Yale University Press, 1982): "Spenser's brilliant 'Epithalamion', a triumph of diachronic poetry, must be weighed against *The Faerie Queene*, where the historical self-consciousness seems sporadic and dim, and where the use of Homer, to take a single example, in the twelfth canto of book 2 lacks etiological firmness" (270); "[Spenser] appears ... as a poet whose loyalty to his own medieval roots limits his room for poetic maneuver, as one unconcerned with the exercise of bridging a rupture and playing with the differences between the separated worlds" (273–74).

Which to late age were neuer mentioned.
Who euer heard of th'Indian *Peru?*
Or who in venturous vessell measured
The *Amazons* huge riuer now found trew?
Or fruitfullest *Virginia* who did euer vew?

Yet all these were, when no man did them know;
    Yet haue from wisest ages hidden beene:
    And later times things more vnknowne shall show.
    Why then should witlesse man so much misweene
    That nothing is, but that which he hath seene?
    What if within the Moones faire shining spheare?
    What if in euery other starre vnseene
    Of other worldes he happily should heare?
He wonder would much more: yet such to some appeare.

                                             (2.Proem.2–3)

This address to the imagined hostile reader grants the implications
of some crucial shifts between the poem's first two books. In leaving
the framework of biblical truth of Book 1, Spenser ventures into
fantastic geographical truths and into the more purely imaginative
realm of Faerie. The stanzas of the Proem, by assimilating imaginative
and visionary truth to geographical truths, hint that he recognizes
and tries to forestall a possible tension in the reader about his accepting this liberty. The capacity for viewing is identical with the
capacity to incorporate his book, as Spenser's characteristic use of
the verb *to read* suggests.[8] The imagination is presented in stanzas 2
and 3 with whole worlds unexpected, exotic, fecund, as well as with
the "venturous" and exhilarating act of exploration itself; the reader/
spectator is invited to participate in visualizing new worlds. The whole
imaginative enterprise here is happily hyperbolic, as when Spenser
entertains the possibility of life on the moon. The anticipated aggressiveness of the reader in stanza 1 is gradually channeled into
tenderer imaginative actions; from the bold "hardy enterprize" of
geographical discovery Spenser moves to the more delicate mental
action of imagining and holding in regard the very hiddenness of
these places and their ancient secrecy of an ongoing life inaccessible to European vision: "Yet all these were, when no man did them

---

[8]See Anne Ferry's discussion of Spenser's use of the verb *to read* in the context of
other Renaissance usages, in *The Art of Naming* (Chicago: University of Chicago
Press, 1988), 9–48 at 10–15.

know; / Yet haue from wisest ages hidden beene." The reader, his energy thus channeled from hostility to exploration and then tamed to appreciative wonder, learns that hiddenness is as desirable a condition as the activity of discovery. The imaginative work that conceives both hiddenness and discovery urges a benign expansion of selfhood through trust in a rectified vision.[9]

Hence it seems to me unlikely that the mirror in which Elizabeth may view herself is the New World simply, or that when Spenser urges her to see her "owne realmes" in "lond of Faery" (2.Proem.4) the wonder of the preceding stanzas is deflected into an act of colonial domination by which American lands are made narcissistic pools for Elizabeth, both suggestions proposed by Stephen Greenblatt.[10] Spenser is at pains to guard the alterity of these marvels, to let neither the reader's potential hostility nor the compelling glow of Gloriana obscure the contours of the world:

> ...ne let him then admire,
> But yield his sence to be too blunt and bace,
> That n'ote without an hound fine footing trace.
>
> · · · · ·
>
> The which [mirror of Faery land] O pardon me thus to enfold
> In couert vele, and wrap in shadowes light,

[9]The sequence of actions from aggression to "hardy enterprize" and exploration to the imaginative regard of hiddenness suggests that Spenser is happy to let the Americas remain hidden territory, in spite of the typical ferocity of colonization of his age. Contrast a passage from Ralegh's *Discoverie of the Large, Rich, and Bewtiful Empyre of Guiana*, which Stephen Greenblatt cites in *Sir Walter Ralegh: The Renaissance Man and His Roles* (New Haven: Yale University Press, 1973) to illustrate the tensions between Ralegh's "primitivism and his plans for the exploitation of Guiana" (112): "To conclude, Guiana is a Contrey that hath yet her Maydenhead, never sackt, turned, nor wrought, the face of the earth hath not beene torne, nor the vertue and salt of the soyle spent by manurance, the graves have not beene opened for gold, the mines not broken with sledges, nor their Images puld down out of their temples" (p. 73). The Ralegh citation is from the edition of V. T. Harlow (London, 1928).

[10]Greenblatt, *Renaissance Self-Fashioning: From More to Shakespeare* (Chicago: University of Chicago Press, 1980), 191: "In an instant the 'other world' has been transformed into a mirror; the queen turns her gaze upon a shining sphere hitherto hidden from view and sees her own face, her own realms, her own ancestry. That which threatens to exist independent of religious and sexual ideology, that is, of what we believe—'Yet all these were, when no man did them know'—is revealed to be the ideal image of that ideology. And hence it need not be feared or destroyed: iconoclasm gives way to appropriation, violence to colonization."

> That feeble eyes your glory may behold,
> Which else could not endure those beames bright.
>
> (2.Proem.4, 5)

The "exceeding light" of the Queen threatens to obscure both the New World of America and the new world of Spenser's poem. The conceit of light in stanza 5 is thus not only a compliment, not only a figure for allegorical poetry, but also an announcement that the precise relationship between author and poem is one of protective custody. The envisioning activity of Gloriana (also Gloriana envisioned) may fuel and inspire but will not be allowed to usurp his poem. Spenser resists colonization of the alien land and the aggressiveness of vision in this book (just the problems he wrestles with in Book 5). Imaginative tools for entering and regarding Faerie are not available to the mind "too blunt and bace"; the reader-adventurer to whom this advice is directed must move delicately. He, and indirectly the Queen, is cautioned to look with a wise passiveness that will not violate the elusiveness of the hidden with a reductive and compulsive teleology.

In the Absence of Belphoebe: Guyon and the Allegorical Epic

Adventurousness, exhilaration, the delight of looking and knowing, eager responsiveness to the promise of the beckoning world—these are astonishing values with which to launch a book the hero of which is encased cap-à-pied in armor, and the moral spokesman of which advocates caution, retraction of the self, mistrust of woman, mistrust of the physical world, mistrust of the temptation to pleasure, and resistance to impulsive response. Guyon is easily the most maligned and least likable of Spenser's protagonists, not excepting even Artegall. He is not brilliant; he does not cut a dashing figure; he misses some of the best episodes in his own book; he has scant access to other characters' affection—a quality that allows us to care for that other difficult hero, Artegall.

It is styles of morality which Spenser is at pains to delineate in this contrast between the values of the Proem and of hero, and it is by means of choices in the exercise of sight, choices divided between hero and narrator, that they are sketched. In a book the opening of which urges the delighted faculty of intelligent vision, Guyon sees little and knows less of delight or of intelligent perception. He does not see Belphoebe, one potent manifestation of feminine power; he cannot see the Angel from the spiritual world; he only dimly perceives (though he responds to) the intense erotic allure of the Bower and the benign venerean power adumbrated momentarily within it. Nor does he see these realms of goddesses, new worlds, and Christian spiritual opulence as they are refracted through the poet's troping power.

By this last statement I do not mean to suggest that Guyon is culpable for some failure to appreciate Spenser's similes and other tropes. I do mean to argue that the diction and moral rhetoric characterizing Guyon's response to spectacle differ noticeably and significantly from that used in some other contexts by the narrator. I do mean to argue that the structure of Book 2 precludes the hero of moralized epic from perceiving important spectacles accessible to other characters, and that this structure is a meaningful commentary on the strengths and limits of Guyon's heroism. The reader/spectator learns to see in a mode sanctioning wonder before objects viewed, a mode that does greater justice to the viewed object than Guyon's moral-allegorical mode of sight can. Guyon can show compassion and endurance, as Aeneas did, but Guyon does not share Aeneas's imaginative sympathy: sight never becomes vision, nor perception apperception, for him. Nor can it do so, in the moralized epic world that he inhabits. In spite of the companionship of the Palmer and occasional encounters with friends like Redcrosse, Arthur, Medina, or Alma, Guyon is generally isolated and stranded in a world of inexplicably threatening forces, working hard to remain self-contained and self-preserved, a little island of firmly guarded humanity amid the beautiful, deadly flux of oceanic chaos.

Sight (like the other senses) in this book is intromissive, as diction repeatedly suggests. In the Bower of Bliss, Guyon allows no delight of the "faire aspect" to "sincke into his sence" (2.12.53). The nymphs' virtuoso performance in the fountain is a "secret pleasaunce" that his "stubborne brest gan . . . to embrace" (2.12.65). When Guyon enters Mammon's house, gazing in wonder, he "[d]id feed his eyes, and fild his inner thought" (2.7.24); to protect himself from the power of these penetrating sights, he makes a barrier out of his own noble ideal, expressed in a visual idiom: "Another blis before mine eyes I place" (2.7.33). Cymochles makes the most of the passivity of intromissive senses, especially sight, and its internal and visceral effects, in an episode to which we will return: "his fraile eye with spoyle of beautie feedes; / ... Whereby close fire into his heart does creepe" (2.5.34). Phaedria "feeds" and "fills" Cymochles' eyes with false delights (2.6.14), and in a positive instance of the same phenomenon which we have already seen, Belphoebe feeds "gazers sense" with "double pleasure" (2.3.22).

Renaissance optics still hung poised among antique theories of extramissive and intromissive sight; it was not until Kepler that a radically new concept of the retinal image cleared the way for redefinition of the terms of the debate. But philosophy, psychology, physiology— all supported the popular causal link between sight and desire. To exchange flirtatious glances was, in a common idiom, "to make babies."[11] One of the most far-ranging and eloquent discourses on sight, the Paris physician André Du Laurens's *A Discourse of the Preservation of the Sight*, presents among the reasons for the pre-eminence of sight among the senses the Platonic argument that the sight of the world's objects "ravishes" the mind; in Richard Surphlet's lovely English translation of Du Laurens we find the primal plots of love and love poetry:

> Yea tell me, how many soules have lost their libertie through the sight of the eyes? Doe not men say that that little wanton, that blind archer doth enter into our hearts by this doore, and that love is shaped by the glittering glimces which issue out of the eyes, or rather by certain subtile and thin spirits, which passe from the heart to the eye through a straite and narrow way very secretly, and having deceived this porter, doe place love within, which by little and little doth make it selfe Lord of the house, and casteth reason out of doores?[12]

And the spirit that fills the eye in love, "(sayth the same Philosopher [Aristotle]) are full of spirit and seede: and this is the reason, why in

---

[11]On "making babies," see W. C. Bolland's note in *Notes and Queries*, ser. 8, no. 63 (11 March 1893), 181–83.

[12]M. Andreas Laurentius, *A Discourse on the Preservation of the Sight; of Melancholike Diseases; of Rheumes, and of Old Age,* trans. Richard Surphlet (1599), with an introduction by Sanford V. Larkey, Shakespeare Association Facsimiles No. 15 (London: Humphrey Milford, Oxford University Press, for the Shakespeare Association), 12. Du Laurens's book is one of a large body of works on vision linked to others in the disciplines of medicine, anatomy, and philosophy in the period. I cite it because it admirably surveys the current theories on its subject, and because it is the most beautiful and ambitious in its language.

new married persons, they bee so much the lesser and as it were languishing."[13]

Du Laurens shows himself to be a selective and optimistic reader of Plato in his adherence to one of Plato's several lines of thought on the value of vision: "Plato for the honour he bare unto this divine part, called it celestiall and heavenly, he beleeveth that the eye is all full of such straines and fire as the starres have, which shineth and burneth not."[14] Plato's legacy to the Renaissance on the relationships of vision and eros is in fact much more mixed. For Renaissance thinkers, Plato's work articulated an ancient understanding of the dangers of the passional, of the erotic madness of attachment to unique and therefore contingent individuals—a madness awakened through the eye—and of passivity or sufferance as a mode of address to the world.[15] These values characterize Plato's anthropology in such works as the *Republic* and the *Phaedo*. On the other hand, he is also the source of the West's most powerful myths on the irreducible value of Beauty, of vision, of the courage to suffer the risk of erotic madness and attachments to unique individuals, as in the choices presented in the *Symposium* or in the *Phaedrus*. In the latter work, as Martha Nussbaum points out, "Beauty is, among the valuable things in the world, the 'most evident' and the 'most lovable' (250D-E). We 'apprehend it through the clearest of our senses as it gleams most clearly' (D1–3); this stirs our emotions and appetites, motivating us to undertake its pursuit."[16]

In the episodes of *The Faerie Queene* 2 which share the classical ethos of moralized epic, intromissive sight is treacherous, and when Acrasia is accused of sucking men's sprights from them, there is a crucial identity, not merely an analogy, between the physical and spiritual actions in that expense of spirit. Images of viewed objects enter the eye and then threaten to undermine the constancy of the identity by awakening destructive drives for perishable and deceptive objects. The model of physical energy in this classical ethos derives from the depiction of the soul in the *Phaedrus*, with the charioteer of the soul trying to control the violent, ugly steed of passion and to encourage the glorious steed of rational aspiration. In Spenser's re-

[13]Ibid., 21.

[14]Ibid., 19.

[15]For a recent and eloquent analysis, see Martha Nussbaum, *The Fragility of Goodness: Luck and Ethics in Greek Tragedy and Philosophy* (Cambridge: Cambridge University Press, 1986), 1–21, 85–233.

[16]Ibid., 214.

daction of this struggle, Guyon notoriously loses his horse and becomes a pedestrian hero, to borrow Northrop Frye's still unhackneyed pun.[17] He struggles with the passions, especially furor, as they are awakened in him, but he tries to prevent their awakening in the first place by hardening himself against intromissive sights. But since Plato also privileges sight as the means of perception of value through love, Guyon also prevents the Platonic divine madness (Spenser's "kindly rage") which finally allows Socrates' charioteer to contemplate the beloved after the *agon* with the steed of passion:

> Humbled in the end, he obeys the counsel of his driver, and when he sees the fair beloved is like to die of fear. Wherefore at long last the soul of the lover follows after the beloved with reverence and awe.[18]

Elsewhere in the *Phaedrus,* intromissive sight is the agent of love, and the passive capacity for visual amazement creates the possibility of recollection of a plenitude of transcendent being:

[17]See Northrop Frye, "The Structure of Imagery in *The Faerie Queene,"* *University of Toronto Quarterly* 30 (1961), 109–27 at 115; rpt. in his *Fables of Identity: Studies in Poetic Mythology* (New York: Harcourt, Brace and World, 1963), 69–87 at 75.
[18]*Phaedrus* 254E, trans R. Hackforth, *The Collected Dialogues of Plato,* ed. Edith Hamilton and Huntington Cairns (New York: Pantheon Books, 1961), 475–525 at 500. For central remarks on the dynamics of vision, see *Timaeus* 45B–D, trans. Benjamin Jowett, ibid., 1151–1211 at 1173: "And of the organs they [the gods] first contrived the eyes to give light, and the principle according to which they were inserted was as follows. So much of fire as would not burn, but gave a gentle light, they formed into a substance akin to the light of everyday life, and the pure fire which is within us and related thereto they made to flow through the eyes in a stream smooth and dense.... When the light of day surrounds the stream of vision, then like falls upon like, and they coalesce, and one body is formed by natural affinity in the line of vision, wherever the light that falls from within meets with an external object. And the whole stream of vision... diffuses the motions of what it touches or what touches it over the whole body, until they reach the soul, causing that perception which we call sight." See also *Theaetetus* 156D–E, trans. F. M. Cornford, ibid., 845–919, which discusses emanations from the object viewed in its long treatment of perception and knowledge.

Plato's theory of intraocular fire includes both extramissive and intromissive movements, in a sequential relation. This formulation of sight, especially when supplemented by that of the *Phaedrus,* eludes any easy attribution of volition or passivity. The motions of objects enter the soul in a process active though unwilled, vis-à-vis both the viewer and the object; these motions *may* then arouse (in the *Phaedrus*) desire and will; but desire and will for access to the beloved viewed object are understood as erotic *sufferings* of the soul, something wished for but also something undergone. This paradox of passion is complicated further by the fusion of eye-fire with daylight, such that the stream meeting the object and bearing its motions back to the soul is not simply an emanation from the self; not only the external object but also the medium of transmission constitutes the not-self borne into the soul.

But when one who is fresh from the mystery, and saw much of the vision, beholds a godlike face or bodily form that truly expresses beauty, first there comes upon him a shuddering and a measure of that awe which the vision inspired, and then reverence as at the sight of a god. ... For by reason of the stream of beauty entering in through his eyes there comes a warmth, whereby his soul's plumage is fostered; and with that warmth the roots of the wings are melted, which for long had been so hardened and closed up that nothing could grow. ... As she [the soul] gazes upon the boy's beauty, she admits a flood of particles streaming therefrom—that is why we speak of a "flood of passion"—whereby she is warmed and fostered; then has she respite from her anguish, and is filled with joy. But when she has been parted from him and become parched, the openings of those outlets at which the wings are sprouting dry up likewise and are closed. ... At last she does behold him, and lets the flood pour in upon her, releasing the imprisoned waters; then has she refreshment and respite from her stings and sufferings, and at that moment tastes a pleasure that is sweet beyond compare.[19]

The actions of eye and soul in this most beautiful of Plato's fables of eros enter Neoplatonism along with the *Symposium*'s account of the ascent of a hierarchy of beauties toward the One; these models of vision and desire are assimilated to the responses of vision to beauty in courtly love lyric and in Dante. This loose alliance underlies and makes possible treatments of love throughout Renaissance culture, from the systematic Platonic commentaries of Ficino and the *trattati d'amore* of those influenced by him, to lyric, dramatic, and narrative genres. It underlies the operations of love in Spenser's *Hymns* and in the romance-epic middle books of *The Faerie Queene*. In its exaltation of sight and the hungers aroused through sight, and in its optimism that the perceived beauty of the beloved is revelatory of divine beauty, it underlies the actions of sight in the blazon of Belphoebe, the Proem, and the description of the Angel.

But the model of desire which exalts sight and the hungers aroused through the eye is opposite to the model upon which Guyon's moral career rests, in which intromissive sight is understood as treacherous. When the narrator is alongside Guyon, so to speak, sharing his adventures and his experience of the hard, hostile world of moralized epic, he becomes a spokesman not for exalted Homero-Vergilian vision but for the harder necessities of resistance to the desires that

[19]*Phaedrus* 251A–E, ibid., 497–98.

sight arouses. Then Spenser quite suppresses the Vergilian narrator's capacities for tenderness.

In Guyon's world, reflected by the language of the poet as well as by that of the Palmer, there is not much alternative except to "bind with briers our joys and desires," as Guyon binds Occasion in chains. In this world it is impossible to suggest the identity of joys and desires, as Blake does, because "Wrath is a fire, and gealosie a weede, / Griefe is a floode, and loue a monster fell" (2.4.35). The only possible response is a stern recoil from the world and from the passions; it is significant that the Palmer's lines just quoted occur in a stanza that joins in a tangled knot "weede...breede...flood...monster fell...Monster filth...decay." There seems no alternative to suppression of human responsiveness to such "filth," because any movement out of the self—toward man, Nature, or woman—makes the self prey to treachery and violence:

> The knight was greatly moued at his [Pyrochles'] plaint,
>   And gan him dight to succour his distresse,
>   Till that the Palmer, by his graue restraint,
>   Him stayd from yielding pitifull redresse;
>   And said, Deare sonne, thy causelesse ruth represse,
>   Ne let thy stout hart melt in pitty vayne.
>
> (2.5.24)

When I discussed Aeneas's meeting with Dido in the underworld in *Aeneid* 6, I purposely neglected the larger context of the passage in order to adduce other points about it. But Aeneas's visit to the underworld reflects in important ways upon Guyon's visit to the House of Mammon, and deserves attention here.

Aeneas's visit to the underworld is an anomaly in the context of the rest of the epic, in one respect at least. For it is the only episode in which sight, so far from existing in tension with a thwarted impulse to action, is instead meant to be a direct inciter of action:

> sic tota passim regione vagantur
> aëris in campis latis atque omnia lustrant.
> quae postquam Anchises natum per singula duxit
> incenditque animum famae venientis amore,
> exim bella viro memorat quae deinde gerenda,

Laurentisque docet populos urbemque Latini,
et quo quemque modo fugiatque feratque laborem.

(Aen. 6.886–92)

[... Thus they wander the whole region in broad and misty fields, and survey everything. After Anchises has led his son through these prospects one by one, and kindled his spirit with the love of fame to come, he tells him what wars were to be waged afterward, and informs him about the Laurentians and the city of Latinus, and about how he might shun or bear each task.]

The meetings that Aeneas has in the underworld affirm rather than block nearly every important relation that he has with other persons (Creusa does not appear). Palinurus addresses him as "dux Anchisiade," a double acknowledgment of relations that persist beyond death. Palinurus also beseeches Aeneas to bury him "per spes surgentis Iuli," "by the rising hope of Iulus" *(Aen.* 6.364) and although Aeneas will not in fact be able to bury his pilot, Vergil's pity for him extends to the Sybil, who consoles him with the prophecy of his eventual role in the life of the living. Even in death, Palinurus is granted a social context *(Aen.* 6.372–83).

The mutual openness of Aeneas and the spirits one to another is the most powerful and surprising thing about the episode, given the pained or shattered personal relations in the world above. For the most part, mutual viewing provides access to real meeting, here as nowhere else in the epic. And the exceptions prove the rule. We have seen the pathos of Dido's refusal to acknowledge Aeneas. But he is shocked into frankness about his feelings toward her; Vergil makes explicit what could not be spoken in Book 4: "demisit lacrimas dulcique adfatus amore est," "he shed tears, and spoke to her with sweet love" *(Aen.* 6.455). Moreover, though the desolation of the scene is paramount, even Dido is granted a permanent reunion with Sychaeus. Repeatedly Aeneas gazes in wonder at the spirits:

constitit Anchisa satus et vestigia pressit
multa putans sortemque animo miseratus iniquam.

(6.331–332)

[Anchises' son stood, restraining his steps, pondering much, and in his spirit he pitied their unhappy lot.]

arma procul currusque virum miratur inanis.

(6.651)

[From far off he marvels at the arms and empty chariots of the men.]

horrescit visu subito.

(6.710)

[(Aeneas) startled at the sudden sight.]

And the fascination is mutual: "nec vidisse semel satis est; iuvat usque morari / et conferre gradum" ("nor is it enough to have seen him once; it pleases them to linger for a long time, and to accompany him," *Aen.* 6.487–88). The appetite of sight, among the living a thirst for reliable contact between persons, is for the spirits a thirst for life and a pleasure in Aeneas's vigor.

In the most elaborate and powerful meeting in the underworld, Anchises and Aeneas fall into a rich and easy version of their relationship in life, only we see more of it, more directly, than we ever did before Anchises' death. In fact, it is only Aeneas's failed attempt to embrace Anchises that brings home the fact of his death, for in other respects Anchises is as lively, vivid, talkative, loving, and in charge as he apparently was in life. Anchises gives more of himself to his son, even as a shade, than Venus can give of herself as a goddess. The long sequence of prophetic sights guided by Anchises confirms Aeneas's role as a son at the same time that it liberates him and enables his role as a leader. These firm placements within familial, historical, geographical, and civic networks are confirming developments in Aeneas's character, and Anchises makes possible this simultaneous discovery of self and role by giving Aeneas a view from a height.

Guyon's sojourn in the House of Mammon is not so much a variation on these salient features of its literary model as a pointed departure from them. Guyon has no personal investment in any of the figures that he sees with Mammon, so one obvious source of pity is denied him. He has no old comrades, no previous history to pull at him; he therefore lacks one claim that Aeneas makes on the sympathy of the reader. Because the visit to the underworld is also a temptation scene in this episode on the threshold between classical and Christian sources of strength, Spenser drastically reduces the roles of the dead, eliminating almost all of the individuals and thereby as well the pity of narrator and reader. The individuals whom Guyon does see are the sinners: Tantalus, Pilate, and other unspecified sufferers. But these compose precisely the one category of souls which Aeneas himself never sees: he never enters Tartarus, and all of Vergil's imaginative concern is directed at Elysium instead.

All of these choices have the effect of minimizing potential narrative space for the protagonist's reactions to the sights that he sees. This is surely a calculated decision on Spenser's part. He suppresses any Aeneas-like responsiveness yet he evokes Vergil's underworld repeatedly. Guyon looks hard, and speaks little. When he does speak, it is in words that are harshly just:

> Nay, nay, thou greedie *Tantalus* (quoth he)
>   Abide the fortune of thy present fate,
>   And vnto all that liue in high degree,
>   Ensample be of mind intemperate,
>   To teach them how to vse their present state.
>
> (2.7.60)

The best that the narrator can do, given the intractable materials of this world, is briefly to acknowledge Tantalus's pain. But the Spenserian narrator is careful to keep his tone neutrally flat, abjuring the pity that Vergil reveals everywhere in his underworld:

> Then gan the cursed wretch aloud to cry,
>   Accusing highest *Ioue* and gods ingrate,
>   And eke blaspheming heauen bitterly,
> As author of vniustice, there to let him dye.
>
> (2.7.60)

No other response is possible to these sights of a harsh and dangerous realm in which even a demonic tempter has so much less awareness of human cultural and social possibilities than the humblest of Vergil's spirits. The Spenserian narrator takes on the harshness of the world that he views with his hero. That this is a deliberate strategy on Spenser's part is clear from his imitative choices, the most fundamental of which is to close off any of the Vergilian realms of Hades and to deny Guyon any old acquaintance there. Guyon's adventure here is of a piece with his struggles against the knights at Medina's house, his futile efforts to restrain the violence of Furor, Pyrochles, and Cymochles, and his deductions from the case of Amavia and Mordant.

The structure of Spenser's second book traces the career of a moralized epic hero but punctuates this narrative with passages depicting or encouraging trust in the nourishments of vision and the exaltations available to beholders. It is as if the working out of a narrative based on classical ethical and psychic ideals released in Spenser equally urgent ethical and psychic ideals of romance errancy, dilation, and wonder, evoked by visions of what Southey called "Muses' mysteries"; both of these sets of ideals can be traced back to Vergil. Generically, that is, working out a moralized Vergilian epic that emerges from the allegorical interpretive tradition of commentary on ancient epic and from the *romanzi* of the Italians provokes Spenser to adduce other strains from ancient epic, notably an elevation of the beheld woman and the capacity for awe before objects beheld, both of which are assimilated, in Spenser's work, to similar romance qualities. These alternating generic possibilities emerge again and again in acts of sight; as in Vergilian and Ovidian texts, looking is synecdochic for possible relations between self and world. Guyon's chastened, subdued, and morally inflected responses to sights, and the narrator's and reader's periodic capacities for extravagance of vision as well as for response to the ontological presence of the viewed object, are twin models for the stance of the self to all that is not the self.

These genre choices allow some large and even breathtaking structural choices. Hence the placement of the Proem and the Belphoebe vignette (canto 3), episodes that privilege the values of expansive vision, trust in the visible, and allow the gratification of the senses and of the wish for access to Belphoebe's presence, these bracketing Guyon's attempts, in the episodes of Amavia and Mordant (canto 1) and the House of Medina (canto 2), to make moral sense of the objects he views. Hence the placement of Phedon's feverish, overstimulated looking just before Guyon's ordeal in the House of Mammon, where he is required to look intently and yet stifle reponse; hence the placement of the Angel just after the claustral oppressions of the House of Mammon. Hence also the occasional discrepancies between Guyon's and the narrator's diction in evaluating things seen.

When Guyon rushes to the scene of Mordant's and Amavia's demise, for instance, Spenser attributes to him the full quota of Aeneas's capacity for compassion: "Pittifull spectacle of deadly smart / . . . / Pitifull spectacle, as euer eye did view" (2.1.40).

> Whom when the good Sir *Guyon* did behold,
>   His hart gan wexe as starke, as marble stone,
>   And his fresh bloud did frieze with fearefull cold,
>   That all his senses seemd bereft attone.
>
> (2.1.42)

The lines suggest Guyon's affinity with his Vergilian predecessor, only to show immediately afterward the limits of that affinity, by contrast with Aeneas's more nuanced mode of address. Guyon's impulses move in the right direction, toward succor and direct action. But the moral terms in which he incorporates experience do not allow responses as subtle as those that the narrator provides. Guyon says to the Palmer:

> Behold the image of mortalitie,
>   And feeble nature cloth'd with fleshly tyre,
>   When raging passion with fierce tyrannie
>   Robs reason of her due regalitie,
>   And makes it seruant to her basest part:
>   The strong it weakens with infirmitie,
>   And with bold furie armes the weakest hart;
>   The strong through pleasure soonest falles, the weake through smart.
>
> (2.1.57)

Guyon pities Amavia, but he moralizes, in terms that are true enough but do not sufficiently acknowledge her anguish; he does not earn them. The language of subjection and hierarchy within the self comes rather too quickly, as the narrator's different responses will show. Guyon, unlike his model Aeneas, has no compelling Vergilian sense of family bonds and the shattering effect of their destruction—one of the chief distinctions between earlier and later hero. Though Guyon speaks from within the tradition of moral commentaries on the *Aeneid,* his own heroism risks glibness insofar as it is empty of Aeneas's passions and internal struggles. Guyon's well-meaning ideas are insufficient to the language of the narrator and of Amavia, who use language that does convey the extremity of the catastrophe, and that gives to the reader a more supple grasp of what has been lost. The losses include the beautiful vigor of the dead youth, the tenderness of her patient devotion while curing him, the promise of her family thwarted at its very inception:

> Besides them both, vpon the soiled gras
>   The dead corse of an armed knight was spred,
>   Whose armour all with bloud besprinckled was;
>   His ruddie lips did smile, and rosy red
>   Did paint his chearefull cheekes, yet being ded,
>   Seemd to haue beene a goodly personage,
>   Now in his freshest flowre of lustie hed,
>   Fit to inflame faire Lady with loues rage,
> But that fiers fate did crop the blossome of his age.
>
> (2.1.41)

One of the chief effects of this stanza is to drive a wedge between Guyon's responses to what he sees and the reader's responses to the pitiful spectacle mediated through language. The reader-spectator re-creates the scene by means of phrases suggesting a ghastly juxtaposition of life with death—"ruddie lips...rosy red...chearefull cheekes...freshest flowre of lustie hed,"—phrases in which the red of life's vigor is the sign of life's loss. There is even a suggestion of the rectified passion that should have been part of his manhood's vocation: "Fit to inflame faire Lady with loues rage." Amavia's own words draw particular attention to the energy and the command of soul now lost to the dark steed of passion through references to horsemanship's guided vigor and to vegetation, all relying on the traditionally medieval vividness of alliteration: "The gentlest knight, that euer on greene gras / Gay steed with spurs did pricke" (2.1.49). This spectacle and the rhetoric with which it is presented ensure that we acknowledge Guyon's pity while recognizing the limitations of his responses. "Tyrannie," "regalitie"—these terms have something real to do with what has happened to Mordant, but the disparity between their user's interest in moral evaluation and the narrator's interest in affect anticipates Shakespeare's depiction of Brutus's response to the news of Portia's death. For Guyon as for Brutus, there is scant distinction between fortitude and numbed resignation: "Patience perforce; helpelesse what may it boot / To fret for anger, or for griefe to mone?" (2.3.3).

The angel who appears to guard Guyon after his collapse outside the House of Mammon is a counterpart to Belphoebe, not only in his androgynous beauty but also in his function as an object of sight evoking wonder from narrator and reader, an object to which Guyon's perceptions simply do not apply. Like that of Belphoebe, the angel's presence suggests what the sensory can reveal of the numinous; the angel's entirely trustworthy and radiant sensual beauty is a sharply conceived alternative to the dark sensuality of Mammon's house in the preceding canto.

In the stanza that prefaces the description of the angel, the narrator risks a certain degree of sentimentality with a rush of gratitude and awe so strong that the following description must earn such a response; as Upton notes, "*And* in the beginning of a sentence is expressive of passion."[20]

> And is there care in heauen? and is there loue
> In heauenly spirits to these creatures bace,
> That may compassion of their euils moue?
> There is: else much more wretched were the cace
> Of men, then beasts. But O th'exceeding grace
> Of highest God, that loues his creatures so,
> And all his workes with mercy doth embrace,
> That blessed Angels, he sends to and fro,
> To serue to wicked man, to serue his wicked foe.
>
> (2.8.1)

With an epic sweep calculated to earn such responsiveness for the reader, the object first presented to our view is not the angel but the imagined spectacle of his home, to which the gratitude and visionary capacity of the narrator make him privy:

> How oft do they, their siluer bowers leaue,
> To come to succour vs, that succour want?
> How oft do they with golden pineons, cleaue
> The flitting skyes, like flying Pursuiuant,
> Against foule feends to aide vs millitant?
> They for vs fight, they watch and dewly ward,
> And their bright Squadrons round about vs plant,

---

[20]I cite from John G. Radcliffe's edition, *John Upton: Notes on "The Faerie Queene*," 2 vols. (New York: Garland, Inc., 1987), vol. 1, 491. On the connection between Cupid and the angel, see Rosemond Tuve, "Spenser and Some Pictorial Conventions, with Particular Reference to Illuminated Manuscripts," *Studies in Philology* 37 (1940), 149–76, rpt. in *Essays by Rosemond Tuve: Spenser, Herbert, Milton*, ed. Thomas P. Roche, Jr. (Princeton: Princeton University Press, 1970), 112–38 at 127–29.

And all for loue, and nothing for reward:
O why should heauenly God to men haue such regard?

(2.8.2)

The Proem's tenderness for hidden worlds and its insistence on the pleasure of imagining the hidden are sustained here; as in the Proem and in the blazon, the tone of this stanza combines confidence in the epic poet's creative powers with a humbler astonishment that such sights answer the human gaze, or that the mind can envision the possibility of such answerability. The reader's privilege of access is emphasized by the intimacy of the phrase "siluer bowers," and by the wonderfully imagined information that to reach earth the angels "cleaue" the skies with their wings. The sky is a tangible substance to be broken through, and its function of separating the human world from the silver bowers underscores the hiddenness of such sanctuaries. The brillant and easy energy of the angels' "golden pineons" which "cleaue / The flitting skyes" helps to create a universe of larger scope and easier penetrability than Guyon's toils have suggested might exist.[21]

The angel's aid to Guyon is an obvious instance of Spenser's Christianizing Vergil's epic form. But though Guyon is the beneficiary of a providential love unavailable to Aeneas, this enfranchisement does not extend to the transformation of either his own moral imagination or the threatening world that he inhabits. The description of the descent from heaven, like the description of Belphoebe, drives a wedge between the hero's perception and the reader's, mediated as it is by highly figured, sensuous, and ornate verse.

Like Belphoebe, the angel is a spectacle of providential and numinous glory that is unavailable to Guyon's vision; he embodies an opulence of being, a largeness of spatial scope, and a physical exuberance that Guyon eschews.

Beside his head there sate a faire young man,
    Of wondrous beautie, and of freshest yeares,
    Whose tender bud to blossome new began,
    And flourish faire aboue his equall peares;
    His snowy front curled with golden heares,

[21]Cf. Berger, *Allegorical Temper,* 42–44; also Bono, *Literary Transvaluation,* 77: "The Christian and neo-Platonic background of *The Faerie Queene* not only assures us of an ultimate order but also reveals it as love, rather than imposing it as authority [as in the *Aeneid*]."

> Like *Phoebus* face adornd with sunny rayes,
> Diuinely shone, and two sharpe winged sheares,
> Decked with diuerse plumes, like painted Iayes,
> Were fixed at his backe, to cut his ayerie wayes.
>
> (2.8.5)

Spectacle here encompasses the sensations of coolness, freshness, and a radiance made up of white and gold: "freshest yeares," "flourish," "snowy front," "golden heares." Spenser plays as well on the tactile qualities of sharp, clean edges: the phrases "sharpe winged sheares" and "to cut his ayerie wayes" convey that sense of easy mastery and joyous efficiency which Spenser always uses to adumbrate his ideal hopes for human transformation.

The description of the angel himself alludes both to the angel of the Resurrection and to Cupid, and draws on the iconographic tradition of Cupid as a symbol of God's love for man.

> Like as *Cupido* on *Idaean* hill,
> When hauing laid his cruell bow away,
> And mortall arrowes, wherewith he doth fill
> The world with murdrous spoiles and bloudie pray,
> With his faire mother he him dights to play,
> And with his goodly sisters, *Graces* three;
> The Goddesse pleased with his wanton play,
> Suffers her selfe through sleepe beguild to bee,
> The whiles the other Ladies mind their merry glee.
>
> (2.8.6)

The mythological simile here abjures specificity of allusion to an earlier narrative in favor of a larger, vaguer allegiance to a syncretistic, Neoplatonic iconography, a shift with implications for the notions of eros intimated here. The Belphoebe episode has pointed to its own poetic resources in Vergil's *Aeneid* and to the potency of a Venus-within-a-Diana, and lightly recalls, in order to transcend them, the Vergilian story's elements of yearning and the neediness of vision. The epic simile describing the Angel, mythic companion piece to the description of Belphoebe, points to its own poetic resources not of story but of visual tableau, to the reliability and nourishment of mythic visual spectacle within a Christian universe.

The salient contrast is with the tableau of violent erotic power which Guyon abstracts from the sight of Amavia and Mordant (2.1.57).

Each of these stanzas sketches a structure of eros, but each belongs to a different genre and reflects a mutually exclusive apprehension of desire. Here is Guyon's tableau:

> Behold the image of mortalitie,
> And feeble nature cloth'd with fleshly tyre,
> When raging passion with fierce tyrannie
> Robs reason of her due regalitie,
> And makes it seruant to her basest part:
> The strong it weakens with infirmitie,
> And with bold furie armes the weakest hart;
> The strong through pleasure soonest falles, the weake through smart.
>
> (2.1.57)

I have cited this stanza previously, but it is worth another look here, held up against the Cupid simile applied to the Angel. Desire in Guyon's tableau is structured as a drive originating within the victim and positing no possible satisfaction by an outside object. Guyon's response to Amavia is less a mythic narrative than a series of *sententiae* positing a statically recurring drive and the deterioration of the victim of the drive. In his stanza the viewer's pity defers to superiority, and Guyon's observations, curiously, apply only to Mordant's fatal erotic susceptibility, not at all to Amavia's story of Mordant's gradual recovery through love or to her account of their child. Guyon's moralized epic ethos acknowledges within eros no positive transformative powers mediated by the feminine; he sees in the dead lovers a visual representation of decay.

But the tableau of the Cupid simile figures the dynamics of positive change within desire—indeed, figures the dynamics of Amavia and Mordant's own history. The simile presents in mythic tropes the power of the feminine to civilize and heal a violent eros; the simile also implies a small-scale sense of historicity in its easy embrace of earlier events in the story. The poet reflects the qualities of the Vergilian observer's sense of depth in time and of the numinous in human life. The Angel containing the image of Cupid is a glamorous, not to say urbane, figure who not only protects Guyon but also awakens the reader's desire for the ontological fullness that he represents. The ornamentation of the verse signals, as in the description of Belphoebe, an eikastic image toward which we turn, as toward a platonic beloved object. Like Belphoebe, the Angel is elusive and yet generous with an abundant presence. Guyon represents fallen human inaccessibility to the opulent regions from which the Angel descends, but Spenser bestows on the reader the gift of the Angel's presence as heaven bestows grace on Guyon. The primal loss that creates desire is acknowledged, but it is contained within the presence of the ideal *imago* (an image meant to be mimetic of the actual), whose silver bowers suggest the possibility of an achieved condition of bliss.

Vision and spectacle in the blazon of Belphoebe, in the Proem, and in the appearance of the Angel represent one kind of relationship between human consciousness and the world, one in which objects of visual perception can be trusted to answer the hungers awakened by vision, one in which wonder is an apt response before objects viewed. Intromissive sight is potentially exalting in Spenser's extensions of Homero-Vergilian visual awe into a Neoplatonic, providential cosmos. This understanding of vision and visual drives contrasts with that of Guyon's career, in which intromissive sight is always dangerous, threatening to enter and undermine the mind's empire by inflaming drives that can have no fulfillment in union with a beloved object, drives that can lead only to death. This understanding of vision and desire is also indebted to Vergil's *Aeneid*, and especially to the moral-allegorical commentary on it.

These two structures of vision struggle most intensely in Canto 12, where they bifurcate in a contest of genres as Guyon struggles to remain the hero of a moralized epic and to avoid the medieval romance and romance-epic elements of his book.

The Pressures of Genre: Canto 12

Those elements have been part of Book 2 from the beginning. Acrasia is an example of the fatal temptresses of allegorized epic, as I said; but in the Renaissance this means that she also belongs to the genre system of allegorized romance-epic; her nearest relations are the enchantresses of Trissino, Boiardo, Ariosto, and Tasso in their sensual gardens. Phaedria is a servant of Acrasia, but generically she is a representative of the world of courtly romance, and the frivolity of her playfulness is echoed in that of the nymphs of the fountain. There is nothing surprising in my saying that nymphs and Phaedria must be left behind, garden and enchantress destroyed. But while the moralized epic hero is achieving these things, Spenser creates in canto 12 an urgent and unresolved tension between moralized epic and romance-epic by pulling their common elements now toward one, now toward the other. The action of canto 12 is divided between a heavily traditional moral-allegorical journey over perilous seas and a heavily traditional romance garden devoted to pleasures "not of the purest kind." Both of these settings are indebted in part to the *Odyssey*, an indebtedness that complicates the tensions at work in the canto, since Renaissance readers could understand the *Odyssey* as an epic with strong affinities to romance.[22]

The *Odyssey* embodies essential features of both epic and romance, notably epic's narrative drive toward a clear and specific goal and the hero's *nostos*, and the narrative drive of the romance toward episodic adventure and wandering. Renaissance apprehensions of the *Odyssey's* hero, in some criticism but more often in epic and romance poetry, reflect this generic doubleness; Ulysses begins as a martial hero from the *Iliad* and escapes Circe and the Sirens by disciplined resistance. But he is also a model of romance adventure and marvel. Spenser begins the last canto of Book 2 with a sea journey imitated from the *Odyssey* 12 and from the *Aeneid* 2–3; its explicit moral significance has been studied at length and annotated with plentiful parallels, that can only aid our understanding of the episode. But, given the argument of the rest of this chapter about a split in Book 2 between a moralized Vergilian strain, somber in tone and epistemologically skeptical, and an Homero-Vergilian strain of wonder before objects viewed, warmer and more awe-filled in tone and epistemologically more optimistic than the moral allegorical strain, we may be able to propose some useful distinctions about imitation and genre in Guyon's journey. Certainly the passage descends from Aeneas's journey, which itself descends from that of Ulysses. But Vergil's imitation argues a much darker view of nature and of

[22]Cinthio says, for example, that "one should realize that in makeup the Romances are much more like Homer's *Odyssey* than the *Iliad*." The translation of the *Discorso intorno al comporre dei romanzi* by Henry Snuggs is published as *Giraldi Cinthio: On Romances* (Lexington: University of Kentucky Press, 1968); the citation is from page 57. The relationships between romance and epic constitute a critical issue of long standing, especially in regard to the Italian *romanzi*, for which see Bernard Weinberg, *A History of Literary Criticism in the Italian Renaissance*, 2 vols. (Chicago: University of Chicago Press, 1961), vol. 2, 954–1073. See also W. P. Ker, *Epic and Romance: Essays in Medieval Literature* (London: Macmillan, 1897); Nohrnberg, *Analogy of "The Faerie Queene,"* 5–22 and passim; A. Bartlett Giamatti, *The Earthly Paradise and the Renaissance Epic* (Princeton: Princeton University Press, 1966).

man's place in it than does the journey of the *Odyssey*. Ulysses's heroism involves not only a struggle to emerge from an engulfing nature into fully human consciousness, but considerable optimism that the human mind can craft the natural world so as to expand consciousness. Ulysses on his journey is chiefly *homo fabulator*, and though he and his crew suffer, he perceives natural threats as opportunities for creative endeavor; Aeneas on his journey is chiefly *homo patiens*, experiencing nature as hostile to human efforts of civilization.[23]

Guyon's journey is much more closely affiliated with Aeneas's dreadful voyage, and with Vergil's mistrust of nature as it appears there, than it is with Ulysses's trouble-plagued but adventurous voyage. Indeed, Guyon's voyage can be seen as Spenser's extension and intensification of a moralized interpretation of the *Aeneid*, and a swerve away from the romance adventurousness of the Proem. Guyon's moralized epic genre grants no expansion or exaljtation through the beholding of wonders; his sea voyage in Canto 12 is a nightmare. Instead of "fruitfullest Virginia," named after the benign woman addressed in the Proem, the brave new world of Canto 12 consists of mouths and abysses threatening to "suck," "engulf," "swallow," "devour." The victims of these disasters are those who have given in to "wanton ioyes" and "lustes intemperate" (2.12.7). Pleasure and the sea are alike in that their movements lead to oblivion. In Guyon's world, desire is a mindless drive from within, like Furor, but it is also figured as the aggressive threat of all nature to devour the self-contained hero. Land itself, used in Homeric similes in the *Odyssey* and in the *Aeneid* to represent the relief of stability after the chaos and homelessness of the sea, is unfixed and untrustworthy:

> For those same Islands, seeming now and than,
> Are not firme lande, nor any certein wonne,
> But straggling plots, which to and fro do ronne
> In the wide waters: therefore are they hight
> The *wandring Islands*. Therefore doe them shonne;
> For they haue oft drawne many a wandring wight
> Into most deadly daunger and distressed plight.

---

[23]Shirley Clay Scott comments on Odysseus as *homo fabulator* in his journey in an unpublished paper, "The Forms of Polyphemos."

> Yet well they seeme to him, that farre doth vew,
>   Both faire and fruitfull, and the ground dispred
>   With grassie greene of delectable hew,
>   And the tall trees with leaues apparelled,
>   Are deckt with blossomes dyde in white and red.
>
>   (2.12.11–12)

The stanzas' diction characterizes the allure of this landscape as erotic and tender; the first line of the second stanza hints at the yearning that this prospect awakens in Guyon, and the fifth line describes its flowers as having the colors of a woman's body. But to identify the land as erotic within Guyon's career is to identify it as threatening to identity, rather than supportive of identity, as land is in the *Odyssey* and the *Aeneid*. When Phaedria turns up on one of these isles, their function as an anticipation of Acrasia's romance garden emerges. Phaedria has throughout Book 2 seemed silly as well as tempting (C. S. Lewis somewhere calls her a flibbertigibbet); her behavior is never more inappropriate than here. The sheer triviality of a romance character in this voyage episode, related as she is to Idleness in *Le Roman de la Rose*, and the inconsequence of woman's merely sexual presence to the Vergilian and masculine *labor* of survival in a hostile world, emerge in Spenser's lines:

> Whom ouertaking, she in merry sort
>   Them gan to bord, and purpose diuersly,
>   Now faining dalliance and wanton sport,
>   Now throwing forth lewd words immodestly.
>   .   .   .   .   .
> That was the wanton *Phaedria,* which late
>   Did ferry him ouer the *Idle lake*:
>   Whom nought regarding, they kept on their gate,
>   And all her vaine allurements did forsake,
>   When them the wary Boateman thus bespake;
>   Here now behoueth vs well to auyse,
>   And of our safetie good heede to take;
>   For here before a perlous passage lyes.
>
>   (2.12.16–17)

When Phaedria first appeared in Book 2, she appeared in a "litle Gondelay" (2.6.2); when Guyon boarded it, he unintentionally strayed from his epic *telos* into a romance adventure.[24] This digression he had found uncomfortable and irrelevant, and he had been glad to escape to the firmer ground of moralized epic:

> She [Phaedria] no less glad, then he desirous was
>   Of his departure thence; for of her ioy
>   And vaine delight she saw he light did pas,
>   A foe of folly and immodest toy,
>   Still solemne sad, or still disdainfull coy,
>   Delighting all in armes and cruell warre,
>   That her sweet peace and pleasures did annoy,
>   Troubled with terrour and vnquiet iarre,
> That she well pleased was thence to amoue him farre.
>
> Tho him she brought abord, and her swift bote
>   Forthwith directed to that further strand;
>   The which on the dull waues did lightly flote
>   And soone arriued on the shallow sand,
>   Where gladsome *Guyon* salied forth to land.
>
>   (2.6.37–38)

Phaedria is trivial within the context of the moral-allegorical epic; but she also descends from chivalric romance, a lineage that she shares with Guyon. Like Sir Gawaine in his medieval chivalric romance, Guyon feels not only desire but also generic and social pressures to entertain the lady and to elevate her femininity as a positive value. But even the anonymous damsel in distress who next appears to Guyon, whom romance knights feel obliged to aid no matter the possible consequences, is in Guyon's world only a bait laid to make the taker mad. Guyon's first chivalric and charitable impulse, says the Palmer, must be suppressed, and Guyon must stay fenced and guarded within himself, denying not only his impulse but also the

---

[24]David Quint expands the implications for the relationship between epic and romance in "The Boat of Romance and Renaissance Epic," in *Romance: Generic Transformation from Chrétien de Troyes to Cervantes,* ed. Kevin Brownlee and Marina Scordilis Brownlee (Hanover, N.H., and London: University Press of New England, for Dartmouth College, 1985), 178–202. Cf. Nohrnberg, *Analogy of "The Fairie Queene,"* 10: "In a Spenserian example of the enchanted boat motif, the voyage provides for both the conveyance of the hero over a psychological threshold of romance and the convergence of two heroes—one a Mars—on an epic battle rendezvous. But the destination, an enchanted island, shows that the affinities of Spenser's treatment are decidedly with romance."

pressure of the chivalric mode that complicates his allegorical Vergilian ethos:

> At last they in an Island did espy
> A seemely Maiden, sitting by the shore,
> That with great sorrow and sad agony,
> Seemed some great misfortune to deplore,
> And lowd to them for succour called euermore.
>   . . . . .
> Faire Sir, be not displeased, if disobayd [says the Palmer]:
> For ill it were to hearken to her cry;
> For she is inly nothing ill apayd,
> But onely womanish fine forgery,
> Your stubborne hart t'affect with fraile infirmity.
>   (2.12.27–28)

In *Le Roman de la Rose* and its character Idleness, the trivial charm of woman is one of the alluring features of courtly life and, indeed, one of the enabling conditions of courtly love. But in *Sir Gawaine and the Green Knight*, a helpful work to compare though Spenser probably did not know of it, Gawaine's heroic values conflict with each other as absolute courtesy and the elevation of woman meet a frivolous and dangerous lady; in the bedroom comedy of *Sir Gawaine*, the lady's triviality is ultimately identical with her dangerousness. Guyon's course is even more problematic, although his first meeting with Phaedria shares the fine comedy of the hero's discomfiture of the earlier work. In Guyon's world even trivial women carry the weight of the moral-allegorical interpretative tradition of the *Aeneid*, in which the tragic nobility and grandeur of Dido are subordinated to the fatal allure of the temptress who enervates the male hero.

The literary history of romance, then, becomes one of the burdens that Guyon bears and has to fight against; it complicates the fulfillment of his quest. I want now to turn to a series of small verbal units— sets of lines and sets of stanzas—for a close look at their small-scale conflicts between the ethos of romance-epic and the ethos of allegorical epic. The first of these records Guyon's first responses to the "aspect" he views, an aspect the tendency of which intromissively to sink in, as we say colloquially today, he resists:

> Much wondred *Guyon* at the faire aspect
> Of that sweet place, yet suffred no delight

To sincke into his sence, nor mind affect,
But passed forth, and lookt still forward right,
Bridling his will, and maistering his might.

(2.12.53)

Guyon's movements here are so conflicted as to merit being called muscular. The pre-eminence of the verb in the first line, a verb laden with affective and literary meanings in the Renaissance, registers an intensity of response seldom welcomed by the characters of Book 2 before this. (The two significant exceptions: Guyon's entrance into the House of Mammon, and the Palmer's reaction on seeing the angel.) Wonder is an affect central to Spenser's romance narratives in the other books of the poem, where it often implies the Platonic dynamic of eros as movement toward a transcendent ideal apprehended in a vision of the beloved, as in Artegall's famous act of falling in love with Britomart when she reveals her face: Artegall "of his wonder made religion."[25] But Guyon's lapse into a romance mode of intense fascination lasts only briefly. Vision here is ominously intromissive, since delights threaten to "sincke into his sence."[26] The sequence of verbs is noteworthy in its movement from the Platonic image of the soul awakening to desire, to the Platonic charioteer model of desire as mere drive: "much wondred" changes to "suffred [not]" changes to "sincke into" and "affect," changes finally to "bridling" and "maistering." Sight awakens desire, but the initial pattern of desire, with its sources in Neoplatonic philosophy and European love lyric, is suppressed immediately in favor of the necessary rigors of the moral-allegorical ethos.

A related set of double assumptions about the movements of desire occurs when Guyon sees the nymphs in the fountain. For the first time, an epic simile of considerable ornamentation is attributed not only to the objects viewed but to Guyon's nascent apprehension of them:

---

[25]*Wonder* can also mean a skeptical and disapproving puzzlement with an element of fascination, as in Guyon's experience in the House of Mammon: "But th'Elfin knight with wonder all the way / Did feed his eyes, and fild his inner thought." But in 2.12.53 it clearly implies amazement and attraction, if evidently to destructive stimuli.

[26]Compare Du Laurens: "The action of every sense is a suffering, and to doe the office of any of the senses, is nothing else but to suffer" (*Discourse of the Preservation of the Sight*, 40–41).

> As that faire Starre, the messenger of morne,
>   His deawy face out of the sea doth reare:
> Or as the *Cyprian* goddesse, newly borne
>   Of th'Oceans fruitfull froth, did first appeare:
> Such seemed they, and so their yellow heare
> Christalline humour dropped downe apace.
> Whom such when *Guyon* saw, he drew him neare,
> And somewhat gan relent his earnest pace,
> His stubborne brest gan secret pleasaunce to embrace.

(2.12.65)

The nymphs may bare their "amarous sweet spoiles" to the fascinated observer, but the simile's ornate style, its subject (a deity of love), and its mythic elements link it to the allusive blazon of Belphoebe and the angel's simile of Cupid, in all of which the pleasure of the prolonged gaze is the taking in of the nourishment of the viewed object's transcendent glory: "Gazers sense with double pleasure fed," as the narrator says of Belphoebe. In the context of this canto, Guyon's appropriation of a Homero-Vergilian wonder before the nymphs assimilates to his idealization of them and makes him momentarily a romance observer. The Palmer quickly pulls him back from this romance wonder: Guyon's guide makes him recognize the wrongness of romance here, and the narrator allows the reader to recognize both Guyon's genuine experience of the nymphs' venerean power and the wild discrepancy between the Venus simile's grandeur and the vulgar reality.[27]

The relatively generous amount of attention that Spenser grants this episode within the Bower is notable, and Spenser uses the narrative expansiveness to emphasize not just the nymphs' sexiness but other qualities that are especially attractive to the epic hero. There are plenty of verbal cues about the ultimate immorality of the nymphs' striptease: "amarous sweet spoiles," "greedy eyes" (st. 64), "melting hart," "bewrayd" (st. 66). But these are not very strongly negative words when considered in the light of the more insidious erotic pleasure of the eye which Cymochles has experienced in the Bower (2.5.33–34). That episode is heavily interlaced with moral diction and

---

[27]See Berger, *Allegorical Temper*, 218–19, for eloquent discussion of the simile. See also Antoinette B. Dauber, "The Art of Veiling in the Bower of Bliss," *Spenser Studies* 1 (1980), 163–75.

describes a corrupt visual-erotic drive. Cymochles' more decadent nymphs are a good deal more interested in self-exposure, and Cymochles himself more interested in living out a fantasy of utter passivity, than in this contrasting episode of Canto 12, where the diction judging against the nymphs of the fountain is relatively gentle. More than that, Spenser takes pains to depict the nymphs' gamesomeness, their canny acknowledgment of their own charm, the tiny differences between them, their capacity to be abashed by Guyon's open gaze at the same time that they court it, their playful competition with each other:

> Sometimes the one would lift the other quight
>   Aboue the waters, and then downe againe
>   Her plong, as ouer maistered by might,
>   Where both awhile would couered remaine,
>   And each the other from to rise restraine;
>   The whiles their snowy limbes, as through a vele,
>   So through the Christall waues appeared plaine:
>   Then suddeinly both would themselues vnhele,
> And th'amarous sweet spoiles to greedy eyes reuele.
>
>   (2.12.64)

> The wanton Maidens him espying, stood
>   Gazing a while at his vnwonted guise;
>   Then th'one her selfe low ducked in the flood,
>   Abasht, that her a straunger did a vise:
>   But th'other rather higher did arise,
>   And her two lilly paps aloft displayd,
>   And all, that might his melting hart entise
>   To her delights, she vnto him bewrayd:
> The rest hid vnderneath, him more desirous made.
>
>   (2.12.66)

> Withall she laughed, and she blusht withall,
>   That blushing to her laughter gaue more grace,
>   And laughter to her blushing, as did fall:
>   Now when they spide the knight to slacke his pace,
>   Them to behold, and in his sparkling face
>   The secret signes of kindled lust appeare,
>   Their wanton meriments they did encreace,

And to him beckned, to approch more neare,
And shewd him many sights, that courage cold could reare.

(2.12.68)

Without minimizing the monitory diction of these stanzas and others like them, we can say, first, that Spenser allows his hero and his readers to enjoy the intermittent revelations bestowed here, not only those adumbrated in the Venus simile but also the more dangerously charming ones of the nymphs' activities. One of these is the pervasive sense of play in the stanzas; with these unlikely characters Spenser edges his way toward the elegant social flirtation that is a frequent characteristic of courtly romance relations, as I suggested in relation to earlier instances of courtly romance. The flirting that the nymphs offer is less silly, more polished, more risky, more charged with erotic attraction, and more enmeshed in literary fields of significance than Phaedria's grosser attempts at a similar game; her sheer inconsequence in Guyon's world now gives way to the nymphs' more textured and subtle romance flirtation.

Second, Guyon's visual and erotic susceptibility to this "faire spectacle" and to no others in the book introduces just a hint of suprasexual pathos in his muted yearning toward the manifestations of Venus before him. The form of their flirtation and the frequent exchange of eye-to-eye gazes perhaps suggest that Guyon is attracted not only by female nudity but also by the spectacle of their mutual sport, their welcome of him into a tiny society, their sense of fun. Hence also the point of having precisely two of them: Guyon inclines not toward the titillation of multiple beauties' fondling, as in Cymochles' James-Bondian experience, but rather toward the different sexual comfort of the nymphs' companionship.[28]

---

[28]C. S. Lewis speaks for many readers when he describes the striptease anonymity of the nymphs by saying "A man does not need to go to faerie land to meet them" (*The Allegory of Love: A Study in Medieval Tradition* [Oxford: Oxford University Press, 1936], 331). It is certainly true that their cousins are ubiquitous in both life and letters. But Lewis himself has, with comic insight, given them specific names, which not only have stuck but have entered discourse about them, despite the occasional protest. It is one of my themes throughout this book that Spenser never homogenizes episodes of voyeurism or exposure in his work, but constantly distinguishes and particularizes them, accommodating a very wide range of motives and impulses in them. In this case, the nymphs' charm, playfulness, and smiles, and Guyon's responsiveness—the situation's potential for recreation—are best contrasted with the

This argument is one way of accounting for the narrative spaciousness afforded the episode. These six stanzas within the longest canto
of the poem provide a romance dilation that allows both Guyon and
reader to speculate not only on the splendor of the Venus simile but
also on the undeniable good humor of the nymphs. (C. S. Lewis named
the nymphs Cissie and Flossie for their lower-class vulgarity, but he
was righter than he knew in the sisterly and cheerful qualities their
names suggest.) The Palmer's stern reminder of the dangers of wandering vision thus comes as something of a shock after the leisurely
expansiveness of these stanzas and the comedy of the nymphs:

> On which when gazing him the Palmer saw,
>   He much rebukt those wandring eyes of his,
>   And counseld well, him forward thence did draw.
>
> (2.12.69)

The tension set up between Guyon's responsiveness and the sharp
exhortation of these three lines persists through the rest of the canto.
The third stanza describing Acrasia, for example, draws on the language of intromissive vision and visual hunger applied to certain other
spectacles in this book, but the specular terms in which she is offered
to the viewer's gaze evoke affects wildly different from those that
Belphoebe invites:

> Her snowy brest was bare to readie spoyle
>   Of hungry eies, which n'ote therewith be fild,
>   And yet through languour of her late sweet toyle,
>   Few drops, more cleare then Nectar, forth distild,
>   That like pure Orient perles adowne it trild,
>   And her faire eyes sweet smyling in delight,
>   Moystened their fierie beames, with which she thrild

---

apparently pleasurable but charmless experiences of Cymochles and his nymphs elsewhere in the Bower, rather than with twentieth-century real-life analogues. And if the
nymphs of the fountain contrast parodically also with Prays-desire and Shamefastnesse, then Guyon's warmth of response to the nymphs may be an echo of his
solace with the demure ladies of Alma's house, with whom he clearly feels the pleasure
of erotically charged social companionship.

> Fraile harts, yet quenched not; like starry light
> Which sparckling on the silent waues, does seeme more bright.
>
> (2.12.78)

The phrase "hungry eies" briefly suggests some pathos of visual desire, but whose eyes are hungry is left unspecified, and their potential action is violence against the vulnerable flesh, "bare to readie spoyle." The beamy light of Acrasia's eyes arouses desire in "fraile harts," but there is no possibility of satisfying this kind of desire: she deceptively appears as an object of ideal eros, as her light imagery suggests, but all her eye-light returns back to her, and the men who desire her exhaust themselves in a compulsive drive that cannot be sated. A phantastic parody of eikastic images like Belphoebe and Gloriana, she and her romance garden falsely imply that a watcher's or a lover's desire for her can become a sustained condition of bliss. That is, she seems to imply the mutual enkindling of the souls of beloved and awed lover in the *Phaedrus*. But in fact Acrasia represents desire as an enervating drive, the enslaving passion of the *Phaedrus*'s dark steed and of allegorical epic's classical ethos. In this stanza it is visual accessibility that arouses desire, but in the stanzas before and after it, the potential conflict of reader response is intensified by displaying Acrasia's victims:

> The young man sleeping by her, seemd to bee
>   Some goodly swayne of honorable place,
>   That certes it great pittie was to see
>   Him his nobilitie so foule deface;
>   A sweet regard, and amiable grace,
>   Mixed with manly sternnesse did appeare
>   Yet sleeping, in his well proportiond face,
>   And on his tender lips the downy heare
> Did now but freshly spring, and silken blossomes beare.
>
> (2.12.79)

Spenser aims to elicit pity from the reader at Verdant's vulnerability; this is one effect of the last lines' emphasis on his youthfulness. More, he elicits the tenderness of the reader by showing Verdant asleep. Indeed, Acrasia is at pains to keep him asleep, in a stanza that complements Cymochles' enacted male fantasy of blissful passivity in a pretense of sleep with Acrasia's enacted female fantasy of male passivity in enchanted sleep:

And all that while, right ouer him she hong,
  With her false eyes fast fixed in his sight,
  As seeking medicine, whence she was stong,
  Or greedily depasturing delight:
  And oft inclining downe with kisses light,
  For feare of waking him, his lips bedewd,
  And through his humid eyes did sucke his spright,
  Quite molten into lust and pleasure lewd;
Wherewith she sighed soft, as if his case she rewd.

(2.12.73)

Eyes and mouths are allied gateways through which desire is roused and the spirit lost. Even for the demonic enchantress, eros is a compulsive hunger, a wound requiring healing; the simile of line 3 suggests her own vulnerability to an intromissive vision that undermines volition and the constancy of the self.

The myths of men who lay down their arms in the arms of a passionate woman—Hercules and Omphale, Bacchus and Ariadne, Aeneas and Dido, Antony and Cleopatra, Mars and Venus—were favorites of Renaissance mythographers of all stripes, amenable as such fables are to a variety of powerful schematic contrasts: love and war, passion and duty, affection and reason—and, in the period's greatest development of the myth of "what Venus did with Mars," Egyptian voluptuousness and Roman militarism, Asiatic and Attic rhetorical styles, romance and epic genres. The full-blown contest of genres of *Antony and Cleopatra* occurs also in Book 2 of *The Faerie Queene*, though in less elegantly diagrammatic form. At the start of the book the sorceress who awakens the hideous steed of uncontrollable bodily appetite has defeated Amavia, who exemplifies a healing and fruitful eros. At the end of the book Acrasia must indeed be destroyed—not because she embodies pleasure but because the particular structure of pleasure she represents is a threat. It threatens not only the ethos of Guyon's moral-allegorical epic but also the emergent form of Spenserian romance-epic, in which the demonic enchantresses of the Italian *romanzi* and of this book give way to numinous nymphs, goddesses, and human women bearing a divine glory to their observers.

But all those pleasant bowres and Pallace braue,
  Guyon broke downe, with rigour pittilesse;

> Ne ought their goodly workmanship might saue
> Them from the tempest of his wrathfulnesse,
> But that their blisse he turn'd to balefulnesse:
> Their groues he feld, their gardins did deface,
> Their arbers spoyle, their Cabinets suppresse,
> Their banket houses burne, their buildings race,
> And of the fairest late, now made the fowlest place.
>
> (2.12.83)

In the end I have returned, if with qualifications and reservations, to C. S. Lewis's formative remarks about the contrasts between the Bower of Bliss and the Garden of Adonis, the sterility of the one and the fertility of the other.[29] Acrasia's Bower is a perversion of Spenserian romance's desire awakened by vision and of romance hopes for a fulfilled state of bliss. Guyon perhaps destroys the Bower because he wants to protect the self-possession of the constant mind. But Spenser destroys the Bower, with considerable pain, because he wants to preserve the poem's movement from allegorical epic to a rectified romance-epic.

[29]C. S. Lewis, *Allegory of Love,* 324–33. In brief, "the one is artifice, sterility, death: the other, nature, fecundity, life" (326). The influence of Lewis's account of the Bower of Bliss is nicely described in Margaret P. Hannay, "Provocative Generalizations: *The Allegory of Love* in Retrospect," in *The Taste of the Pineapple: Essays on C. S. Lewis as Reader, Critic, and Imaginative Writer,* ed. Bruce L. Edwards (Bowling Green, Ohio: Bowling Green State University Popular Press, 1988), 58–78.

Chapter Three

The Human Form:
Surfaces and Secrets

The form that receives the most frequent, sustained, and various visual attention in *The Faerie Queene* is the human body. This may seem a fundamental so obvious as to preclude comment: of course characters perceive each other, and experience each other, as bodily creatures. But Spenser focuses his notions of human nature in the bodily form in ways that cannot be said of all narrative artists; Vergil, for example, is uninterested in awakening the reader's awareness of bodily form to the degree that Spenser consistently does. There are often extraordinary bodily circumstances: Duessa's revolting lower extremities, Serena's nakedness before the cannibals, Amoret's gaping hole where her heart should be. But there are also more mundane roles for the human form. Spenser is especially concerned with the social decorums, and sometimes the social comedies, of human figures impinging on each other; we can think of the various, often well-intentioned intruders on lovers of Book 6, or of knights who meet and narrowly avoid undesirable battles when they discover each other's identity. Some of these we shall see in subsequent chapters; here I want to focus on episodes in which women become visible to men in some context that fixes attention on sexual identity. What are the possible ways in which men can be present to women, or watch women, and vice versa? What attracts male viewers to the visual contemplation of female characters? What ethical circumstances make such contemplations wrong or right? How do such episodes affect the social relations between male and female characters? These questions can best be answered by recourse to Spenser's imitations of Ovid, and in the sections that follow I want to adduce from Spenser's work qualities of bodily experience with an Ovidian origin, an Ovidian thematic interest in the ways that male characters watch female, and a stylistic interest in the problems of depicting such Ovidian episodes and characters.

But first I turn to Petrarch, who occasions a departure from my general rule of not discussing authors who mediate Spenser's responses to Vergil and Ovid. Petrarch's poetic techniques, and his structures of love and desire, so permeate Elizabethan poets' work that a few comments about Spenser's apprehensions of Petrarchan poetry and gender relations will considerably clarify subsequent discussions about the English poet's depictions of male characters regarding female. Petrarchanism presents a steady challenge throughout Spenser's work, not least in episodes of male viewers smitten by the sexual vision of women, and it is these episodes, which are one concern of this chapter and which are shaped not only by Ovidian models but also by their Neoplatonic and Petrarchan antecedents, which reveal Spenser's efforts to challenge the Petrarchan contemplation of woman without sacrificing access to the visionary.[1]

Spenser responds to four problems in the Petrarchan syntax of erotic relations. The first and most familiar is the risk of hypostatization and rhetorical dismemberment of the beheld woman.[2] It is this consequence of blazon that Spenser parodies and critiques most memor-

[1] For his argument about Petrarchanism, I am indebted to Joseph Loewenstein's essay "Echo's Ring: Orpheus and Spenser's Career," *English Literary Renaissance* 16 (Spring 1986), 287–302.

[2] On Petrarchan frustration and fragmentation of identity in lover as well as beloved, see Nancy Vickers, "Diana Described: Scattered Woman and Scattered Rhyme," *Critical Inquiry* 8 (1981), 265–79, rpt. in *Writing and Sexual Difference*, ed. Elizabeth Abel (Chicago: University of Chicago Press, 1982), 95–110; Gordon Braden, "Beyond Frustration: Petrarchan Laurels in the Seventeenth Century," *Studies in English Literature* 26 (Winter 1986), 5–23, and "Love and Fame: The Petrarchan Career," in *Pragmatism's Freud: The Moral Disposition of Psychoanalysis*, ed. William Kerrigan and Joseph H. Smith (Baltimore: Johns Hopkins University Press, 1986), 126–58; John Freccero, "The Fig Tree and the Laurel: Petrarch's Poetics," *Diacritics* 5 (Spring 1975), 34–40, rpt. in *Literary Theory/Renaissance Texts*, ed. Patricia Parker and David Quint (Baltimore: Johns Hopkins University Press, 1986), 20–32; Guiseppe Mazzotta, "The *Canzoniere* and the Language of the Self," *Studies in Philology* 75 (1978), 271–96.

ably in the visual cannibalization of Serena's naked body by the savages who plan her literal cannibalization (6.8.37–51). The cannibals' ethical failure in this legend of courtesy lies less in their plan to eat their victim than in their more fundamentally indecorous exposure and display of her. This display degrades her and shows the risks to both humans and language of even the loveliest rhetorical features found in traditional languages of love, for instance, catalogue, religious diction, allusiveness to the Song of Songs:

> Her yuorie necke, her alablaster brest,
>   Her paps, which like white silken pillowes were,
>   For loue in soft delight thereon to rest;
>   Her tender sides, her bellie white and clere,
>   Which like an Altar did it selfe vprere,
>   To offer sacrifice diuine thereon;
>   Her goodly thighes, whose glorie did appeare
>   Like a triumphall Arch, and thereupon
> The spoiles of Princes hang'd, which were in battel won.
>
>   (6.8.42)

Serena's response to her ordeal suggests a second problem in the Petrarchan tradition: she naturally responds to exposure with shame. The sheer publicity of display violates inward identity, the reserve of the body's "inward parts," and she can offer her rescuer Calepine only a radical reticence throughout the night on which he protects her. Calepine's rescue of Serena from the cannibals reflects Spenser's wish to rescue the beloved woman from the intense publicity of the Petrarchan sexual gaze, since this gaze risks the appropriation of the woman by the male imagination in a denial of her otherness, her separateness from him.[3]

Petrarchan sexual vision is risky for the male viewer, as well, who needs to be rescued from endless frustration—the third problem Spenser confronts in Petrarchanism. Petrarch's *Canzoniere* regularly acknowledge that the deprivation which initiates the potency of artistic creativity also threatens to deprive the poet of his creative flow of poems; the lover in the Petrarchan tradition suffers the experience of

---

[3]This consciousness of the danger of solipsism exists throughout Petrarch's work, where the danger is accepted as a complement of sublimation. Spenser, whose characters struggle to establish active relationships with their lovers, needs to find ways to keep the male imagination from making feminine life an *imago* of male desire.

woman as both desired and inaccessible. Spenser attempts various ways of representing women observed so as to avoid both this frustration of inaccessibility and the unhappily complete sexual access of vulnerable Ovidian nymphs, by redefining what about the woman observed could satisfy desire and by rectifying desire itself by making its ideal form not Ovidian but Vergilian. The blazon of Belphoebe is the paradigm: Braggadocchio tries to ravish her, in a parody of Ovidian pursuit and rape, but the reader and the hypothesized gazers of the episode may benignly feast on her beauty and numinous potency, her simple accessibility, when the gaze is not Ovidian and possessive but Homero-Vergilian and based on wonder.

Another frequent danger to the male viewer contemplating feminine beauty in Spenser's work is the arresting power of that beauty, as Joseph Loewenstein observes after commenting on the bride in the *Epithalamion* and the astonishment that she evokes, just as the Medusa's head did: "Renaissance neoplatonic symbolism is regularly invoked to contain the shock of the simile: the 'astoneying' effects of Medusa's head figure the arrest of sensuality achieved by great Beauty. ... Throughout Spenser's work, the *arresting* power of beauty constitutes both a narrative and a poetic problem."[4] Spenser is deeply ambivalent about this Petrarchan arrest. In the splendid recognition scene of Book 4, when Artegall and Britomart first consciously meet, Artegall's response to his unexpected vision of Britomart radiantly transforms his abashment into Neoplatonic contemplation: the movement within the phrase "of his wonder made religion" (4.6.22) finely carries his own surprise at himself. And Scudamour's parallel response to her includes a transformation of fear into a Vergilian openness to "celestiall vision" (4.6.24). But in Artegall's similar experience during his battle with Radegund in Book 5, the Neoplatonic power of feminine beauty unmans him:

> But when as he discouered had her face,
>   He saw his senses straunge astonishment,
>   A miracle of natures goodly grace.

· · · · ·

[4]Loewenstein, "Echo's Ring," 291. See also Kenneth Gross, " 'Each Heav'nly Close': Mythologies and Metrics in Spenser and the Early Poetry of Milton," *PMLA* 98, 1 (January 1983), 21–36, partially rpt. in *Edmund Spenser: Modern Critical Views*, ed. Harold Bloom (New York and New Haven: Chelsea House, 1986), 211–18, for a discussion, to which I am indebted in the following paragraphs, of Spenser's sense of time.

At sight thereof his cruell minded hart
  Empierced was with pittifull regard,
  That his sharpe sword he threw from him apart,
  Cursing his hand that had that visage mard.

(5.5.12–13)

The paralysis of the male viewer/victim before "his senses straunge astonishment" and its link with the obsessive sexual gaze (in Petrarch, a gaze directed inward to the *image* of the woman) appear throughout the *Amoretti*, a sequence that depicts Petrarchan love as periodically ensnaring the poet-lover in spite of efforts to transform and escape it:

My hungry eyes, through greedy couetize,
  Still to behold the obiect of theyr payne:
  with no contentment can themselues suffize,
  but hauing pine, and hauing not complayne.
For lacking it, they cannot lyfe sustayne,
  and seeing it, they gaze on it the more:
  in theyr amazement lyke Narcissus vayne
  whose eyes him staru'd: so plenty makes me pore.

(*Amor.* 83)

This sonnet follows Petrarch in the psychologizing of the Ovidian myth, in the application of the myth to a female beloved, and in its grasp of the inherently frustrated solipsism of fashioning the beloved in the image of the lover's own soul. But the disruptive movements of Petrarch's own love lyrics emphasize the violence of psychic transformation: the self is in an agonizing and fascinating exile from itself, risking permanent loss of identity in its self-alienating journey, risking a real paralysis by beauty's image.

Spenser's departures from this radical disruption of selfhood, in the sonnet above and elsewhere, point to the fourth great problem Petrarchanism poses for him. The arresting power of beauty is a drastic disruption, a breaking of time's continuity by a rupture that Spenser is ever anxious both to acknowledge and to overcome. Not only is the vision of the feminine numinous a providential gift; it is also a compelling and potentially dangerous object of wish. The heaven of Neoplatonic wonder before the beheld woman also threatens to paralyze the lover, as Artegall learns to his cost in Book 5, or to wrench him from his own identity. Therefore Spenser consistently elides the self-estranging violence of Petrarchan eros in the direction of gradual change or sustained transformation, acknowledging but defusing the threat of rupture in time. Just so he responds to the arresting power of sexual vision, a power submission to which Petrarch had understood to risk selfhood itself: Spenser laments mutability, one aspect of change within time, but he craves continuity, a concept that can accommodate change within time. Even the radiant stasis of bliss carries the risk that it will disruptively transcend the quotidian, so it is necessary that Glauce's comic voice, a voice from "in the middest" of time, interrupt Artegall and Scudamour's celestial wonder as they gaze on Britomart and draw it back to earth; necessary that Calidore's brief happiness on Mt. Acidale enter the daily, labyrinthine world through the more humanly reliable pleasures of knowledge and conversation. Spenser attempts to circumvent not only the limits of Petrarchan representations of woman but also the crisis of radical disruption of time and identity which Petrarchan sexual vision poses.

The Integrity of the Female Form: Virginity in Ovid and Spenser

The virginity of Ovidian nymphs is a model for many of Spenser's characters, male and female alike: in its vulnerability and its desire for self-preservation, in its originary hiddenness and its inevitable exposure. We might first discern what Spenser responds to in Ovid's depictions of human identity by addressing one of Spenser's own Diana stories, stories which are meditations on the Roman poet's tales of the virgin goddess and those whose lives intersect with hers, especially Ovid's Actaeon and Callisto.

Although Diana's inviolability is in part a resistance to the accommodation of male sexuality, it is not solely or even primarily so, for either poet. Spenser's Diana, discovered by Venus during her search for Cupid (3.6.17–20), makes this clear. As in Ovid's tale of Diana surprised by Actaeon, the integrity of the self here is defined by boundaries, particularly by geographical boundaries that are intended to preserve privacy, freedom from the presence of undesired beings. That Spenser changes the traditional intrusion of Actaeon (mortal, male) to an intrusion of Venus (divine, female) marks Spenser's self-conscious variations on Ovid—especially the ascendancy of Venus, in Spenser's middle books, as presiding goddess and principle, and the shift of the perceived threat from masculine invasion to feminine interruption—and marks the difference, too, between Ovid's painful and Spenser's more benign comic modes. For the fact that Spenser's Venus is the intruder obviates any possible scene of punishment—one goddess does not directly punish another—and converts the social and psychic dynamics from those of Ovid. Not, here, the moral danger of viewing the goddess naked, nor the ancient Theban tragedies of human consciousness shattered by contemplation of divinity; rather, social disarray and embarrassment, two social peers in a comic squabble. Given the popular Petrarchan and Neoplatonic allegorical interpretations of the Actaeon story in the Renaissance, it is an act of some originality for Spenser to turn away from these dominant interpretations in order to focus on the social dynamics of sight and embarrassment.[5]

Diana's assumption of privacy makes possible an utter self-possession in nakedness, a self-possession that is also a perfect self-forgetting:

> Shortly vnto the wastefull woods she came,
>   Whereas she found the Goddesse with her crew,
>   After late chace of their embrewed game,
>   Sitting beside a fountaine in a rew,
>   Some of them washing with the liquid dew
>   From off their dainty limbes the dustie sweat,
>   And soyle which did deforme their liuely hew;
>   Others lay shaded from the scorching heat;
> The rest vpon her person gaue attendance great.
>
> She hauing hong vpon a bough on high
>   Her bow and painted quiuer, had vnlaste
>   Her siluer buskins from her nimble thigh,
>   And her lancke loynes vngirt, and brests vnbraste,

[5]For the history of those interpretations, see Leonard Barkan's rich essay "Diana and Actaeon: The Myth as Synthesis," *English Literary Renaissance* 10 (Autumn 1980), 317–59. The Petrarchan line of interpretation, which came to pervade Renaissance love poetry, derives from the climax of Petrarch's *Rime* XXIII, in which "the lover's identity is finally split between the helpless victim and the poetic lamenter" (337); later "the association between self-inflicted love torment and the destruction is almost a cliché" (339). In the Neoplatonic interpretive tradition, the ancient link between feminine mysteries and ecstasy is revived: "Actaeon becomes the hero *par excellence* of heroic frenzies, the exemplar of the enthusiast who can attain divinity through love and contemplation" (342).

> After her heat the breathing cold to taste;
> Her golden lockes, that late in tresses bright
> Embreaded were for hindring of her haste,
> Now loose about her shoulders hong vndight,
> And were with sweet *Ambrosia* all besprinckled light.
>
> (3.6.17–18)

This bathing of the goddess is beautifully and surprisingly non-narcissistic for Diana, and non-voyeuristic for the reader. It can be so for two reasons. First, the initial athleticism of Diana and her troop sanctions the relief of the bath and its ideal of bodily joy, a sensory rather than a sexual happiness that Ovid also depicts often. What Spenser represents is not naked women as the object of a male gaze, or even of their own regard, but the purified voluptuousness of those bodily sensations after strenuous and disciplined exertion, of inhabiting one's body fully. Second, the assumption of Diana's and nymphs' perfect harmony with the natural world saves them from the self-regard that is a threatening possibility for fully human sexual consciousness. Disrobing, for goddess and nymphs, marks an ease of relationship with nature which human beings can know only in wish and in myths of a golden age.

This episode is one of Spenser's ventures into imagining scenes of female life, and it is notable that he chooses to depict moments of both secrecy and vulnerability—moments the more vulnerable, and the more attractive to putative viewers, for being private. To such privacy belong the post-hunt leisure and the heightened intensity of the senses ("After her heat the breathing cold to taste") which Venus upsets when she innocently enters:

> Soone as she *Venus* saw behind her backe,
>   She was asham'd to be so loose surprized,
>   And woxe halfe wroth against her damzels slacke,
>   That had not her thereof before auized,
>   But suffred her so carelesly disguized
>   Be ouertaken. Soone her garments loose
>   Vpgath'ring, in her bosome she comprized,
>   Well as she might, and to the Goddesse rose,
> Whiles all her Nymphes did like a girlond her enclose.
>
> (3.6.19)

The perfect bodily self-possession and sensory fineness of the bath are prerogatives of divinity—indeed, the very manifestation of her godhead: the composure of privacy, and the full extension of identity into that private space, are what define Diana's divinity to mortals. After the chase she is extended into bodily sensation—bodily consciousness *is* her consciousness—only this, in Diana, is not a bestial but a divine state. Her consciousness is likewise fully expanded into the sequestered grove that she inhabits, so geographical boundaries are coterminous with personal boundaries. As in the *Metamorphoses*, the entry into the grove by another is therefore not just an interruption of privacy but an invasion of identity. Self-possession and sensory fineness are fragile things, and they collapse immediately into fluster, defensiveness, and physical awkwardness; even Diana must counter invasion by setting up another form of protective boundary: "... all her Nymphes did like a girlond her enclose." These emphases on the private feminine scene and its invasion, and on the bodily experiences of athleticism and the bath, are especially Ovidian and Spenserian; other writers about Diana both antique and Renaissance show more interest in her victim.

The bodily and psychic vulnerability of Spenser's characters derives in part from Ovid's depictions of vulnerable nymphs, exemplary characters who may appear in Spenser's work either in their pure form or assimilated to other character types, for example, the distressed damsel of medieval romance.[6] Most nearly Ovidian are certain minor characters populating Faerie Land, characters like Agape, a "Fay" who shares with Ovidian nymphs a taste for "priuie place": "But she as Fayes are wont, in priuie place / Did spend her dayes, and lov'd in forests wyld to space" (4.2.44). Agape is raped casually by a passing knight, as she sits, just short of narcissism, on that Ovidian threshold between natural and human consciousness:

> There on a day a noble youthly knight
>   Seeking aduentures in the saluage wood,
>   Did by great fortune get of her the sight,
>   As she sate carelesse by a cristall flood,
>   Combing her golden lockes, as seemd her good:
>   And vnawares vpon her laying hold,

---

[6]Northrop Frye speculates on the symbolic significance of threatened virgins in romance, especially the line of romance from Sidney to Milton, in *The Secular Scripture: A Study of the Form of Romance* (Cambridge: Harvard University Press, 1976), 83–86.

> That stroue in vaine him long to haue withstood,
> Oppressed her, and there (as it is told)
> Got these three louely babes, that prov'd three champions bold.
>
> (4.2.45)

Cymoent conceives Marinell in a similar encounter, where the schematic lack of specific details verbally supports the casual triviality of the rape: Dumarin

> ...on a day
> Finding the Nymph a sleepe in secret wheare,
> As he by chaunce did wander that same way,
> Was taken with her loue, and by her closely lay.
>
> (3.4.19)

It is always the secrecy of the place that, so far from guaranteeing virginity, allows its loss; seclusion and defenselessness *invite* invasion or entrance by other characters in this Ovidian-romance world of random aggressions.[7]

This is true not only of creatures easily placed as Ovidian, but also of characters, even male characters, whose Ovidian shape has been influenced by later romance affinities, in whom Ovidian characteristics undergo expansion or development. Serena, like Ovid's Proserpina

---

[7]Recently, the work of Mikhail Bakhtin has prompted analysis of social symbolisms of the "grotesque body"—a notion that might usefully be considered as the alternative to Spenser's depiction of the body as I describe it here. This Spenserian depiction might perhaps be called an aristocratic body, except that this term seems to do justice to the image's cultural status (e.g., its relationship to the Queen and to the cult of Eliza) at the expense of its equally interesting generic affiliations. Peter Stallybrass and Allon White describe Bakhtin's "classical body," which has an ideological privilege over the "grotesque body": "To begin with, the classical statue was always mounted on a plinth which meant that it was elevated, static, and monumental.... The radiant centre of a transcendent individualism, 'put on a pedestal,' raised above the viewer and the commonality and anticipating passive admiration from below. We *gaze up* at the figure and wonder. We are placed by it as spectators to an instant—frozen yet apparently universal—of epic or tragic time" (*The Politics and Poetics of Transgression* [Ithaca: Cornell University Press, 1986], 21). See also Stephen Greenblatt's "Fiction and Friction," in *Reconstructing Individualism: Autonomy, Individuality, and the Self in Western Thought*, ed. Thomas C. Heller et al.(Stanford: Stanford University Press, 1986), 30–52, for an analysis of medical discourse in the period and its modes of understanding female sexual anatomy with categories of internal and external. See also Jean Starobinski, "Je hais comme les portes d'Hadès...," *Nouvelle Revue de psychanalyse* 97 (1974), 7–22, trans. by Frederick Brown as "The Inside and the Outside," *Hudson Review* 28 (Autumn 1975), 333–51.

who invites disaster in a protected grove with female companions, wanders gathering flowers; though Spenser uses moral diction to imply a vague culpability of her own, the foremost effect is that of Ovidian innocence attacked, when the Blatant Beast seizes her (6.3.23—24). The romance figure of Arthur, waiting for Turpine, sleeps "loosely displayd vpon the grassie ground" (6.7.18—19), a formula used also for Spenser's very Ovidian Chrysogonee. Aladine and Calepine, knights and lovers of Book 6, are each caught off guard in a sheltered place to which they have retired with their respective ladies for intimacy and solace, their defenselessness inevitably leading to invasion: "that proud Knight in his presumption / The gentle *Aladine* did earst inuade, / Being vnarm'd, and set in secret shade" (6.3.8). Even Redcrosse, whose roots are native English and biblical, not classical, is a beneficiary of Spenser's sensitivity to the vulnerable human form in an unpredictably dangerous sylvan landscape. Although the dangers are in this case cast as Christian, and are interior and moral, the landscape of the protected grove, its attendant spirit, and the tone of threat are Ovidian (drawn from *Met.* 4.285–386, 15.319–21); as Hamilton notes in his edition, Spenser fuses Diana's vigorous athleticism with the Christian ideal of running the good race:

> Vnkindnesse past, they gan of solace treat,
>   And bathe in pleasaunce of the ioyous shade,
>   Which shielded them against the boyling heat,
>   And with greene boughes decking a gloomy glade,
>   About the fountaine like a girlond made;
>   Whose bubbling waue did euer freshly well,
>   Ne euer would through feruent sommer fade:
>   The sacred Nymph, which therein wont to dwell,
> Was out of *Dianes* fauour, as it then befell.
>
> The cause was this: one day when *Phoebe* fayre
>   With all her band was following the chace,
>   This Nymph, quite tyr'd with heat of scorching ayre
>   Sat downe to rest in middest of the race.
>
> (1.7.4—5)[8]

Psychic and bodily vulnerability is expanded to human nature in general, on the many occasions when Spenser contemplates the in-

---

[8] We know of Spenser's unease with indolence, an unease that Joseph Loewenstein identifies with pastoral *otium* as the source of Spenser's "enduring ambivalence to

vadable condition of the body. Busyrane's tapestry, a concentration
of mythic seductions described in a catalogue like that used by Ovid
to describe Arachne's tapestry (*Met.* 6.103–28), repeatedly structures
raptus as invasion into a generative space, an action simultaneously
beautiful and violent, as in the Roman poet's work. Body and guarded
tower are confounded in the story of Danaë:

> Soone after that into a golden showre
>   Him selfe [Jove] he chaung'd faire *Danaë* to vew,
>   And through the roofe of her strong brasen towre
>   Did raine into her lap an hony dew.
>
> (3.11.31)

Leda is herself invaded, while sleeping—or sleeping and watching
covertly—in the shade:

> O wondrous skill, and sweet wit of the man,
>   That her in daffadillies sleeping made,
>   From scorching heat her daintie limbes to shade:
>   Whiles the proud Bird ruffing his fethers wyde,
>   And brushing his faire brest, did her inuade;
>   She slept, yet twixt her eyelids closely spyde,
> How towards her he rusht, and smiled at his pryde.
>
> (3.11.32)

Nor is the violability of the body in Spenser's work limited to sexual
invasions of women; Spenser's diction points attention to this vulnerability in many other contexts. It is the body that is wounded
internally, in its tender inner parts, regardless of whether a wound is
physical or psychic and regardless of the victim's gender: knights
fighting "tryde all waies, how each mote entrance make / Into the life
of his malignant foe" (6.1.37). Sclaunder's actions wound the inner

---

the pastoral mode" (*Responsive Readings: Versions of Echo in Pastoral, Epic, and
the Jonsonian Masque* [New Haven: Yale University Press, 1984], 131–32). It may
be partly this dissatisfaction with pastoral leisure which draws Spenser to his ampli-
fications of the sylvan, Ovidian cousin to pastoral and his plentiful descriptions of
Diana and her nymphs absorbed in the athleticism of the hunt. Such athleticism
legitimizes the subsequent rest and pleasures of the senses which Spenser bestows
upon them; it also allows Spenser's Diana to be representative of both pastoral *otium*
and pastoral energy, and enemy of those who are "dull and slow" (1.7.5).

parts (4.8.26); the parallel wounding of Serena and Timias by the Blatant Beast releases an inward poison that can be opposed only by the strictest censoring of the exterior of the body (6.6.7–8, 13–14).

One unexpected implication of this argument for the Ovidian descent of Spenser's virgins, and the frequent extension of Ovidian vulnerability to other kinds of characters, is that Spenser gives relatively little resonance to virginity as a Christian moral ideal. Of major characters, Belphoebe alone is devoted to virginity per se, but her depiction is complicated by her being partially a representation of Elizabeth, and even Belphoebe's story tugs her toward some kind of transformed consciousness of eros. All the other virgins are more precisely steadfast lovers. Or, among minor characters, there are nymphs, like Cymoent, who come all but directly from the *Metamorphoses*, beings on the threshold between natural and human consciousness, as we have seen. Virginity in *The Faerie Queene* is more often conceived on an Ovidian model than on any other, as integrity of selfhood, intimacy with the natural world, and the fragile pleasure of bodily and psychic sensation allowed by invisibility to the social world.

A fundamental fact about the human body both male and female in Spenser's work, a development from his Ovidian characters, is that it has a hallowed interior space and an eloquent, if vulnerable, exterior. This fact about the human form has always been obliquely recognized, as in comments about Spenser's situating of the creative act "deepe within the mynd," or about the secret, hidden centers of the psyche in Books 3 and 6, or in treatments of allegorical castles like the House of Alma.[9] The relationship between the visible, eloquent surface and the hidden, secret space within takes a variety of forms. Leonard Barkan has, for example, documented the implications about microcosm and macrocosm which inhere in the allegorical and iconographical traditions.[10] Sometimes Spenser relies on a traditional, Christianized Neoplatonic sense of the soul encased in the body, as when the souls of Priamond and Diamond flit from one body

[9]David L. Miller's *The Poem's Two Bodies: The Poetics of the 1590 "Faerie Queene"* (Princeton: Princeton University Press, 1988), 25–26, 113–15, and passim, discusses the interior space of the body in the first half of the epic. His book appeared too late to have any direct consequences for my arguments; we often arrive at similar observations about passages discussed, though our larger arguments reflect different interests.

[10]See Barkan's *Nature's Work of Art: The Human Body as Image of the World* (New Haven: Yale University Press, 1975).

to the next (4.3) or when Britomart fears that the tormented Scudamour's "wearie soule" "from her cage...would flit" (3.11.12), or when Serena's body is called the "fraile mansion of mortality" (6.3.28). But bodily life is often less a matter of soul within body, spirit caged in flesh, than of interior and surface or shape, as a continuum, as different kinds of spaces through which identity is known.

The "inner parts," only rarely differentiated as organs (with the exception of the heart), are in both sexes a space of generativity, both artistic and biological, and of the authentic self. Guyon, addressing Shamefastnesse, refers to "the secret of your hart" (2.9.42), and unknowingly describes the central quality within himself; it emerges to visibility with her blush. Britomart, literally containing her joy on hearing Artegall praised, is like a mother who bears a child "[i]n the deare closet of her painefull side" (3.2.11). Tristram, dubbed squire, unfurls the joyfulness that had been hidden, infolded within him:

> Like as a flowre, whose silken leaues small,
> Long shut vp in the bud from heauens vew,
> At length breakes forth, and brode displayes his smyling hew.
> (6.2.35)

Amoret is the "sweet lodge of loue and deare delight" (3.12.45, 1590 ed.), and Spenser's love in the *Amoretti* is "the lodging of delight" and the "bowre of blisse" (*Amor.* 76); the speaker's interior is the site of amorous and epideictic writing: "Deepe in the closet of my parts entyre, / Her worth is written with a golden quill" (*Amor.* 85). This sense of the bodily self as a continuum between hallowed interior and eloquent, vulnerable surface in Spenser's work has its roots, yet once more, in Ovid's depictions of virginal and defenseless nymphs whose vulnerable surfaces visually inflame the gods and allow violation. Spenser will privilege the interiority of the individual in a way foreign to Ovid, giving it psychic shadows and historical depths; but Ovid makes this move possible with his creation of an imagined bliss of privacy, an invisibility in which the self can unfold in safety.

An ideological commitment to a different relationship of outer shape and inner space, and hence to a notion of virginity not particularly strong in Spenser's work, occurs in Milton's Spenserian *Mask*. The Lady's condition in that work can clarify by way of contrast how

Spenser conceives the body's inner and outer parts, and how Ovidian metamorphosis figures in Spenserian human nature. The Elder Brother voices notions to which his sister also subscribes:

> So dear to Heav'n is Saintly chastity,
> That when a soul is found sincerely so,
> A thousand liveried Angels lackey her,
> Driving far off each thing of sin and guilt,
> And in clear dream and solemn vision
> Tell her of things that no gross ear can hear;
> Till oft converse with heav'nly habitants
> Begin to cast a beam on th'outward shape,
> The unpolluted temple of the mind,
> And turns it by degrees to the soul's essence,
> Till all be made immortal: but when lust
> Lets in defilement to the inward parts,
> The soul grows clotted by contagion,
> Imbodies and imbrutes, till she quite lose
> The divine property of her first being.
>
> (453–69)[11]

"Outward shape" and "inward parts," for Milton early in his career, form a contrast, not a Spenserian continuum, and this contrast is equivalent to the contrast between body and soul. The ideal is to turn the body into "the soul's essence"; the threat is that the soul may turn into the essence of flesh. William Kerrigan's discussion of the *Mask* identifies the Platonic and Orphic anthropology that supports the confidence of the Lady and the Elder Brother: "Virtue begins, as it has always begun in the Orphic cosmos, with the gnosis of this estrangement, teaching us that we are the same as the soul and other than the body."[12]

These traditional dichotomies compel Spenser very little in his depiction of virginity; virginity's valence lies rather in its proximity to "first being," understood not as the soul's existence before its "imbruting" in flesh but as the natural ground and the initial integrity

[11]All citations from Milton are from Merritt Hughes's edition, *Complete Poems and Major Prose* (New York: Bobbs-Merrill, 1957).

[12]William Kerrigan, *The Sacred Complex: On the Psychogenesis of "Paradise Lost"* (Cambridge: Harvard University Press, 1983), 31. Kerrigan's full discussion of the *Mask*, 22–72, bears on my points here.

of its possessor.[13] The great examplar of this mode is Belphoebe, whose origins are described in Book 3. She is "Pure and vnspotted from all loathly crime, / That is ingenerate in fleshly slime" (3.6.3). Spenser has used a variant of the final phrase before, to describe Orgoglio as "this monstrous masse of earthly slime" (1.7.9). But although he acknowledges the consequences of the Fall with such a phrase, his imagination is not particularly compelled by a dichotomy of decadent flesh and immortal spirit, as these stanzas about Belphoebe's conception suggest:

> On her they [the heavens] poured forth of plenteous horne;
> *Ioue* laught on *Venus* from his soueraigne see,
> And *Phoebus* with faire beames did her adorne,
> And all the *Graces* rockt her cradle being borne.

> Her berth was of the wombe of Morning dew,
> And her conception of the ioyous Prime,
> And all her whole creation did her shew
> Pure and vnspotted from all loathly crime,
> That is ingenerate in fleshly slime.

$$(3.6.2-3)$$

The opposite of "fleshly slime" in these lines is not "transcendent spirit." It is rather the vitality and freshness of the early—a time within nature, within culture, and within individual life which Spenser wishes to preserve throughout psychic development. The earliness of Belphoebe is most evidently a matter of time in the natural world, a freshness and a "glittering chastity of form"[14] guaranteed by her dawn conception. But her nearness to origins is suggested as well by her access to the generosity of the antique gods; the abundance of ancient poetry accrues to her along with the gods' gifts, a belated explanation of her suitability for large-scale imitation in Book 2. She is early vis-à-vis Judaeo-Christian poetry, too: as Thomas Roche points out, the allusion to Psalm 110 ("Thy birthes dew is the dew that doth from wombe of morning fall") was typologically read as a reference to the

---

[13]Florimell, fixed in her resistance to Proteus (3.8.42–43), most closely resembles Milton's Lady, and Spenser praises her as "Fit song of Angels caroled to bee." But her fixed resolve is a matter also of her steadfastness to Marinell; her love for him has already changed the direction of her original, purely virginal, psychic energy.

[14]Camille Paglia, "The Apollonian Androgyne and the *Faerie Queene*," *English Literary Renaissance* 9 (Winter 1979), 42–63 at 42.

begetting of Christ.[15] The Judaeo-Christian earliness of the lines is in fact twofold: the Psalms, as elsewhere in Spenser and later, profoundly, in Herbert and Vaughan, evoke a world of nearness to the origins of the patriarchs and to divinity itself, a world of vigor and clarity; and the Incarnation is the nativity par excellence, which Belphoebe's miraculous birth echoes. The lines dilate the earliness of "first being," in the biological individual, in the Graeco-Roman and Judaeo-Christian cultures, and in nature.

The potency of Spenser's structural apprehension of the body as hallowed interior and living external shape, and the relation of this bodily structure to Ovidian metamorphosis, we can see in the negative instance of the false Florimell's creation (3.8.6–8), which is Spenser's clearest inversion of his sense of the body as eloquent surface and generative interior. The false Florimell is best seen against the poem's proliferating and luxuriant descriptions of natural, living nymphs and virgins. Lacking a generation that situates her in nature's time of the "ioyous Prime" and nature's substance the "Morning dew" (3.6.3)— the blessings of Belphoebe's nativity—the false Florimell is compounded of construction materials (snow, mercury, wax) which, although natural substances, are removed from the natural cycles that give a context to Chrysogonee's and Belphoebe's natural worlds. This "carkasse dead," the mechanical surface of which *is* its substance, is the treasury of no animating plenitude stored within, but only the hollow container of an inserted spirit adept at making the thing's eyes "stirre and roll" (3.8.7). The thing is a mechanistic container and void interior, a bogus imitation of the quick Spenserian body with its warmly eloquent surface and protected interior. It is made of unmelting snow and malleable mercury and wax, natural objects detached from nature to construct a simulacrum of virginity from the outside—an inversion of the Spenserian maiden's rootedness in the natural world. In particular, the false Florimell's witch creator uses pure snow gathered in hills "from all men conceald" (3.8.6); the hidden places of nature are not, here, the sheltered places of sanctuary or of virginal privacy but the secret source of the power of black magic. The false Florimell's pliancy to men is only the inevitable mark of the absence of that primal integrity that characterizes Spenserian virgins—and that integrity is, precisely, the unbroken continuum of

[15]Thomas P. Roche, Jr., *The Kindly Flame: A Study of "The Faerie Queene" 3 and 4* (Princeton: Princeton University Press, 1964), 105–6.

interior and surface, the unity of psychic consciousness with bodily consciousness.[16]

The greatest exemplar of that integrity is Belphoebe; Spenser's long treatment of her tests and expands the qualities of Ovidian virginity for which he has the greatest affinity. I suggested in Chapter Two that the blazon of Belphoebe in Book 2 succeeds in part because her eloquently visible body bears signs that can be read by an appropriate viewer, which is to say a Vergilian one. Until her discovery of Timias in Book 3 opens the possibility of self-consciousness in her, her very candor is the mark of her undivided identity and of her Ovidian solitude.

Spenser is of two minds about this un-self-consciousness in Belphoebe, his most Ovidian nymph but also a character strongly linked to the non-literary world, since she bears various figural relations to the Queen. I have suggested that he privileges the qualities that attend virginity: its integrity, its perfect consonance of inner bodily space and exterior, its earliness, its pristine emergence from nature. But he has an equally strong sense that the possible bliss of erotic adulthood demands an entry into history and a turbulent, tormented, risky break with the *circumstances* of nature, nature as that which encompasses her. Virginity permanently embraced, although he needs it in Belphoebe for Elizabeth's sake, he finds atavistic, a standing within nature at the expense of adult consciousness. Hence one generic and ethical source for the dwindling of narrative possibilities in the relations of Belphoebe and Timias.[17] One solution to this problem of a conceptual conflict between virginity and maturation is to multiply heroines who expand the notion of virginity to chastity, as passionate married love—the chief solution of Books 3 and 4.

Another, which I want to emphasize here, is to nudge the fixed aspects of virginity into more flexible, not to say paradoxical, redefinitions. This is what happens in the tricky iconographical doubleness of a stanza about the Queen:

[16]Anne Ferry discusses the description of the false Florimell as a perverse blazon in *The Art of Naming* (Chicago: University of Chicago Press, 1988), 166–68.

[17]Cf. Angus Fletcher on Milton's *Mask:* "Metaphysically the virgin state, which is defined by its beginning as an unspoiled oneness, seems to tend, as an idea, toward a virtual disorder. Virginity, like paradise, needs to be lost—preserved, it gradually loses its springlike nature. Virginity is a fountain from whose perfect source the stream can only move away into less limpid channels" (*The Transcendental Masque: An Essay on Milton's "Comus"* [Ithaca: Cornell University Press, 1971], 212).

To such therefore I do not sing at all,
   But to that sacred Saint my soueraigne Queene,
   In whose chast breast all bountie naturall,
   And treasures of true loue enlocked beene,
   Boue all her sexe that euer yet was seene;
   To her I sing of loue, that loueth best,
   And best is lou'd of all aliue I weene:
   To her this song most fitly is addrest,
The Queene of loue, and Prince of peace from heauen blest.
                          (4.Proem.4)

The image of Diana is made to accommodate a Venus within it: if virginity is a state in which something is contained and hidden within, inviolate, then the contained is to become the abundance of eros, here sanctified by propinquity to Christian images of love. Elizabeth's virginity is sanctioned insofar as she can exemplify both Venus ("Queene of loue") and Messiah ("Prince of peace"), but, as in Ovid's work there is a conflict between the "maiestas" and "amor" of Jove, so Spenser is uncomfortable with the "vse of Maiestie" untransformed. Elizabeth becomes, in Spenser's wish at least, a treasury of love. The forbidding aspects of Diana are acknowledged only to be expelled, as the wished-for identification with Venus becomes bolder in the next stanza:

Which that she may the better deigne to heare,
   Do thou dred infant, *Venus* dearling doue,
   From her high spirit chase imperious feare,
   And vse of awfull Maiestie remoue:
   In sted thereof with drops of melting loue,
   Deawd with ambrosiall kisses, by thee gotten
   From thy sweete smyling mother from aboue,
   Sprinckle her heart, and haughtie courage soften,
That she may hearke to loue, and read this lesson often.
                          (4.Proem.5)

The dew of pristine virginal earliness is now assimilated to the kisses that are the emblem of Venus's power, and the reticence of virginity defined wholly negatively as fear and *hauteur*. By the end of the Proem, the potential rigidity of virginity has virtually been reversed: Diana remains, but her inner content is now Venus, her inner consciousness love. In effect, Spenser's stanza is a prayer, on behalf of his Ovidian nymph, to the god who can metamorphose her by means of a magic love potion. This paradoxical metaphoric transformation, along with the narrative of Belphoebe and Timias, is Spenser's most subtle effort to extend to Elizabeth the potency of psychically transformed human nature. Belphoebe's cautious acceptance of Timias is an obvious first step in the process, but the fact that the metamorphosis-as-maturation cannot be fulfilled in married sexuality gives Spenser notorious problems of plot development. His recourse is to turn to figurative language, as in the stanza above, for both Belphoebe and the Queen.

"So many heauenly faces": The Envisioning of Women

The blazon of Belphoebe and the description of the false Florimell's creation repeatedly stress the fascination of the eye which the presence of these characters arouses in other characters or in a more abstract, hypothesized spectator. In the former case the gaze of one watcher is assumed to be a rectified one, by virtue of its Vergilian awe and by virtue of the narrator's protection of Belphoebe's assumption of solitude. Spenser creates the passage's multiple decorums and tactfulnesses toward Belphoebe, the Queen, Vergil, and Ovid, and among characters, narrator, and readers, with a range of poetic resources which argues considerable subtlety in his awareness of the problems of beholding women. These are representational and ethical problems, and they are problems for the author, the observer characters, the observed characters, and the audience of Spenser's work alike. But the complex awareness of the blazon of Belphoebe is not consistently found throughout Spenser's epic.

The display of the false Florimell herself (or itself) and the entire exhibition of ladies following the tournament, both contests for the girdle of chastity (4.5.10–17), do not much clarify ethical matters about viewing the female body. There is no recognition that such ethical distinctions can even be made; the passage is, for Spenser, a relatively perfunctory adaptation of romance competitions. If the contest has an ethical tone at all, it is a sporadic irony directed toward the spectacle of men and women behaving themselves so, mixing up as they do chastity and greed—a tone not inconsistent with other works published in 1595 and 1596. Duessa reappears after her ignominy in Book 1, restored to her former glamor and in Paridell's company, but she does not function as a marker of the duplicity or inappropriateness of the contest. Even Britomart is there, displaying Amoret, and Spenser gives no indication that the process of display, elsewhere so carefully evaluated and placed, is morally and socially complex.

The Faerie Queene demonstrates the diverse difficulties of bringing male presence before a feminine or erotic scene. Given the blind spots in our knowledge of the poem's composition, it is impossible to prove a detailed development in its representations of women viewed. The teleological impulse of the critic is strong, though, and I will be suggesting at the very least that the pertinent episodes manifest a gradually increasing range of narrative mastery and grasp of the implications for the rest of a particular canto or book. Except in rare instances, moreover, Spenser embraces the intertwined problems of representing and beholding women, and experiments with ways of solving them without denying the motives and hungers of the eye.

Duessa is so wicked that she merits two exposures, through each of which Spenser probes the otherwise infrequent viewer response of disgust. The first occurs when Fradubio tells how he accidentally came upon Duessa bathing:

> I chaunst to see her in her proper hew,
> Bathing her selfe in origane and thyme:
> A filthy foule old woman I did view,
> That euer to haue toucht her, I did deadly rew.

> Her neather partes misshapen, monstruous,
>   Were hidd in water, that I could not see,
>   But they did seeme more foule and hideous,
>   Then womans shape man would beleeue to bee.

> (1.2.40–41)

What Fradubio describes is a grotesque twist on the topos of the numinous woman at her bath. Like Actaeon, Fradubio "chaunst to see" the taboo sight. But Duessa's power is demonic rather than divine: she represents sexual excess rather than virginity; the herbs that she applies were used to heal skin disorders, and thyme, as A. C. Hamilton notes, was a treatment for syphilis.

The second exposure of Duessa, when Una, Redcrosse, and Arthur strip her after her defeat, is considerably more detailed, erotic, and filled with disgust than Spenser's brief scriptural sources (Isa. 3.17–

24, Rev. 17.16, 18.16) or the similar moment in *Orlando Furioso* when Ruggiero discovers Alcina's true nature (7.72–74).

> So as she [Una] bad, that witch they disaraid,
>   And robd of royall robes, and purple pall,
>   And ornaments that richly were displaid;
>   Ne spared they to strip her naked all.
>   Then when they had despoild her tire and call,
>   Such as she was, their eyes might her behold,
>   That her misshaped parts did them appall,
>   A loathly, wrinckled hag, ill fauoured, old,
> Whose secret filth good manners biddeth not be told.
>
> Her craftie head was altogether bald,
>   And as in hate of honorable eld,
>   Was ouergrowne with scurfe and filthy scald;
>   Her teeth out of her rotten gummes were feld,
>   And her sowre breath abhominably smeld;
>   Her dried dugs, like bladders lacking wind,
>   Hong downe, and filthy matter from them weld;
>   Her wrizled skin as rough, as maple rind,
> So scabby was, that would haue loathd all womankind.
>
> Her neather parts, the shame of all her kind,
>   My chaster Muse for shame doth blush to write;
>   But at her rompe she growing had behind
>   A foxes taile, with dong all fowly dight;
>   And eke her feete most monstrous were in sight;
>   For one of them was like an Eagles claw,
>   With griping talaunts armd to greedy fight,
>   The other like a Beares vneuen paw:
> More vgly shape yet neuer liuing creature saw.
>
>   (1.8.46–48)

Fradubio could only guess at the monstrosity of Duessa's "neather parts," submerged in water as she bathed; a man who has been her lover hardly needs more explicit knowledge than he already has to be shocked and repelled. But Fradubio's was an accidental encounter, and he had no purpose in seeing Duessa's nakedness. In Canto 8, she is intentionally exposed and degraded. Spenser provides a vigorous parody of blazon, as the sequence of hair, teeth, mouth, breasts, and "neather parts" suggests. This is an appropriately witty literary punishment, parallel to the punishment of stripping within the action of the story, for the witch whose power over men has relied on an opulent and sensuous sexuality. This is the temptress whose friends and allies have throughout the book been the sophisticated, charming, and decadent representatives of courtly love; it is through one more structure of courtly love, the literary blazon, that Spenser describes her exposure.

Moreover, she does not only pervert feminine beauty in her effort to undermine Redcrosse's quest for sanctification. She also distorts and brings shame upon the *old* female body. John Upton's commentary cites Chaucer's *Knight's Tale* ("eld hath great avauntage, / In eld is both wysedom and usage") and suggests that "Chaucer seems to have Ovid in his eye. —Seris venit usus ab annis (*Met.* 6.29)."[18] We might also adduce the tale of the Wife of Bath, in which Chaucer exploits the knight's revulsion from old women only to turn the tables on him with the hag's powerful arguments for gentilesse. In Spenser's description, Duessa's own body is naturally expressive of contempt for age: "Her craftie head was altogether bald, / And as in hate of honorable eld, / Was ouergrowne with scurfe."

The prurience that this spectacle may encourage in the reader-viewer exists along with a good deal of understandable fascination with the monstrous, as well as something of the moral desideratum to see and know evil fully in order to expel it completely. But such moments are infrequent in the greater part of the poem. As I have suggested, Spenser is alive to the nature of man's attentiveness to woman, and more precisely the male artist's attention to the bodily presence of woman, and how he might place himself visually in relation to her. Most broadly, it is not only the Homero-Vergilian awe but also the reticence or invisibility of the viewer which may redeem the male contemplation of the woman. In the *Metamorphoses*, the hoped-for guarantor of the self is hiddenness, freedom from the implicitly interested gaze of another. But of *The Faerie Queene* it is more precise to say that what private female characters need is not liberation from a male gaze, but innocence of the knowledge of that gaze, of

[18]Cited from John G. Radcliffe, ed., *John Upton: Notes on "The Faerie Queene,"* 2 vols. (New York: Garland, 1987), vol. 1, 278–79. James Nohrnberg draws another important comparison with Duessa's exposure—the exposure of Serena in Book 6: "Exposure in the context of courtesy [in Book 6] means a very different thing from exposure in the context of revelation [in Book 1]" (*The Analogy of "The Faerie Queene"* [Princeton: Princeton University Press, 1976], 714–16).

the knowledge that others desire their sexual presence. Spenser wishes to grant them circumstances that permit them the freedom to be perfectly present only to themselves, in the candor that, as we saw in the case of Belphoebe, permits them to exist as if "independently of any audience."[19]

It seems to have been Spenser's large-scale development of Ovid's *Metamorphoses* that empowered Spenser to begin making just the kind of social and ethical discriminations that appear only briefly in Book 1 with the stripping of Duessa, and to perceive that an encyclopedic survey of such scenes could be made in the first place. That it is Spenser's responses to Ovid—imitative expansion of episodes, character types, and ethical norms—which lead to his proliferating watchers of the female sexual body is most evident in the adapted tales of Diana (one of which we have already seen), in which the majesty and terror of taboo are redirected into social fluster and embarrassment. Embarrassment is not trivial in *The Faerie Queene*, as we shall see; as a sudden awareness of the gaze of another it is a loss of innocence. The stories about Diana and Venus, and Diana and Faunus, derived from Ovid's stories of the sexual body revealed which we saw in Chapter One, report not only others' observations of Diana but also the flustered loss of her usual self-possession when she becomes aware of the watcher, a condition that destroys the possibility of candid solitude. The goddess surprised at her bath is doubly undone, for her vulnerable bodily nakedness is coterminous with her divinity. This is why Diana in all her tales tries to protect her bodily freedom from visibility to all but her own nymphs. Diana's nakedness interests representational artists insofar as it exists precisely *not* to be present to the gaze of others (a gaze always problematically present, for artists, in the act of depicting her), but rather insofar as it marks her full presence only to herself and to her nymphs. Modesty or shamefastness in Spenser's poem, therefore, is often a protective social habit that veils the private enclosed territory and secrecy of interiority. Concomitantly, to expose one's body or to have it exposed creates a

---

[19]Stanley Cavell, *The World Viewed: Reflections on the Ontology of Film*, enlarged ed. (Cambridge: Harvard University Press, 1979), 111. The discussion that follows in the rest of this chapter—indeed in the rest of the book—owes a large debt to Cavell's development of acknowledgment, especially in "Knowing and Acknowledging" and "The Avoidance of Love: A Reading of *King Lear*," both in *Must We Mean What We Say? A Book of Essays* (Cambridge: Cambridge University Press, 1976), 231–66 and 267–353, respectively.

fallen self-consciousness, the human parallel to Diana's embarrassment, which intrinsically sullies. Spenser's own limited anti-theatrical prejudice derives from his regret over the loss of innocence inherent in one's awareness of oneself as object of another's view.

The relative clarity of these ethical, psychological, and aesthetic principles does not inevitably simplify Spenser's representational difficulties in bringing male presence before a sexual or a feminine scene. In fact, Spenser attempts complex balancing acts between his efforts to create the innocent eye and his understanding of the evident fact that the eye cannot be innocent in any simple sense. This is true, for instance, of the beautiful and disturbing episode of Chrysogonee's impregnation by the sun (3.6.3–10). A preliminary reading, one that acknowledges the best motives of the text, could make the following points.

Spenser's Ovidian nymph bathes in a fountain in a forest, "farre from all mens vew"—a phrase by which we are reminded simultaneously of her assumed solitude and of the watching presence of an Ideal Spectator:

> It was vpon a Sommers shynie day,
> When *Titan* faire his beames did display,
> In a fresh fountaine, farre from all mens vew,
> She bath'd her brest, the boyling heat t'allay;
> She bath'd with roses red, and violets blew,
> And all the sweetest flowres, that in the forrest grew.
>
> (3.6.6)

The sense of watching the naked and the private, in this adaptation of the ancient motif of the goddess surprised at her bath by a fascinated man, is emphasized by Chrysogonee's utter lack of self-consciousness: here and throughout the episode she expresses an innocent, open solitude that sharpens our awareness of watching her.

Her vulnerability to the possible dangers of the male gaze intensifies when Spenser tells us that she lays herself down on the grassy ground and sleeps: Spenser says a slumber "upon her fell," using a locution that suggests her passive openness to events. She commits herself to the earth trustingly, like a child; but Spenser's phrasing recalls Ovid, whose Callisto had done exactly the same thing just before Jove's possessive, powerful gaze aroused his violent desire for her (*Met.* 2.417–24). Spenser raises these undercurrents, anticipations of dreadful things to come, only to dismiss them gently. No terrible harm can come to Chrysogonee, dwelling as she does in a protective space that the narrator opens for her. The depiction of the god's descent upon her swerves from Ovidian aggression and rape to a natural, engendering process of fructification. And the sun, the male viewer in the episode, not only is not present to Chrysogonee's consciousness (a move by which Spenser preserves her candor), but entirely lacks any kind of bad faith in his relation to the woman, because by not assuming human form he also does not assume fully human male volition:

> The sunne-beames bright vpon her body playd,
> Being through former bathing mollifide,
> And pierst into her wombe, where they embayd
> With so sweet sence and secret power vnspide,
> That in her pregnant flesh they shortly fructifide.
>
> (3.6.7)

Chrysogonee is "all naked bare displayed" in her sleep, her bodily surface eloquent of her imperturbable simplicity. The notion of display here carries no ominous ethical undertones, being as completely without the will to be seen as it is possible to be. (Contrast Cymochles' posturing nymphs in the Bower of Bliss, 2.5.32–35.) Furthermore, we have already seen Titan benignly displaying his beams (3.6.6), and for the sun, the act of seeing is identical with the act of displaying; seeing and being seen are superimposed on each other as the reflexive, beautiful, and natural activity of the eye of heaven. So Chrysogonee's display is as innocent as that of the sun, and both are aspects of fully natural, sanctioned processes. She is further assimilated into the world of nature when the ground welcomes her, one of the flowers already spread naturally to the sun. That her impregnation might prove a sexual wounding that leads to transformed consciousness, as sexual wounding does diversely in the *Metamorphoses,* Spenser hints when she laments her pregnancy, but she delivers the twins unawares, and slips out of Spenser's purview. In fact, this sustained unawareness of Chrysogonee Spenser has chosen for specific reasons, interesting insofar as they show his intentions in this episode and insofar as they suggest why the episode cannot fully satisfy the desires that it evokes.

What the narrator does throughout his contemplation of the nymph is to focus on her bodily life of sensation, her self-contained presence depicted to appear as much flower-like as human. By suppressing an Ovidian appearance of the god in anthropomorphic form, he goes out of his way to avoid depicting a male viewer who might disrupt this mode of sensation. The maintenance of her bodily otherness allows Spenser to depict in Chrysogonee something of what man may respond to or find represented in women, and this depiction is certainly moving. Her flesh is proleptically called "pregnant" before it conceives; though consciously she has no love for the twins, and sleeps through their birth, the babies are taken from her "louing side" (st. 27). She is essentially creative, again on the threshold between natural and human forms of creativity. We get glimpses of qualities that Spenser finds valuable when we see her easy surrender to sleep after bathing, and when she plants herself down to cheer herself up: "wearie of long trauell, downe to rest / Her selfe she set, and comfortably cheard" (3.6.10). The role of the hallowed inner space of Chrysogonee's body suggests that the most private, inward, and incommunicable of phenomena is made naturally manifest without any act of conscious display: the sun beams "pierst into her wombe, where they embayd / With so sweet sence and secret power vnspide..." (3.6.7), and during her pregnancy the twins "were enwombed in the sacred throne / Of her chaste bodie" (3.6.5).

It is simultaneously Spenser's implication of an Ideal Spectator of her, and his preservation of her unconsciousness of any viewer, which creates the possibility for this kind of revelation, the revelation of a life candid, complete, and apart from the watcher. Chrysogonee is depicted with an emphasis on her independent bodily life, as if to suggest the poet's attempt to acknowledge a feminine experience of selfhood, including the mysterious generativity of pregnancy and birth.

One indication that Spenser's creative impulse here is to honor the otherness of feminine bodily life is that Chrysogonee, notwithstanding the miracle of her impregnation, notably departs from the splendor of many of his female characters, who have either the numinous radiance of a Belphoebe or the darker glamor of a Lucifera or a Radegund. Chrysogonee is no sister of Beatrice, and her sexual body bears no radiant glory. In the terms of Wallace Stevens's late reflection on the numinous woman, she is

> Not, for a change, the englistered woman, seated
> In colorings harmonious, dewed and dashed

By them: gorgeous symbol...rainbowed,
Piercing the spirit by appearance.[20]

What Spenser reaches for instead of the glory of the englistered woman
is a fullness and self-sufficiency of quotidian bodily life, either
viewed or experienced. Chrysogonee's fruitfulness and stability,
like that of the natural world that takes her in, bespeak a human desire, imagined and gratified by the author, to contemplate the plenitude and contentment of the physical world. As in the Proem of
Book 2, Spenser evidently wishes to acknowledge and then dispel
the hungry imagination's possessiveness and narcissism, its temptation to colonize the alien and to make it over in the image of its possessor.

But it is exactly this fact that admits more disquieting implications of Spenser's depiction of Chrysogonee's solitude. As we shall see
more fully, women viewed in *The Faerie Queene* often evoke the pathos or nostalgia of the male viewer's desire, not so much for possession as for a full, prolonged access to the mysterious otherness of
woman's bodily presence. This wish, found throughout Spenser's
work, most often takes either a Vergilian or an Ovidian mythopoeic form.

Spenser gratifies this wish for benign access with the pleasure of
the Chrysogonee episode, set apart with mythic and fairy tale diction.
But it is the mythic license by which Chrysogonee's bodily experience is made into miracle which also threatens to denude that experience of mortal significance. Her birthing of the twins can by no
stretch of the imagination be called labor, "which means that she
is oblivious to the mortalities of birth."[21] She is unaware equally
of the bodily pleasure and the pain that her experiences ought to
provide, and Spenser makes parallel and balanced syntactic structures of the absence of consciousness and the absence of bodily
sensation:

[20]Wallace Stevens, "The Sail of Ulysses" VIII, in *Opus Posthumous: Poems, Plays,
Prose,* ed. Samuel French Morse (New York: Alfred A. Knopf, 1971), 99–105.

[21]Joseph Loewenstein, in remarks delivered as a response to an early discussion
of mine on Chrysogonee, at the Sixteenth-Century Studies Conference in St. Louis,
October 1986. I owe much of this chapter's argument about female awareness
to the pressure of Loewenstein's initial unease with Chrysogonee's "summery mind-
lessness."

> Vnwares she them conceiu'd, vnwares she bore:
> She bore withouten paine, that she conceiued
> Withouten pleasure.
>
> (3.6.27)

The tone of these lines, like that of all the other stanzas in the episode, is one of romance wonder before a marvel viewed. But such wonder in *The Faerie Queene* is most apt when it is a response to an eikastic image of what should be (for example, the lovers at the heart of the Garden of Adonis, both mythic and natural), or when it is a response to an eikastic image of what may be (for example, Britomart, in whom Spenser unites human and natural images as an ideal of human life). Chrysogonee, marvelous as she is, is also without awareness, and so she can never be presented as an ideal to be made real; she represents a dream of "female bodily experience as a corporeal utopia," an atavistic desire to escape pain, pleasure, and consciousness altogether.[22] Spenser depicts his understanding of this powerful attraction of Chrysogonee's plantlike life. But although he places her in circumstances that usually force human consciousness in the poem, he seems not to register that it is *because* he cherishes her unawareness that she slips out of his purview.[23] The dirt and danger of Duessa evoke a gaze of disgust, but the particular purity of Chrysogonce aborts the drive of narrative.

As a contrast to this charmingly and deceptively simple Ovidian passage, sanctioning the gaze of the narrator and of the reader as well as of the sun, and sanctioning natural and therefore innocent display, we might turn to the episode of Phedon and Claribell (2.4.17–33), which works out its ethical norms in the neo-Vergilian context of Book 2 rather than in an Ovidian context, and which consequently

[22]Ibid.

[23]But Stevie Davies finds an interesting reason for Chrysogonee's condition of unawareness: "This [Book 3] is the Book of Love, where what happened to Amavia would never be allowed to happen. Whereas the Book of Temperance kills Amavia and she cannot be revived, the Book of Love visits on Chrysogonee an experience of nightmare horror which, as if in a benign dream, is resolved below the level of consciousness.... God's vindictive curse on womankind is thus [in Chrysogonee's painless delivery] evaded in the feminine universe.... There is no husband; there are no labour pains, no multiplication tables of sorrow to daunt her, but rather a birth of new selves from the unconscious psyche" (*The Feminine Reclaimed: The Idea of Woman in Spenser, Shakespeare, and Milton* [Lexington: University Press of Kentucky, 1986], 85–86).

draws around the notion of display far more malign passions than are found in the tenderer effort of the Chrysogonee passage.

Phedon, like Ariodante in *Orlando Furioso* (5.5–74) and Claudio in *Much Ado about Nothing*, has been easily misled by a friend into doubting the fidelity of his espoused, Claribell. The friend, Philemon, has ostensibly provided ocular proof of this accusation by dressing Claribell's maid in her mistress's clothes and posing himself as the other man. It is the passion aroused by this episode which sends Phedon home in a rage, instantly to slay Claribell. The crucial stanzas invoke the philosophical and ethical issues of identity, integrity, and sincerity in drama. Philemon, Phedon says,

> Me leading, in a secret corner layd,
> The sad spectatour of my Tragedie;
> Where left, he went, and his owne false part playd,
> Disguised like that groome of base degree,
> Whom he had feignd th'abuser of my loue to bee.
>
> Eftsoones he came vnto th'appointed place,
> And with him brought *Pryene*, rich arayd,
> In *Claribellaes* clothes. Her proper face
> I not descerned in that darkesome shade,
> But weend it was my loue, with whom he playd.
>
> (2.4.27–28)

Phedon is first bitter about Philemon's betrayal, his "false part." But Philemon plays a part in the narrower sense that one does in drama, the rhetorical motives of which are here corrupt. Phedon speaks of himself as spectator of his own tragedy; in general we can see how this expresses his bitter irony at the ultimate discovery that he was indeed watching something staged. But the theatrical metaphor also exposes the bad faith of this viewer (and not just the bad faith of the performer, as he thinks). Intent looking, at a performance, is a privilege not accorded us upon encountering the dramas of others in daily life. This intent looking is acceptable in drama, where the understood separation between audience and players implies a distance that bears meaning, and implies the players' acknowledgment of the viewers' presence, and the viewers' acknowledgment of their presence before a fiction. These motives of dramatic action simply do not work if Phedon is, as he thinks, spying on Claribell. Phedon's casting of himself as a public, recognized audience—even complaining

that he has a bad seat in a dark corner where he cannot see clearly—
implies a mode of visual address which is inappropriate as a way of
viewing, as he thinks, his own intimates. His angle of vision, both
literally and figuratively speaking, allows him to see not the maid
who is really there, dressed as Claribell, but the body of his wife. He
claims himself as both audience and subject of his tragedy (a curious
selfishness when one considers that Claribell might more properly be
considered the subject of his tragedy), so the distinction between
audience and players which makes possible the viewed performance
is collapsed.

Display is the central moral notion of this story. Phedon sees the
clothes of the woman, assumed as a theatrical costume by her maid;
but he cannot see her "proper" face, as he admits with a crucial choice
of adjective. That is, he not only confuses those distinctions between
public and private, observer and observed, which make drama a sanctioned means of visual address, but also confuses sartorial with bodily
tokens of identity. (This is a point in which he interestingly violates
the narrative conventions of identity tokens, the most incontestable
of which are always marks on the body, marks of earned or revelatory
identity, like Odysseus's scar or Pastorella's rose mole.) The apparently conclusive display of the body in fact conceals its real identity
by obscuring the face, which is the threshold between interior and
surface of the bodily self. Phedon willingly turns Claribell's putative
actions into a display, an act that breaks their mutual trust. Her
identity and her guilt are confirmed for him not by reference to the
surface of the body or its hallowed interior (notions that do not arise
in this non-Ovidian tale), but by reference to a gown, veiling the body
in order to conceal identity.

Inner identity always becomes manifest in *The Faerie Queene*, but
ideally it does so as a natural or unintentional process, even an accidental process, which Spenser understands as revelation. Wilfully
to exhibit identity by exhibiting the body is to act against the integrity
of "the inward parts." This is the case, for example, in the frank and
detailed description of Cymochles' fantasy of blissful passivity with
the nymphs in the Bower of Bliss.

> There he him found all carelesly displayd,
>   In secret shadow from the sunny ray,
>   On a sweet bed of lillies softly layd,
>   Amidst a flocke of Damzels fresh and gay,

That round about him dissolute did play
  Their wanton follies, and light meriments;
  Euery of which did loosely disaray
  Her vpper parts of meet habiliments,
And shewd them naked, deckt with many ornaments.

And euery of them stroue, with most delights,
  Him to aggrate, and greatest pleasures shew;
  Some framd faire lookes, glancing like euening lights,
  Others sweet words, dropping like honny dew;
  Some bathed kisses, and did soft embrew
  The sugred licour through his melting lips:
  One boastes her beautie, and does yeeld to vew
  Her daintie limbes aboue her tender hips;
Another her out boastes, and all for tryall strips.

(2.5.32–33)

I have cited these two stanzas fully because it is important to emphasize not only Spenser's ethical discriminations but also his accommodating inclusion of explicit and pornographic pleasures. Troubled
male conscience there certainly is—in the initial warning hint of the
watcher "carelesly displayd" and, in the stanza following these two,
in phrases such as "like an Adder, lurking in the weeds"; "wandring
thought"; "fraile eye"; "spoyle of beautie" (2.5.34). But Spenser objects, I think, less to the distinct pleasures depicted than to the sole
and unimaginative emphasis on the body's surface at the expense of
any acknowledgment of its interiority. The nymphs compete with each
other, but competition here hardly functions to distinguish them from
one another. Their actions are completely explicit and completely
anonymous. One sign of the trouble is that Cymochles, the male
viewer, is *visibly present* to the nymphs. Legitimate visual enjoyment
depends partly, as I have suggested, upon preserving the observed
character's assumption of solitude and therefore her privacy; Cymochles' own visibility and the nymphs' pleasure in his watching
negate any potential for the narrator's or the reader's unguilty enjoyment of the scene. To be present to another's gaze is these nymphs'
only life; there is no hint of an absorbed, disregarding, ongoing life
in the woods, for example, as there is with Ovid's nymphs or with
Spenser's Belphoebe or Chrysogonee. Though Spenser shows some
open regret at not being free to enjoy their fair looks, "glancing like
euening lights," he finally rejects this representation of woman's bod-

ily presence which fails to include a masculine attempt to imagine and acknowledge her otherness, her interiority. He recognizes Cymochles' experience as a male fantasy, self-aggrandizing; this he tries to avoid in the Chrysogonee episode, where the reasons for his failure, as we have seen, are as interesting as a different kind of success might have been.

In the episodes from Book 2—Phedon, Cymochles, and Guyon with the nymphs Cissie and Flossie, whom we saw in Chapter Two—there is always a voice that acknowledges the potential guilt or bad faith of the male viewer. Phedon castigates himself, and the Palmer corroborates with some tendentious, metrically monotonous statements on the evils of passion; the narrator compensates for his own remarkable indulgence in contemplating Cymochles' nymphs with a subsequent crackdown of punitive rhetoric leveled against Cymochles; the Palmer, as we have seen, suddenly and harshly tightens the restraints that Guyon has gradually loosened. I want now to return to the scene of Guyon's fascination with the nymphs in the Bower, in light of my Ovidian and mythic emphases here. Rebuking Guyon (2.12.69), the Palmer becomes a representative of the unease with which some male viewers can contemplate certain kinds of female scenes. But what kinds of male viewers, and what kinds of scenes of women?

I said in Chapter Two that Guyon's attraction to the nymphs of the fountain may include the hint of a supra-sexual wish to be part of their tiny, comic society. Among Ovidian nymphs in *The Faerie Queene*, this sense of camaraderie is recurrent, as in the tales of Diana. Venus assumes as old knowledge their supposed social and sexual habits (3.6.16); they relax in an easy intimacy after the hunt (1.12.7, 3.6.17); with one mind they attack Faunus (7.6.49—50). All of these characters and episodes are traceable to Ovidian origins: Spenser expands the feminine society of Ovid's nymphs, perhaps drawing as well on the several sets of sisters and sister-storytellers in the *Metamorphoses*, and extends it to his moving scenes of feminine bonds. Episodes depicting Diana's votaresses occur repeatedly; many of these we have seen. Diana and her nymphs refresh themselves after a hunt just before Venus interrupts (3.6.17—18) and just before realizing that Faunus spies on them (7.6); they appear as companions of Belphoebe (3.5.37—40); they appear even in a simile describing Una after the Dragon's death, when she watches the celebrants

As faire *Diana* in fresh sommers day
Beholds her Nymphes, enraung'd in shadie wood,
Some wrestle, some do run, some bathe in christall flood.

(1.12.7)

We might think of other communities of women. There is the friendship between Amoret and Britomart after the latter is revealed as a woman (4.1.7–16). And our first sight of Pastorella (6.9.8) as a girl ringed by other girls adumbrates the grander vision of Mt. Acidale; the two relatively stable neighborhoods of the pastoral community and Mt. Acidale reveal a ceremonious feminine society. The male wish to be part of or near to these easy female intimacies is one attitude that can legitimize or make sympathetic the role of the male viewer. The nymphs of the fountain represent a perverse version of such feminine intimacy in the choreography of their highly eroticized play; what they display is not simply their sexual bodies but also their dance of mutual understanding. It is in part this invitation, friendly and mocking at once, which tantalizes Guyon and which must be renounced in Book 2 with its iron world of allegorized Vergilian necessity.

We see another community of women in Book 4, when Scudamour enters the precincts of the Temple of Venus (4.10.21–52). Once he has reached the island, the only men whom he meets are the friends and lovers (who have nothing to do with the running of the place) and the brothers Love and Hatred—who are kept firmly in check by their mother, Concord. In fact, the whole place is an orderly maternal system, the damsel priestesses and the allegorical figures together representative of eros tempered by ideal feminine qualities. Scudamour sees

... an hundred brasen caudrons bright,
To bath in ioy and amorous desire,
Euery of which was to a damzell hight;
For all the Priests were damzels, in soft linnen dight.

(4.10.38)

—and later he finds Womanhood, Curtesie, Cherefulnesse, Silence, Obedience, Modestie, and Shamefastnesse surrounding Amoret in a ring. These attendants of Venus Hermaphroditus, both erotic priestesses and the damsels surrounding Amoret, suggest an august power of feminine and even maternal *protectiveness*, largely because they function to guard against Scudamour's entrance. This very protectiveness, in the histories of the two protagonists here, invites or requires not contemplation (as Calidore contemplates the rings of maidens on Mt. Acidale) but a vigorous and healthy invasion by the male viewer. And this makes sense in the development of erotic vision from Book 2 through the middle books of the poem. Scudamour enters what is in effect a powerful women's college—mysterious, creative, fecund—a place which the heroine, aided by the hero, must leave in order to enter adulthood. Feminine society, imagined as more benign and more complex than in Book 2's sketch of the corrupt nymphs of the Bower or Book 3's brief glimpse of Diana's nymphs, and containing the very source of all created life in the form of the Venus Hermaphroditus, is, within Scudamour and Amoret's tales, a nursery that must be abandoned. It is the hero whose shield bears the sign of Cupid who can lead the virgin into her central metamorphosis, as Ovid's Cupid inflames the gods who press the nymphs into erotic consciousness through the mysteries of metamorphosis.

By Book 6, however, and Calidore's vision on Mt. Acidale, feminine group life is more pervasive (if more fragile) and is freed from the constraints of the maternal; the wish for a vision of feminine society, a society uninterrupted by male intrusion but accessible to male presence, triumphs briefly. It is one of Spenser's greatest efforts to imagine visual bliss and, along with the Garden of Adonis, his greatest success in imagining the gratification of masculine and feminine presence to each other. Furthermore, it overgoes the Garden of Adonis in its encompassment of human consciousness, which alone allows the recognition of candor's possibility and candor's necessity in relations liberated from the tyrannies of the gaze. But the resolutions and releases of Mt. Acidale we must suspend here. Its vision beautifully if briefly transcends some of the tensions of defensiveness in the poem, but these need to be addressed more explicitly—hence the next chapter. The achievement of Mt. Acidale will not be accessible to Spenser until he explores some particularly difficult political and literary events of the 1590s. The works published in 1595 and 1596 show serious strains and anxiety, and contemplate not only the loss of the vision of woman but also, more sadly, a decline of the very desire for proximity to the feminine. This loss and the events that occasion it are the burden of Chapter Five; only at its end will the pressures of the poem be clear enough to evoke the fleeting triumph of Mt. Acidale.

Chapter Four

Vision and Defense

The notions of defense and defenselessness appeared frequently in the previous chapter, and this is not accidental. Virginity as conceived by Ovid and Spenser, resting as it does on the condition of candid hiddenness, is the paradigmatic defenseless state; in this condition, being seen is the fundamental intrusion on selfhood. *The Faerie Queene*'s most spectacular instance of the defenselessness of exposure occurs, of course, in Serena's grisly adventure with the cannibals (*FQ* 6.8.31–51), an episode that extends Spenser's usual interest in relatively mundane or numinous visual encounters to the grotesque, melodramatic, and extreme case of Serena's visual consumption by admirers whose connoisseur-like scrutiny of her beauty makes them uncomfortably analogous to conventional writers of blazon in love poetry. Donald Cheney noted in 1966 that the cannibals confuse "the two appetites of hunger and lust with the language of a love-religion"; the parody of blazon in this canto serves Spenser's understanding that the love conventions of his culture may expose a woman and her vulnerability to scrutiny, and deny her affective life and her subjectivity.[1] The aspect of Spenser's critique relevant here is his emphasis

---

[1] Donald Cheney, *Spenser's Image of Nature: Wild Man and Shepherd in "The Faerie Queene"* (New Haven: Yale University Press, 1966), 106. On Serena and the cannibals, see also Paul Alpers, *The Poetry of "The Faerie Queene"* (Princeton: Princeton University Press, 1967), 321–24, and James Nohrnberg's fine comments in *The*

on Serena's intense and terrible embarrassment; the degradation and humiliation that form her distress are a natural outcome of the cannibals' elevation of her. Following a line occasionally found in the criticism, Hamilton notes that "the episode treats the sexual phantasies of a woman in love," and he uses the adjectives "ungrateful" and "unloving" to describe Serena's silence and withdrawal when Calepine rescues her. This is surely a case of blaming the victim, and Paul Alpers is closer to Spenser's real interests and tone when he speaks of Spenser's "solicitude" for Serena and his narrative means of protecting her by covering her figuratively with nightfall.[2] The point is that although Serena's is a particularly violent case, it is unexceptional insofar as it expresses the epic's pervasive topics of exposure and abashedness and of the need for defensiveness in its social world; these are among the qualities that Spenser chooses to develop no matter what generic models he turns to.

The Ovidian wish for candid solitude in the woods is precisely a wish to be freed of the need for defenses and defensiveness; and though wood nymphs and fays like Chrysogonee and Agape have apparently dwelt in this free condition for some time, their stories begin at the very moment when defense would be useful, when their solitude is broken. The same is true for the sets of interrupted lovers of Book 6: the bliss of privacy which they enjoy enters the narrative only at the moment when it turns into defenselessness.

To consider defenses, in fact, is to consider some of Spenser's most pervasive concerns, both about ethics and about how narrative is constituted. What he seeks is a way of persons watching persons which simply does not require defensiveness on either side, and yet this way of watching must acknowledge the possibility of defensiveness, so that watching can become part of a narrative. So, as we saw in the last chapter, he wants to defend candid solitude and virginal innocence against predatory eyes. But also he wants to defend the desire for vision, including sexual vision, and to make possible both candor and awareness in the presence of men and women to each other. This dual wish, which is both ethical and representational, affects most of the episodes which I have discussed. It is possible, for example, to see Book 2 generally as a book of defensiveness against threatening stim-

---

Analogy of "The Faerie Queene" (Princeton: Princeton University Press, 1976), 655–63 and 710–15.
  [2]Alpers, *Poetry of "The Faerie Queene,"* 324.

uli; so Spenser structures his hero's temperance in heroic action. Both the desire for access to the feminine, cast in morally unacceptable forms, and the accusation of that desire, occur from within the book; Spenser thus both expresses and defends against the desire. It is hard to escape the legitimacy of the moral judgments brought against Phedon and Cymochles; even the dour Palmer fills a necessary role as censor of misdirected or degraded sexual vision. But, as we saw in the Proem to Book 2, the hostile or bad-faith watcher can sometimes be gradually transformed into a potential friend, and this conversion of watcher from enemy to friend is one of Spenser's means of anticipating and disarming antagonism.[3] In the episodes of Belphoebe and Chrysogonee, the narrator has become not only friend but protector of the observed character's vulnerable solitude. But by protecting the candor of these characters against a threatening world, he limits the possibility of consciousness in them, as in the Chrysogonee episode.

At every step it is Vergil's and Ovid's works that enable Spenser's negotiations of defense and defenselessness. Vergil and Ovid are great poets of human vulnerability and of human needs for or apprehensions of defenses in a hostile and violent cosmos. In *The Faerie Queene* 2, the neo-Vergilian, moral-allegorical mistrust of sight and sense is interrupted by the great Ovidian comic set piece of Belphoebe with the braggarts, which itself contains the imitative description of her Vergilian numinous splendor and her Ovidian candor, her comic and sublime transcendence of mere defensiveness against the likes of Braggadochio. And Trompart's echo of Aeneas's awestruck response to Venus's epiphany in the *Aeneid* is an early sanction in *The Faerie Queene* of the viewer's response of open wonder, one of Aeneas's salient strengths. At the other end of the book, Vergil and Ovid together preside over the Bower of Bliss, its lasciviousness and its sporadic perceptions of the feminine numinous. In the middle books,

---

[3]Margaret Ferguson discusses a similar movement in Freud's *New Introductory Lectures*, in her *Trials of Desire: Renaissance Defenses of Poetry* (New Haven: Yale University Press, 1983), 172. Frank Whigham's *Ambition and Privilege: The Social Tropes of Elizabethan Courtesy Theory* (Berkeley and Los Angeles: University of California Press, 1984) and Annabel Patterson's *Censorship and Interpretation: The Conditions of Writing and Reading in Early Modern England* (Madison: University of Wisconsin Press, 1984) are also useful contributions to social, literary, aesthetic, and political aspects of defensive behavior in a vying or hostile environment; I am indebted to them for my general comments on defensiveness.

it is Vergil's *Aeneid*, especially Aeneas's warmly admiring responsiveness to Venus and to Dido, which opens to Spenser the possibility
of retaining access to the visionary wonder sparked by sexual vision
while jettisoning the riskiest effects of the Petrarchan imagination for
male and female alike. And it is Ovidian landscape and social life,
and defensive Ovidian nymphs, as I argued in the last chapter, which
everywhere direct Spenser's apprehension of bodily life and his mod-
ulations of Petrarchan vision into a full psychology of erotic process
for both male and female characters.

Vision in both Vergil and Ovid involves a wish to be free of outside
threats, that is, a wish on the part of the beheld to be free of defensiveness. It is this freedom from any shadow of defensiveness which
distinguishes Homer's Nausikaa, and which Vergil's Venus bears into
the *Aeneid* as a condition poignantly unavailable to the frequently
threatened mortals in that poem. The treatments of vision in both
Vergil's and Ovid's great poems also include a wish on the part of
the viewer to be able to feast on sexual vision, though in the *Metamorphoses* the prerogatives of sexual watchers are consistently more
violent and aggressive than in the *Aeneid*. Spenser sustains both sets
of wishes, those of the beheld and those of the beholders, and as the
last chapter indicated, moves toward a way of granting them without
arousing censuring voices like the Palmer's, that is, without arousing
defensiveness within himself or within characters.

The greatest expression in *The Faerie Queene* of intimate love freed
from defensiveness and of the privilege of sexual vision is the Garden
of Adonis (3.6.29–52). In its freedom from shame, abashedness, and
the inimical effects of the world's gaze, as in so many other respects,
the Garden depicts an ideal that in its fullness is inaccessible to human
beings "in the middest," but toward which we forbear aspiration at
our peril. Ideal candor emerges in details about various groups of
lovers. The song of the "ioyous birdes" sheltered "emongst the shadie
leaues" transforms their natural behavior to an ideal for human lovers:
the birds, unconfined by the reticences of humans, "their true loues
without suspition tell abrode" (3.6.42). Nor does shame complicate
relations between members of loving couples of any species in the
Garden: "Franckly each paramour his leman knowes" (3.6.41).[4]

---

[4]Carol Kaske has suggested to me in a note a parallel between the medieval notion
of frankness and the idea of candor I develop in this book from Stanley Cavell's notion
of candor in *The World Viewed: Reflections on the Ontology of Film*, enlarged ed.
(Cambridge: Harvard University Press, 1979), 111.

Shame plays no part in the depiction of Venus and Adonis, either; indeed, they seem to function as an encouragement and a gratification of the wish to behold intimacies. It is Spenser's very acknowledgment of this wish, and his bold accommodation of it in his description of the lovers, which help to account for the powerful sexual attractiveness of the episode. More particularly, we may follow Isabel MacCaffrey's splendid remarks about the reader's experience of the Garden and its chief lovers.[5] Spenser leads us "through a labyrinth of foliage, among trees that tower over us, dropping their 'precious deaw.' 'In the thickest covert of that shade' is the arbor itself where, again, the spectator has the sense of an approach from below to within" (261). By this stage of the journey inward, the reader/spectator has left behind envy, "fell rancor," and "fond gealosie" (3.6.41), and has participated instead in Spenser's celebration of the frankness of the other lovers; the consequence should be a rectification of visual and erotic desire, so that we may contemplate the lovemaking of Venus and Adonis with as much trust in the rightness of the impulse to look as we were granted in Belphoebe's epiphany. This is a considerably different impulse from that with which the reader sees the "exposed and exhibitionist sensuality of the Bower" (MacCaffrey, 260) and of Acrasia and Verdant. For the reader to look at Acrasia and her lover (and I work from the premise that this is most often how we do understand and speak of that episode) is an experience of uncovering, uncasing, and seeing things exposed; it is a satisfaction of hungers easily gratified by sights "bare to readie spoyle / Of hungry eies" (2.12.78). But to regard Venus and Adonis is an experience of "coming into a small, protected, intimately enclosed space... penetrating layer after layer as one approaches a center" (MacCaffrey, 262).

I take it as true that "the sense of coming into a small, protected, intimately enclosed space probably satisfies an atavistic urge in all of us" (MacCaffrey, 262) and, more, that the erotic experience imaged in Venus and Adonis appeals to a deeper level of human consciousness than that imaged in Acrasia. If these things are so, then we may go some way toward accounting for the fact that the reader's act of imaginative looking in the Garden is a powerful sexual impulse for

---

[5] Isabel MacCaffrey, *Spenser's Allegory: The Anatomy of Imagination* (Princeton: Princeton University Press, 1976), 258–63; specific page references are given in the text.

the ideal reader-spectator, regardless of gender, while looking in the Bower of Bliss, an act mediated through the eyes of Guyon and the Palmer, may be more specifically inflected toward only one of the two great sexes. The eroticism of moving inward to the center hardly allows notions of exposure and shame or shamelessness even to arise, as they so readily do in discussions of Acrasia.

I said above that the lovers enjoying candid privacy in Book 6 enter the narrative only at the moment when their privacy is lost. The same may be said of Faunus's spying on Diana in *Mutabilitie*. His failure of decorum literarily speaking lies in his ignorance of Vergilian wonder before a numinous woman; socially speaking, it lies not only in his peeping but in his interruption of Diana's ongoing life with a crude jest and a private joke. But in the Garden of Adonis, Spenser can go very far indeed in acts of visualizing privacies, just because he wishes in this case not to interrupt their candor. Venus and Adonis, while subject to Time, seem to exist outside the mortal times depicted within the poem; this is due in part to Spenser's time markers, which grant the lovers an eternal present ("There now he liueth . . . Ioying his goddesse," 3.6.48), but also it is due to the fact that Spenser depicts no spectator's interruption of them.

All of these elements—Spenser's liberation of the lovers from intrusion; his delineation of erotic vision as a compelling movement into a protected space and into deep levels of human consciousness; the structural contrasts of the Garden with the Bower; the frankness of the minor lovers in the Garden—attest to the tact of the poet and to the freedom from abashedness which contributes to the ideal quality of the Garden.[6] In the mortal world of most of Spenser's characters, however, the prerogatives to gaze and to be gazed upon, acts liberated from defensiveness, are often achieved only after some conflict—a breakthrough to love and poise after the turbulence of defensive struggles. This sort of breakthrough occurs for Spenser himself, as he moves from the troubled and defensive erotic visions of Book 2 to the briefly poised and elegant vision of Mt. Acidale. And it occurs within characters in the poem. The recognized need for defense implies a con-

---

[6]Similar points could be made about other lovers' paradises in Spenser's work, e.g., the lovers in the garden outside the Temple of Venus whom Scudamour "beheld with gazefull eye" but who themselves are "free from feare and gealosye" and "frankely there their loues desire possesse" (4.10.28), and the lovers who love "without rebuke or blame, / And in her [Pleasure's] snowy bosome boldly lay / Their quiet heads, deuoyd of guilty shame" (*Hymne to Loue* 288–90).

dition of potential weakness and exposure, a condition in which the self is necessarily defined in relation to a threat, often the threat of possible hostility in another. There are several possible responses for the defensive character in Spenser's poem; some of these we have seen. There is flight or hiddenness: the combination of defensive help-lessness and flight is the very essence of Florimell's actions, as it is of the actions of Ovid's nymphs. But both Spenser and Ovid recognize the inadequacy of flight as a response to threat, as well as the im-possibility of hiddenness in an intricate social world. Another possible response—this time not only to threats from the outside world but also to threats from within the self—is to harden resistance to all such stimuli, as Guyon's neo-Vergilian career illustrates. The moral-allegorical tradition of Vergilian interpretation rests on an under-standing of human life in this world as fundamentally defensive. This is true as well of the neo-Stoic ethos underpinning Book 2, an ethos that Spenser comes to understand less as a virtue than as one necessary mechanism for human survival in society, figured visually as a capacity to *gaze unmoved*. This ability, I think, accounts for the opacity of Guyon's visual responses in the House of Mammon, and of Brito-mart's visual response to the pageants in Busyrane's castle. In the pages that follow, I look at defensiveness in three characters who experience its psychological concomitants of shame or abashedness, and then at abashedness and its implications in relation to one of Spenser's great subjects: wedding.

A major threat to the individual in *The Faerie Queene* is that of exposure, with its two elements of being forcibly revealed or discov-ered and then being perceived. The tension of Belphoebe's meeting with Braggadochio in Book 2 arises from the power of the Ovidian pattern of nymphs exposed and violently handled; its comedy arises from Braggadochio's wildly inadequate perception of her. In no way is her identity truly exposed to his observation. It is this fact, and not only her superior strength and courage, which makes him incapable of being a real threat, and which frees Belphoebe from the need for the defensiveness that characterizes her literary sisters. But Serena stripped by cannibals is the very image of the human need for defense; her exposure to their greedy, even epicurean sight reflects Spenser's understanding of man as a poor, bare, forked thing, though his char-acteristic note is poignance rather than tragedy. To suffer unwillingly the observation of one's person, one's proper self, is to invite mis-understanding, invasion, violation, or appropriation. Even the redoubtable Britomart disguises herself as a knight as a cautionary protection of her precious inner part and its secrets, and not simply as a plot device allowing her access to masculine adventure and to the fusion of masculine and feminine qualities.

The exposure of selfhood arouses the possibility of defensiveness insofar as it arouses an intense self-awareness through the presence of observers. Spenser charts two possible responses of the self-conscious character. One is shame—or, to use Spenser's word embracing a spectrum of notions from mere embarrassment to the humiliation of shame—abashedness. Abashedness bespeaks a vulnerability to defensiveness, in which the self is defined wholly as an object observed, and implicitly judged wanting, by another. Characters feel this as a lapse from an ideal that they hold of themselves, though the lapse need have nothing to do with morality: Diana is "abasht" when Venus unexpectedly enters without ringing first. Spenser's single favorite emblem for this condition of discomposure is the blush. Any of his characters who are capable of change or of education have the grace to blush, and Britomart is the greatest blusher of all.

The first two sections that follow attend to diverse responses to threat and the need for defense. The first is a discussion of abashedness in Belphoebe and Britomart and its connections with Ovid's treatments of shame and erotic change. The second section considers Malbecco, in whose tale the shame of an interior privation like that of Ovid's Aglauros is structurally contrasted with the imagined repletions offered by vision.

"All suddenly abasht she chaunged hew"

Angus Fletcher argues that "virtue, the positive ideal of moral allegory, needs to be given its original sense of 'power,' and moral fables need then to be reinterpreted as having to do chiefly with polarities of strength and weakness, confidence and fear, certainty and doubt."[7] This is pre-eminently true of Spenser, whose moral allegory often shows characters struggling through the complexities of a defensive weakness toward the simplicity of a confident, even jubilant mastery. The weakness may be no more than the inexperience

[7]Angus Fletcher, *Allegory: The Theory of a Symbolic Mode* (Ithaca: Cornell University Press, 1964), 295.

that allows a character early in his quest to be undone by the unexpected; the uncertainty and surprise of such circumstances manifest themselves as abashedness. This is true of Redcrosse, Guyon, Britomart; the new self-consciousness of abashedness eventually gives these characters access to greater poise and possession of their respective virtues. But the intense abashedness of exposure and humiliation can also destroy or transform identity, as we have seen it do in Ovid's works and as it does in the Ovidian metamorphosis of Malbecco.

The use of the word *embarrassment* to signify the momentary fluster and self-consciousness we feel in an awkward situation did not begin until the late seventeenth century, but the phenomenon, being the result of an unexpected breach in social expectations, might be expected in any society as reliant on ceremony and elaborate codes of conduct as Elizabethan England.[8] The wish to remain unwitnessed and unseen, which I have argued is a strong wish in *The Faerie Queene*, is complemented by the social reality of frequent exposure to the gaze of others; Spenser's sense of himself, readers, and characters alike as audience is pervasive. I have already suggested that to be an audience, a privileged watcher, is one of the desires that Spenser hopes to legitimize partly because it is experienced as unsanctioned intrusion, arousing defensiveness in himself as well as in the object of sight. Moreover, he has a finely tuned and defensive awareness of his poem's images as subjects of a watching, judging, courtly audience, as we might deduce simply from the permutations of wooing and aggressive stances in the proems.

Frank Whigham argues that socio-political interaction in the complex courtly world that Spenser inhabited created pressures on the individual through the creation of an internalized audience:

> The cramming of recreative activities with intensely serious political maneuver significantly altered the psychological character of the experience.... In effect this posture interiorized a social conscience, an internal witness of privacy concerned not with moral injunctions but with social ones.... And the arbiter of such manipulation will be a hypothetical internal witness of the sort before whom one would publicly perform—an internal courtly Other. Anything like "really" unwitnessed

---

[8]Christopher Ricks, *Keats and Embarrassment* (Oxford: Oxford University Press, 1976), 3–4. See also John Bayley's comments on embarrassment and on Ricks's treatment of it, in *The Uses of Division: Unity and Disharmony in Literature* (New York: Viking, 1976), 145–56.

experience becomes scarce, but the fiction of such behavior remains crucial because of the epistemological privilege it supposedly offers to an unseen viewer.[9]

To argue the presence of an "internal courtly Other" is to suggest tension between one's membership in an inescapably observing social world and one's internal distance from it, which Spenser represents as the wish for a candid hiddenness. But if characters are steadily vulnerable to unwanted exposure before an audience, they are also themselves apt to become audiences or witnesses—to moments of unguarded candor, intimate exchanges, others' exposed vulnerabilities, romance marvels. Challenges in social decorum and ethics arise from the condition of being an unprepared witness as well as from the condition of being seen; both can lead to the exposure and discomposure that constitute abashedness.

The sixteenth-century term *abashedness* or *abashment* (both forms of the noun were used, as well as *abashance*) is a stronger word and a more various one than our word *embarrassment*. To "abash" can mean simply to destroy self-possession momentarily; to shock with the unexpected, so that the abashed person is confused, astonished, or checked with a sudden consciousness of shame, presumption, or error. To be "abashed" can mean to flinch or recoil with surprise, shame, or humiliation (*OED*). Abashedness manifests inwardness, insofar as it is the consciousness of public and private, witness and witnessed, impinging on each other. The deepest interior response becomes public through physical manifestations (blushing, trembling, nervous gestures, and, for knights, a rush to aggress); the very circumstance of this exposure or confrontation triggers an acute discomfort of self-consciousness through a new and surprising awareness of the other. Such awareness threatens to undermine assumptions about one's own selfhood, to make precarious the elaborate social and relational identity that structures character in the courtly world and in the generic world of romance.[10]

Spenser's phrase for that core of identity is "the secret of your hart" (2.9.42), and it appears in the episode of *The Faerie Queene* that provides the prototype of what we now call embarrassment, the mild-

[9]Whigham, *Ambition and Privilege*, 90–91.
[10]See Erving Goffman's work in *Interaction Ritual: Essays on Face-to-Face Behavior* (New York: Doubleday, 1967), 107–8, a book whose insights illuminate encounters in many kinds of romance.

est form of abashedness."¹¹ In the House of Alma in Book 2, Guyon meets Shamefastnesse and is "abashed" to discover that she is part of himself, indeed, the very aspect of himself which would be concealed, unknown, unrecognized:

> ... *Alma* him bespake, Why wonder yee
> Fair Sir at that, which ye so much embrace?
> She is the fountaine of your modestee;
> You shamefast are, but *Shamefastnesse* it selfe is shee.
>
> (2.9.43)

The reflexive confusions and involutions of Guyon's meeting, embarrassing, and being embarrassed by his own bashfulness or modesty finely suggest the dynamics of self-consciousness, a comic and witty function of an allegorical figure. A character meeting a personification of himself finds his essential reticence suddenly externalized, and this unsettles Guyon's composed self, that is, his composure. His social discomfiture and the comedy of the encounter are the stronger, moreover, because Spenser makes the personification an attractive courtly lady with whom Guyon engages in a decorous "solace" (2.9.44). The precise nature of their conversation goes unrecorded until Guyon is compelled to remark the lady's blushes; then the language of both Guyon and the narrator (Shamefastenesse cannot bring herself to speak) is all of the embarrassment-arousing phenomena of mistaken erotic intentions, flashes, and inflamings.

Guyon's social discomfiture is matched by that of Shamefastnesse, whose regular fury of blushing intensifies with every verse:

> ... too oft she chaung'd her natiue hew.
>
> (2.9.40)

> ... euer and anone with rosie red
> The bashfull bloud her snowy cheekes did dye.
>
> (2.9.41)

---

¹¹Robert A. White discusses this episode, and the traditions relating to shamefastness, in "Shamefastnesse as *Verucundia* and as *Pudicitia* in *The Faerie Queene*," *Studies in Philology* 78 (1981), 391–408. The phrase "the secret of the hart" appears as well in the Geneva Bible, Psalm 51, noted by Anne Ferry in her useful survey of sixteenth-century words describing the inward life in *The "Inward" Language: Sonnets of Wyatt, Sidney, Shakespeare, Donne* (Chicago: University of Chicago Press, 1983).

> She answerd nought, but more abasht for shame,
> Held downe her head, the whiles her louely face
> The flashing bloud with blushing did inflame.

$$(2.9.43)$$

All the principals recover themselves with the graceful social tact which Spenser develops most fully from medieval romance, and each of them demonstrates this tact in particular ways. Guyon turns away, blushing, until he can reassemble himself before this charming embodiment of his own modesty. Alma graciously "faynd to ouersee" (2.9.44) Guyon's social lapse, an elegant and oblique acknowledgment of abashedness and of the importance of countenance, and an acknowledgment as well granting Guyon the dignity of his composure. The personification of Shamefastnesse, the blushes, and the social decorums of face-to-face encounters are all apt treatments of abashedness to depict within Alma's house, a large-scale allegory of bodily structure and processes.[12]

Abashedness in Spenser usually encompasses some notion of shame, which tends to emerge when the self-possession of a romance character is unsettled because of the sudden discrepancy between former notions and ideals of identity, and the newly revealed reality of identity. "Shame occurs," says one early psychoanalytic theorist of shame, "whenever goals and images presented by the ego ideal are not reached," and an ashamed condition is by definition the awkwardness that attends an apparent lapse of the ego ideal.[13] Shame and embar-

---

[12]Another "fayning to ouersee" occurs at 3.9.19, when the knights admitted so grudgingly to Malbecco's castle tactfully "dissembled, what they did not see"—that is, they overlooked his churlishness and glowering. This overlooking, coupled with their relief at being protected from the elements (Spenser pays unusual attention to their shedding of wet and uncomfortable clothing and armor), contributes to the conviviality and the happiness taken in simple creaturely pleasures, qualities that pervade their stay with Malbecco.

The model of the temperate body in Alma's house differs in many ways from the model that I have been adducing, derived in large part from Ovid's nymphs. For useful discussions of bodily life in the House of Temperance, see Harry Berger, *The Allegorical Temper: Vision and Reality in Book 2 of Spenser's "Faerie Queene"* (New Haven: Yale University Press, 1957), 65–88, and, on Shamefastnesse, 195–202; David L. Miller, *The Poem's Two Bodies: The Poetics of the 1590 "Faerie Queene"* (Princeton: Princeton University Press, 1988), 168–91. At 172–74 Miller discusses the blushes of Guyon and Shamefastnesse in an argument about the displacement of language for erotic genital expression.

[13]See Gerhart Piers's essay on shame in the book, which he wrote with Milton B.

rassment can occur together and reinforce each other, as they do in Britomart's humiliation when she first falls in love. She is shocked by and ashamed of the discovery of her sexual nature; what she is turns out to be different from what she has known herself to be. The new intensity of self-attention is part of what destroys her equanimity, and the new power of the involuntary aspects of eros makes her ashamed, until Merlin's recognition and prophecy offer her a new conceptual structure with which to understand her identity and the place of eros in it.

The sources of the Renaissance understanding are, not surprisingly, both classical and Judaeo-Christian. Shame had long been understood in terms of its origin in the Fall, as in Genesis 3.7–10, where Adam and Eve know their nakedness and clothe themselves. Commentators on Genesis inevitably remarked on the link between the Fall, sexuality, and shame, and expressed nostalgia for the prelapsarian lack of shame. Abraham Ross's *Exposition on the Fourteene First Chapters of Genesis* (London, 1626) is representative: "Question: Why did [Adam and Eve] cover their privy members? Answer: Because their inordinate lust began most to appear here: secondly, these are the instruments of generation, which then became sinfull; therefore all people are ashamed to see those parts, because sinne comes by generation. Hence circumcision (the signe of generation) was on this part of the body."[14] Classical sources also fed into Renaissance notions of shame in its sense as a decency or rectitude or honor that can prevent unrestrained behavior. This positive ethical quality, the fear of dishonor, was powerful throughout Renaissance culture, particularly in genres and forms concerned with ideals of human achievement and goodness.

Spenser's work certainly reveals these assumptions about shame,

---

Singer, *Shame and Guilt: A Psychoanalytic and a Cultural Study* (New York: Norton, 1953; rpt. ed., 1971), 23–24 and passim. See excellent suggestions on shame, autonomy, and control in the quest for temperance in Book 2, and a survey of the phenomenon of shame in Books 1 and 6 of Spenser's epic, in Nohrnberg's *Analogy of "The Faerie Queene,"* 299–301 and 704–8. See also Maurice Evans on shame in Book 6, in *Spenser's Anatomy of Heroism: A Commentary on "The Faerie Queene"* (Cambridge: Cambridge University Press, 1970), 210–12, 216–17.

[14]See Arnold Williams, *The Common Expositor: An Account of the Commentaries on Genesis, 1527–1633* (Chapel Hill: University of North Carolina Press, 1948), 109, 126.

but his emphasis is most often on shame as affective event, the painful and humiliating emotion that acompanies any exposure of what is or ought to be unseen. In *The Faerie Queene*, characters are vulnerable to shame because the romance fiction posits for them extraordinary ego ideals—ideals of true knighthood, glory, holiness, chivalry—toward which they continually strive. Dramatic interest often lies in a character's efforts and shortcomings and his consequent sense of shame. Characters who strive after goals or ideals are implicitly aware of the potentialities of the self, experienced as challenges, and Spenser constantly presents us with images of what the self wishes to be, as well as of its humiliations. Shame as an affect of this kind either puts the character who experiences it on the defensive or is itself a mark of defensiveness. Britomart suffers the debilitating humiliation of prolonged exposure to her own new experience of eros; Diana reacts defensively against Venus because her characteristic strength or *virtù* of self-possession fails her.

These psychic aspects of abashedness and shame interlock with social aspects of the genre, as well. In romance narrative, characters are continually meeting marvels and unexpected events. In interlaced stories, where plot is based on wandering and fortuitous coincidence, characters are perpetually recombining in different constellations of social groups. Any character at any moment can find himself challenged to maintain his poise and bearing in uncertain circumstances. The characters continually intrude upon each others' self-contained worlds, or upon marvels; they are then surprised, astonished, and abashed at what they see.[15] At the very least, Spenser wishes to observe passing moments of poise or its loss, and individuals confronted with the unexpected:

> Greatly thereat was *Britomart* dismayd,
> Ne in that stownd wist, how her selfe to beare.
>
> (3.11.22)

> Soone as she [Diana] *Venus* saw behind her backe,
> She was asham'd to be so loose surprized.
>
> (3.6.19)

[15]See, e.g., in Book 3 alone: 4.32, 5.3, 6.27, 7.7, 7.13, 9.23.

And euer and anone the rosy red,
Flasht through her [Britomart's] face, as it had been a flake
Of lightning, through bright heauen fulmined.

(3.2.5)

I now turn to several episodes of Spenser's third book, the book in which he most fully develops the mysterious inwardness of selfhood. We have already considered the implications of Diana's shame, which is to say her loss of her essential *virtù*, when surprised by Venus, and Belphoebe's comically grand incapacity for loss of composure when surprised by Braggadochio. The closure of Belphoebe's inviolate condition, though, benefits by the abashedness of her discovery of Timias (3.5.28–36)—a shift signalled by a blush when the sufficiency of her Ovidian huntress's life gives way to solicitude for a vulnerable other, as we shall see. The rigidity of Malbecco, whose cautiously circumscribed selfhood cracks under the pressure of exposure, turns into a desire to escape the shame of his own being which paradoxically imprisons him within the inescapable privacy of his own identity. The means by which this fixation of identity takes place is Ovidian metamorphosis; it is Spenser's darkest interpretation of Ovid, and the reduction of selfhood which Ovidian sexual shame effects is brought up against specifically Vergilian expansions of identity. Vergil and Ovid thus provide inflections on Spenser's vocabulary of sexual vision, exposure, defensiveness, and shame. And in Britomart's story Spenser most fully sketches the benign abashedness of a nascent erotic awareness, the emergence of new impulses within the self which insist on being acknowledged and accommodated. The structural importance of abashedness to the book thus hinges on the issue of the self's hidden inwardness and its exposure to the larger world.

Belphoebe's discovery of Timias, like Chrysogonee's fructification or impregnation by the sun, is an episode at once charming and, in its limitations, provocative. The Ovidian freshness of her conception becomes, in her adult life, the independent competence and self-possession that also characterize Diana's nymphs elsewhere in *The Faerie Queene*. The beginning of Belphoebe's adventure in Book 3, potentially a movement from virginity to chastity more broadly defined, sets up her preoccupation with the hunt and the focus of all her energies in a gay bloodlust:

> ...the same along did trace
> By tract of bloud, which she had freshly seene,
> To haue besprinckled all the grassy greene;
> By the great persue, which she there perceau'd,
> Well hoped she the beast engor'd had beene,
> And made more hast, the life to haue bereau'd.

(3.5.28)

The closure of this solitary and focused concentration ends, and her "expectation greatly was deceau'd," when her eager search finds Timias instead of her prey. She responds with a momentary recoil: "All suddeinly abasht she chaunged hew, / And with sterne horrour backward gan to start." The clash between expectation and reality makes her suddenly self-conscious. Her self-containment is upset here, when the mortal world in its most defenseless form impinges, and this leads to abashedness. Moreover, this unexpected development in the history of an avatar of Diana's neatly reverses the dynamics of Ovid's tale of Actaeon and Diana, and of Spenser's own episode of Diana discovered by Venus. Here the virgin-huntress blushes with the discomposure not of being discovered by, but of herself unexpectedly discovering, the vulnerable youth.

For Belphoebe it is a necessary and maturing experience of discovery and abashedness. Spenser's long description of her in Book 2, as we have seen, has established that placid, easy, and magnificent privacy that is the source of her early self-possession. Although we find her attractive partly because of such poise, it is a kind of obliviousness, a virginal immersion in her own being, which is challenged when she finds Timias. She accepts the challenge that abashedness offers: herself defensive, she next draws toward Timias and has a moment of suffering for a fellow creature:

> But when she better him beheld, she grew
> Full of soft passion and vnwonted smart:
> The point of pitty perced through her tender hart.

(3.5.30)

"Meekely she bowed downe": Spenser moves lightly from this moving gesture to the gritty details of saving Timias's life. She rises to the event's demand for a capable response by moving outward from her literal intactness.

Spenser's delicate observation of poise and its surrender ends by balancing that picture of the competent healer with a picture of the blushing girl who receives a compliment—in fact, the compliment of both Odysseus and Aeneas, "Angell, or Goddesse do I call thee right?" (3.5.35)—and turns it away:

> Thereat she blushing said, Ah gentle Squire,
>   Nor Goddesse I, nor Angell, but the Mayd,
>   And daughter of a woody Nymphe, desire
>   No seruice, but thy safety and ayd.
>
>   (3.5.36)

Belphoebe's abashedness, signaled by her blush, has modulated from the early and simple shock of the unexpected sight of vulnerability to a personal feeling of self-consciousness evoked by the intensity of another person's regard. Her blush identifies a tension between inner self and outer world which is quite absent from her description in Book 2; her sudden awareness of an other opens her to discomposure as well as to human community. She is forced to leave the privacy of her own mind and to take the first steps toward participation in the larger social and erotic realities that govern encounters in the legend of chastity.

But, given Belphoebe's fictive identity and her royal referent in Spenser's own historical world, such expansion cannot go very far, and the rest of the story reveals these intrinsic limits in spite of Spenser's best efforts to make imagery circumvent them. The language used to describe Belphoebe's bodily life raises conflicts between Ovidian virginity and erotic Petrarchan rose, and conflicts between Queen Elizabeth's politic self-presentation as adored mistress and as virgin. When Belphoebe blushes, she bashfully tries to turn aside Timias's Homero-Vergilian response to her (o dea certe!) by speaking of their common creatureliness. But Timias has already carried his vision of nymph and numinous woman in the direction of Petrarchan love and its despairing stasis. The blush, usually in *The Faerie Queen* an image of internal erotic metamorphosis, is in this case an aborted transformation. This is partly because of Spenser's conflicted sense that virginity is atavistic as well as beautiful. But it is more especially because we now perceive Belphoebe not only as a nymph with her independent integrity but also, through Spenser's sympathy with Timias, as the cruel fair of Petrarchan love. Once this conceptual gap occurs in her representation, there arises a conflict between her fully evoked sylvan life, with other feminine companions, and her cruelty as lover. The

Petrarchan opacity of feminine consciousness takes over, and Belphoebe can only seem dim in her failure to perceive Timias's desire:

> Which [Timias's lauguishing] seeing faire *Belphoebe*, gan to feare,
> Least that his wound were inly well not healed,
> Or that the wicked steele empoysned were:
> Litle she weend, that loue he close concealed.
>
> (3.5.49)

The conflict between Belphoebe as Petrarchan mistress and Belphoebe as nymph whose proximity to origins and to nature, whose candor, and whose strength identify her as a literary descendent of Diana extends to Spenser's efforts to commend her virginity—a quality, like hiddenness, the characteristics of which mean one thing in the rhetoric of courtly Petrarchanism and quite another in the syntax of Spenser's Ovidian poetics and character values:

> That dainty Rose, the daughter of her Morne,
> More deare then life she tendered, whose flowre
> The girlond of her honour did adorne:
> Ne suffred she the Middayes scorching powre,
> Ne the sharp Northerne wind thereon to showre,
> But lapped vp her silken leaues most chaire,
> When so the froward skye began to lowre:
> But soone as calmed was the Christall aire,
> She did it faire dispred, and let to florish faire.
>
> Eternall God in his almighty powre,
> To make ensample of his heauenly grace,
> In Paradize whilome did plant this flowre;
> Whence he it fetcht out of her natiue place,
> And did in stocke of earthly flesh enrace,
> That mortall men her glory should admire:
> In gentle Ladies brest, and bounteous race
> Of woman kind it fairest flowre doth spire,
> And beareth fruit of honour and all chast desire.
>
> Faire ympes of beautie, whose bright shining beames
> Adorne the world with like to heauenly light,
> And to your willes both royalties and Realmes
> Subdew, through conquest of your wondrous might,
> With this faire flowre your goodly girlonds dight,

> Of chastity and vertue virginall,
> That shall embellish more your beautie bright,
> And crowne your heades with heauenly coronall,
> Such as the Angels weare before Gods tribunall.

(3.5.51–53)

These stanzas are worth quoting in full because of the internal conflicts in their imagery.[16] The rose image of stanza 51 is largely one of Ovidian shrinking purity, with the tender impulse to hide from rough treatment, and the impulse to open candidly when safety is restored, which characterize both Ovid's solitary nymphs and Spenser's Diana. But the shyness of the rose that closes itself up is oddly matched with the glorious and terrible power of the anglicized Petrarchan lady to conquer and "subdew," to radiate heavenly light like a forceful beam. The dominant Petrarchan woman, who perforce controls the distance of the relationship and whose consciousness remains opaque, unbroken, cannot be vulnerable to the sudden exposure of inner life which abashment involves.

Britomart has an examplary blush, that Paul Alpers calls "both grand and charming," when Merlin reveals his recognition of her in Book 3:[17]

> The doubtfull Mayd, seeing her selfe descryde,
>   Was all abasht, and her pure yuory
>   Into a cleare Carnation suddeine dyde;
>   As faire *Aurora* rising hastily,
>   Doth by her blushing tell, that she did lye
>   All night in old *Tithonus* frosen bed,
>   Whereof she seemes ashamed inwardly.

---

[16]Spenser uses this imagery also at *Faerie Queene* 2.12.74, in the *carpe diem* song in Acrasia's bower, where diction and context make the rose's movements seem first coy and then sexually inviting—an implication that further complicates the rose image when used five cantos later for Belphoebe. For discussions of contradictions in this imagery, sometimes attributed to Spenser's intentional irony, see Miller, *Poem's Two Bodies*, 224–35; Judith Anderson, " 'In liuing colours and right hew': The Queen of Spenser's Central Books," in *Poetic Traditions of the English Renaissance*, ed. Maynard Mack and George deForest Lord (New Haven: Yale University Press, 1982), 47–66 at 52–54; Cheney, *Spenser's Image of Nature*, 101–3.

[17]Alpers, *Poetry of "The Faerie Queene,"* 394.

> But her old Nourse was nought dishartened,
> But vauntage made of that, which *Merlin* had ared.

>   (3.3.20)

This stanza depicts one of a series of reddenings in Britomart's experience, either blushes or flushes of exertion; they are always charming, as Alpers says of this blush, and all are important. For they mark specific revelations of her identity not only to others but also, and more especially, to herself, through an experience of discovery and abashment. The simile of Aurora's hasty rising and her failed attempt to hide the shame of sexual inactivity with Tithonus is apt, for Britomart's comic embarrassment springs precisely from the force of her sexual feelings, before which she has been ashamed and helpless. The simile here makes Britomart's own current lack of fulfilled love seem part of a natural and benign process. The dawn has a cooling effect on the blush, so that we are distanced from the hot awkwardness of it and of Britomart's suffering. The same effect emerges from the color words in the stanza: the change from "pure yuory" to "cleare Carnation" seems healthy, simple, and transparent—we are not implicated in the hot confusion and congestion of a sexually embarrassed blush.[18]

Natural analogies for blushes have formed a *topos* since antiquity, when Ovid adapted reddenings from Homer, Sappho, Vergil, and others in virtuosic imitative passages in the *Amores* and the *Metamorphoses*. Ovid crystallizes the tradition in which the bodily sign of preserved single identity is virginity; its psychic sign, the candor of the sole self's assumption of privacy; and its color, the white of undisturbed innocence. The colors of love in European literature, red and white, reside in the arousing alternatives of innocence and experience, candor and shame, the quotidian complexion of white broken into by the rising blood of erotic self-consciousness.[19] To repeat

---

[18]This argument I adapt from Ricks's analyses of blushes in Keats's work, in *Keats and Embarrassment*, 198–211 and passim.

[19]Homer, *Iliad* 4.141–47: "As when some Maionian woman or Karian with purple / colours ivory, to make it a cheek piece for horses; /...it is laid up to be a king's treasure, /.../ so, Menelaos, your shapely thighs were stained with the colour of blood" (trans. Richmond Lattimore [Chicago: University of Chicago Press, 1951]); Sappho, fr. 105a: "As the sweet-apple reddens on the bough-top, on the top of the top-most bough; the apple-gatherers have forgotten it—no, they have not forgotten it entirely, but they could not reach it" (trans. David A. Campbell in *Sappho, Alcaeus*: vol. 1 of *Greek Lyric*, 4 vols. [Cambridge: Harvard University Press, 1982–   ]); Vergil,

two important facts about blushes which I made earlier: first, to observe the rising blood in the face is to observe the most deeply internal being made external and visible against the will; second, as an opening up of interior identity, the blush in Ovid's work generally has the effect of arousing tenderness or desire for intimacy in any observer, even against the consent of the blusher, as when Hermaphroditus's blush inflames and exacerbates Salmacis's attraction to him. This is why, in Vergil and Ovid, blushes are so often both arousing and a result of arousal. They are arousing also in sixteenth- and seventeenth-century epyllia, where blushes and flushes appear in profusion, flourishing their indebtedness to Ovid and to the use of

---

Aen. 12.64–69: "accepit vocem lacrimis Lavinia matris / flagrantis perfusa genas, cui plurimus ignem / subiecit rubor et calefacta per ora curcurrit. / Indum sanguineo veluti violaverit ostro / si quis ebur, aut mixta rubent ubi lilia multa / alba rosa, talis virgo dabat ore colores" ("Lavinia heard her mother's voice, her burning cheeks bathed with tears; their profuse blushing cast a glow over her face. As when one stains Indian ivory with the color of blood; or when white lilies blush, mixed with many roses: the maiden's face revealed such colors"); Ovid, *Met.* 4.329–33: "pueri rubor ora notavit; / nescit, enim, quid amor; sed et erubuisse decebat: / hic color aprica pendentibus arbore pomis / aut ebori tincto est aut sub candore rubenti, / cum frustra resonant aera auxiliaria, lunae" ("A blush marked the boy's face, for he did not know what love was; but blushing became him. Such a color as have apples hanging on a tree, bathed in sunlight, or painted ivory, or the moon, red under white, when brazen vessels ring in vain"); Ovid, *Amores* 2.5: "Haec ego, quaeque dolor linguae dictavit; at illi / conscia purpureus venit in ora pudor, / quale coloratum Tithoni coniuge caelum / subrubet, aut sponso visa puella novo; / quale rosae fulgent inter sua lilia mixtae, / aut ubi cantatis Luna laborat equis, / aut quod, ne longis flavescere possit ab annis, / Maeonis Assyrium femina tinxit ebur" ("Thus I spoke whatever grief dictated; but crimson shame came to her conscious face, like the sky reddening with the color of Tithonus's spouse, or like a girl gazed on by her new bridegroom; as roses gleam mixed with lilies, or as when the Moon drives her celebrated steeds, or when a woman of Maeonia dyes Assyrian ivory, so that long years cannot yellow it").

I cite these passages here in order to demonstrate their interlocked allusiveness and to suggest the way literary blushes tend to attract bunched similes. They are discussed at more length in my "Sappho's Apples: The Allusiveness of Blushes in Ovid and Beaumont," *Comparative Literature Studies* 25 (March 1988), 1–22. See also Catherine Campbell Rhorer, "Red and White in Ovid's *Metamorphoses* : The Mulberry Tree in the Tale of Pyramis and Thisbe," *Ramus* 9 (1980), 79–88; Linda Woodbridge, "Black and White and Red All Over: The Sonnet Mistress amongst the Ndembu," *Renaissance Quarterly* 40 (1987), 247–97. Relevant discussion of the Latin *conscius* is found in Jean Hagstrum, "Towards a Profile of the Word *Conscious* in Eighteenth-Century Literature," in *Psychology and Literature in the Eighteenth Century*, ed. Christopher Fox (New York: AMS Studies in the Eighteenth Century, 1987), 23–50 at 24–26.

metamorphic myth which he made possible. Spenser is one of the beneficiaries of the tradition of psychologizing Ovidian myth. His domestication of classical, mythic blushes, making them English, pastoral, and part of a benign natural process rather than an Ovidian prelude to violence, makes his mythopoeic blushes not only charming but also a legacy to later erotic writers.

The Aurora simile describes both goddess and girl as "ashamed inwardly," and Britomart unhappily compares herself, at the start of her story, to Biblis and Pasiphae, who were "shamefull and vnkind" (3.2.43). Her initial shame she herself describes by reference to stories of unnatural mythic lovers from the pseudo-Vergilian *Ciris* and from Ovid. Shame is the keynote of her first experience of eros; she recoils from an apparent internal monstrosity that cannot be hidden indefinitely. Her story, marked by such shame, and by blushes and flushes, is a passage from shame to embarrassment to revelation.

The aptest of these analogues that Britomart draws is Narcissus, who in the *Metamorphoses* fails to understand that his lover's visual fixation is reflexive—effectively intromissive and extramissive simultaneously. He cannot look *into* the hidden depths of an other, since he gazes only *on* a surface image. He is disclosed only to himself; he is his only self-witness; his erotic consciousness is self-aborting. It is significant that Ovid uses, as a simile to describe Narcissus, Sappho's lovely fragment comparing a new bride to a reddening apple just out of reach, a fragment Ovid imitates also in Hermaphroditus's blush to adumbrate the charm of innocence ripening toward experience and being abashed at the prospect. The simile for Narcissus purposefully departs from the issues of sexual abashedness and reticence, which are conspicuous by their absence, since Narcissus is exposed only to himself. Instead, the reddening apple reflects the youth's perturbation, and a minor violence directed against himself, when his image in the pool is disrupted by a perturbation of the water:

> "quo refugis? remane nec me, crudelis, amantem
> desere!" clamavit; "liceat, quod tangere non est,
> adspicere et misero praebere alimenta furori!"
> dumque dolet, summa vestem deduxit ab ora
> nudaque marmoreis percussit pectora palmis.
> pectora traxerunt roseum percussa ruborem,
> non aliter quam poma solent, quae candida parte,

> parte rubent, aut ut variis solet uva racemis
> ducere purpureum nondum matura colorem.
>
> (Met. 3.477–85)

["Where do you flee? Stay, cruel one, and do not desert me, your lover!"
he cried. "What is impossible to touch, let me see, and feed my wretched
passion!" And while he grieved, he tore his upper garment from its
border and beat his naked breast with his palms, white as marble. His
breast when struck took on a rosy blush, just as apples, white in part,
become red, or as grapes in variegated clusters redden, not yet ripe.]

The reddening of the beloved's face traditionally inflames the lover.
But it is not primarily the aesthetic appreciation of mingled red and
white which generally melts the lover, as it melts Narcissus, but the
implications of vulnerability, passion, bashfulness, and sometimes
pain within the beloved—all internal activities bespoken by the blush,
which makes the lover suddenly and sharply aware of the presence
of the beloved. Narcissus's simile applies not to a facial blush, with
its revelations and its eloquent relations to sexuality, but simply to
the flush of the skin when blood rushes to the surface, a result of his
beating himself in frustration. Such a flush is an image of his paradoxical and claustral situation. The blush is normally an act and a
consequence of regarding or being regarded by an other, and Narcissus's failure to perceive a real other means that the powerful simile
of reddening apples is perforce displaced from the face to the breast.
It shows by its allusiveness how his love misfires. This is doubly true
if his words are meant to echo Aeneas's words to Venus in the *Aeneid*,
when she turns away from him after her epiphany: "quid natum
totiens, crudelis tu quoque, falsis / ludis imaginibus? cur dextrae iungere dextram / non datur ac veras audire et reddere voces?" (*Aen.*
1.407–9). The answer to Aeneas's question—"Why do you delude
your son with false images?"—is that his mother is elusive and fickle,
and that the combined potency of her numinosity and motherhood
evoke from him a yearning for full mutual presence between them, a
yearning for an ontological repletion that he is never vouchsafed in
the poem. The answer to Narcissus's imitative question to his own
image is more comic, paradoxical, and hopeless: one's presence to
oneself necessarily differs in its possible satisfactions from the satisfactions of one's presence to and for an other; he cannot make contact
with the phantom, though he invests it with the same plenitude of
being which Venus more properly has for Aeneas.

This is precisely the fear that Britomart voices, that she is obsessed with a phantom or a mere surface reflected in glass:

> I fonder, then *Cephisus* foolish child,
> Who hauing vewed in a fountaine shere
> His face, was with the loue thereof beguild;
> I fonder loue a shade, the bodie farre exild.
>
> (3.2.44)

She is ashamed first of the force and violence of her erotic drives, before which she must be uncharacteristically passive. In her abashedness she discovers one of the powers of eros: that it threatens identity and one's own assumptions about one's identity. The self-consciousness thus aroused is at the least unpleasant; if intense and lasting, it can lead to terror and shame; if it enforces the passivity and helplessness that Britomart feels, she will scourge herself into guilt. Her native tendency to direct action exacerbates her guilt at being trapped, being able to envisage no course of action. She can only endure her new drives and the abashedness to which they lead.

But it is Britomart's very capacity to blush which marks her as safe from the fate of Narcissus; she not only is aware, eventually, of Artegall, as an other, but is also bound to other members of the social world, others who witness her shame and self-consciousness, notably Glauce, Merlin, and Redcrosse. The potential nightmare of entrapment in an obsession, which she fears partly because of her knowledge of tales from Vergil and Ovid, simply drops away when her identity is *acknowledged* by Merlin in the stanzas surrounding her Aurora blush, in the same gesture that transforms her descent to Merlin's underworld, imitative of Aeneas's quest and equally fraught with terror, into a comic and providential discovery of herself:

> The wisard could no lenger beare her bord,
>   But brusting forth in laughter, to her sayd;
> *Glauce,* what needs this colourable word,
>   To cloke the cause, that hath it selfe bewrayd?
> Ne ye faire *Britomartis,* thus arayd,
>   More hidden are, then Sunne in cloudy vele.
>
> (3.3.19)

Merlin's act of acknowledgment, the recognition that triggers her blush, and his subsequent prophecy, together absorb and redirect her shame by sanctioning her erotic drive and locating it in history; his acknowledgment removes her need for defensive caution. To observe a solitary character without revealing one's watching presence can be, in *The Faerie Queene*, a bestowal of love, a gesture of tact which tries to preserve the otherness of the observed. But to witness and to acknowledge Britomart's shame: these are the tactfulnesses required between characters of explicit intelligence and awareness, whose very consciousness is Spenser's subject. Merlin's shrewd and kindly acknowledgment here turns the torment of Britomart's shame into the milder fluster of embarrassment.

Such acknowledgment of her inward sources of shame by the kindness of parental figures (Glauce, Merlin) is the initial step in the emergence and eventual revelation of her erotic identity. That identity is forcibly revealed in the farcical disaster with Malecasta; after steadfastly refusing to suffer the gaze of others in the house of courtly love by removing her armor, she finally suffers a more drastic exposure as she stands only in her shift, defensively brandishing a sword across from the fainting Malecasta:

> But the braue Mayd would not disarmed bee,
> But onely vented vp her vmbriere,
> And so did let her goodly visage to appere.
>
> (3.1.42)

> (For she her sexe vnder that straunge purport
> Did vse to hide, and plaine apparaunce shonne:)
>
> (3.1.52)

> Tho when the Britonesse saw all the rest
> Auoided quite, she gan her selfe despoile,
> And safe commit to her soft fethered nest.
>
> (3.1.58)

> On th'other side, they saw the warlike Mayd
> All in her snow-white smocke, with locks vnbownd,
> Threatning the point of her auenging blade.
>
> (3.1.63)

Exposed, Britomart is immediately wounded by a character named Gardante, and the ensuing melée is a compact image of the inner chaos that besets her when the protective and defensive disguise of her armor fails her.

But even this turmoil issues in the increased friendliness between herself and Redcrosse, as they ride off from Castle Joyous. One barrier of defensive hiding, her disguise, no longer stands between them; although she lies about her reasons for searching out Artegall, her erotic desires and joys disclose themselves more openly than before, through the literal and metaphoric expressiveness of her body. At the thought of speaking of Artegall,

> ... with hart-thrilling throbs and bitter stowre,
> As if she had a feuer fit, [Britomart] did quake,
> And euery daintie limbe with horrour shake;
> And euer and anone the rosy red,
> Flasht through her face, as it had been a flake
> Of lightning, through bright heauen fulmined.
>
> (3.2.5)

The elaborate lie that she constructs for Redcrosse's benefit is another defense, one devised to preclude his awareness of her real interest, which to her own consciousness seems not hidden but painfully evident. But the fearful anticipation of discovery takes a comic and jubilant turn when her joy at the independent confirmation of her mental image of Artegall is compared to the joy of a mother just giving birth from the private compartment of her body:

> The royall Mayd woxe inly wondrous glad,
>
> . . . . .
>
> How euer finely she it faind to hide:
> The louing mother, that nine monethes did beare,
> In the deare closet of her painefull side,
> Her tender babe, it seeing safe appeare,
> Doth not so much reioyce, as she reioyced theare.
>
> (3.2.11)

Britomart has two more reddenings in her journey to Artegall; both occur in the great recognition scene among Britomart, Artegall, Scudamour, and Glauce (4.6.2–32). This is the first conscious meeting between Britomart and Artegall—a meeting that splendidly resolves the suspense that Spenser has built by keeping us waiting for this occasion since early in Book 3. The episode begins with a characteristic interest in the simplest social decorums of sight. Scudamour, wandering pensively away from the house of Care, sees in the distance a knight in armor; battle between them is narrowly avoided when he and Artegall recognize each other. They perceive their common enemy (who will turn out to be Britomart) at a distance, and prepare to attack. This is a common enough pattern from romance, and Spenser uses it elsewhere, for example, when Arthur and Timias prepare to attack the Wild Man (6.5.25), and when Guyon readies himself to attack Redcrosse (2.1.25–26). Passionate hostility in this case issues in the crucial battle of the lovers Artegall and Britomart, and as in other battles throughout the poem, Spenser is at pains to emphasize the vulnerability and penetrability of the whole body, the human reality of "tender flesh" unseen beneath mail and plate. He mentions Britomart's weapon

> Whose raging rigour neither steele nor bras
> Could stay, but to the tender flesh it went,
> And pour'd the purple bloud forth on the gras;
> That all his mayle yriv'd, and plates yrent,
> Shew'd all his bodie bare vnto the cruell dent.
>
> (4.6.15)

But if the rage of weapons normally and shockingly reveals tender flesh and spilt blood, in this instance it beautifully transforms shock into surprise by next revealing Britomart's identity:

> The wicked stroke vpon her helmet chaunst,
>   And with the force, which in it selfe it bore,
>   Her ventayle shard away, and thence forth glaunst
>   A downe in vaine, ne harm'd her any more.
>   With that her angels face, vnseene afore,
>   Like to the ruddie morne appeard in sight,
>   Deawed with siluer drops, through sweating sore,
>   But somewhat redder, then beseem'd aright,
> Through toylesome heate and labour of her weary fight.
>
> (4.6.19)

The stanza is justly famous for its process of humanizing Britomart's divinity with drops of sweat and with the reddening caused by her efforts in battle. In this flush we recognize, along with Scudamour, that her virginal beauty is of heaven but also emergent from nature:

Which when as *Scudamour*, who now abrayd,
   Beheld, whereas he stood not farre aside,
   He was therewith right wondrously dismayd,
   And drawing nigh, when as he plaine descride
   That peerelesse paterne of Dame natures pride,
   And heauenly image of perfection,
   He blest himselfe, as one sore terrifide,
   And turning his feare to faint deuotion,
Did worship her as some celestiall vision.

                                                    (4.6.24)

   The numinous woman viewed here has a fit audience in Scudamour and Artegall: their visionary wonder, a quality elsewhere in the poem capable of an Ovidian turn into cupidity of the eye, is in this episode sanctioned by its grounding in a fully human sense of sheer astonishment, emerging as an inevitable step in the plot. Both the wonder and the astonishment signal again Spenser's affinity with the crucial Homeric and Vergilian tones that we noted in Chapter One. The visionary rapture, moreover, is carefully supervised by Glauce, who insists that the luminous joy of the moment become naturalized, part of the quotidian scene, and that it be extended to the revelation of male identity as well:

But *Glauce*, seeing all that chaunced there,
   Well weeting how their errour to assoyle,
   Full glad of so good end, to them drew nere,
   And her salewd with seemely belaccoyle,
   Ioyous to see her safe after long toyle.
   Then her besought, as she to her was deare,
   To graunt vnto those warriours truce a whyle;
   Which yeelded, they their beuers vp did reare,
And shew'd themselues to her, such as indeed they were.

                                                    (4.6.25)

Glauce, with a fine sense of dramatic closure, "gan wisely all vpknit" (4.6.30) by presenting all the characters to one another as spectators of one anothers' turbulent emotions, thus making possible the concord of friendship and leading the poised moment of celestial wonder back to the mundane issues of social and bodily decorums: "Thereat full inly blushed *Britomart*; / But *Artegall* close smyling ioy'd in secret hart" (4.6.32).

When Shakespeare's lovers unite in his romantic comedies, they are notably poised and triumphant, pleased to be securing their loves ceremonially and publicly, unabashed by the nighttime rites to come. Spenser's lovers evince a different awareness of the publicity of their intimacy: it abashes them. But abashment is liberating for Britomart, coming as it does as a result of all the cumulative disclosures and revelations that we have seen. These disclosures are a progress from the complex, tortuous, tangled miseries of shame, through increasingly open sublimities of joy and the easy poise of self-revelation in Malbecco's castle, to a refreshingly simple and momentary embarrassment, depicted in one line, when Glauce unites the lovers.

The Wary Eye, the Spying Eye: The Defensiveness and Exposure of Malbecco

Two instances of prolonged gazing, with extraordinary effects on the watchers, frame the story of Malbecco (3.9–10), and together they provide the terms by which we can apprehend the diversity contained within Spenser's fabliau. The first occurs when Britomart takes off her armor, openly revealing herself as a woman to the assembled company—the unlikely mix of Paridell, Satyrane, Malbecco, and the Squire of Dames:

> Which whenas they beheld, they smitten were
>   With great amazement of so wondrous sight,
>   And each on other, and they all on her
>   Stood gazing, as if suddein great affright
>   Had them surprised. At last auizing right,
>   Her goodly personage and glorious hew,
>   Which they so much mistooke, they tooke delight
> In their first errour, and yet still anew
> With wonder of her beauty fed their hungry vew.
>
>   (3.9.23)

It is of course one of the many moments of Vergilian revelation of the feminine numinous, piercing radiantly "through veils or clouds of shining faces and hair," of the kind that has appeared throughout these pages.[20] Its possible functions in the harsh comedy of cantos 9 and 10 bear some consideration, particularly given its ideals of gratified pleasure fused unproblematically with religious awe, and the bestowal upon its characters of candor within a social setting rather than in solitude.

Spenser devotes five stanzas (3.9.20–24) to the description of the prolonged pleasure of fully sanctioned sexual vision. They are entirely and remarkably without any of the warning voices that elsewhere call into question the dynamics of such sight. Even Paridell, crass and flippant, simply surrrenders the cranky malice aroused by his earlier blow from Britomart, and "Through gracious regard of her faire eye, / And knightly worth, which he too late did try, / Yet tried did adore" (3.9.25). The unqualified simplicity of this happy gaze allows us to read the gaze as a gratification of the intense wish we have seen at work elsewhere in the poem, the desire for sustained access to the presence of a woman who arouses and fulfills hunger simultaneously: "they . . . Stood gazing"; "yet still anew / With wonder of her beauty fed their hungry vew"; "note their hungry vew be satisfide"; "seeing still the more desir'd to see"; "firmely fixed did abide / In contemplation" (stanzas 23–24). This fulfillment is a significant change from the elusiveness of numinous beauty embodied in Vergil's Venus, a change effected partially by the echo of a Vergilian epiphany along with an adaptation of an image from the *Metamorphoses* which Upton cites:

> Haec ubi nequiquam formae deus aptus anili
> edidit, in iuvenem rediit et anilia demit
> instrumenta sibi talisque apparuit illi,
> qualis ubi oppositas nitidissima solis imago
> evicit nubes nullaque obstante reluxit.
>
> (Met. 14.765–69)

[When the god in the form of an old woman had spoken, he returned to his youthful form, took off his old woman's things, and appeared to her as when the sun's most brilliant face has dispersed the clouds before it and, with nothing to obstruct it, shines again.]

---

[20]A. Bartlett Giamatti, "Spenser: From Magic to Miracle," in *Four Essays on Romance,* ed. Herschel Baker (Cambridge: Harvard University Press, 1971), 17–31 at 24; rpt. in Giamatti's *Exile and Change in Renaissance Literature* (New Haven: Yale University Press, 1984), 76–88.

Spenser juxtaposes Vergilian and Ovidian echoes in order to create an iconic moment not of yearning but of fulfillment, a gratification that is ideal not only in its pleasure but in its social ease and in the way it arises naturally, not in an enchanted bower but within the less glamorous necessities of the quotidian world:

> Each gan vndight
> Their garments wet, and weary armour free,
> To dry them selues by *Vulcanes* flaming light,
> And eke their lately bruzed parts to bring in plight.
>
> And eke that straunger knight emongst the rest,
> Was for like need enforst to disaray:
> Tho whenas vailed was her loftie crest,
> Her golden locks, that were in tramels gay
> Vpbounden, did them selues adowne display,
> And raught vnto her heeles; like sunny beames,
> That in a cloud their light did long time stay,
> Their vapour vaded, shew their golden gleames,
> And through the persant aire shoote forth their azure streames.
>
> (3.9.19–20)

   Spenser turns the images of desire in Vergil's and Ovid's central episodes of men and women regarding each other to images of ideal repletion; he also acknowledges and then masters the Petrarchan danger, to the male viewer, of stasis before transcendent feminine beauty, with its threat of radical disruption in identity and in time. We have just seen that Britomart's revelation emerges (literally, out of ordinary wet clothes and heavy armor) rather than erupts into the consciousness of the viewer. Fixation does loom as a momentary threat in the simile about the Medusa-head shield that allows Minerva to "transfix" her enemy:[21]

> Like as *Minerua,* being late returnd
> From slaughter of the Giaunts conquered;
> Where proud *Encelade,* whose wise nosethrils burnd

---

[21]The goddess of war is identified as Bellona in the 1590 edition, Minerva in 1596. Hamilton's note suggests that the change to Minerva was made because her name, associated with wisdom, "is preferable to Bellona's which is associated with aggressive violence." For the other mythological references in the stanza, see Hamilton, and the *Variorum* 3.279.

With breathed flames, like to a furnace red,
Transfixed with the speare, downe tombled ded
From top of *Hemus*, by him heaped hye;
Hath loosd her helmet from her lofty hed,
And her *Gorgonian* shield gins to vntye
From her left arme, to rest in glorious victorye.

(3.9.22)

The simile describes the temporary arrest of Britomart's witnesses, and so acknowledges this Petrarchan danger that Spenser tries to defend against throughout the poem; here he succeeds by modulating that arrest into the shared pleasure of surprise. Her companions jointly realize that they had mistaken her before, but see her truly now, and this understanding both of her true nature and of their error is an active pleasure. They "delight" in their knowledge, and it allows them to indulge vision fully. They feast on a "diuinitie" not elusive but fully present and sustaining; they take in her "cheualree" and "prowesse," demonstrated earlier outside Malbecco's castle; they enjoy the pleasant surprise of their own mistake.

Admiring as they do not only her divinity but her individual humanity, and responding as they do to a surprise, the viewers have the added pleasure of candor in open and legitimate gazing. Such candor extends as well to Britomart, whose prior caution in guarding her disguise disappears here, as she openly and even "carelessly" lets herself be known as a woman:

She also dofte her heauy haberieon,
    Which the faire feature of her limbs did hyde,
    And her well plighted frock, which she did won
    To tucke about her short, when she did ryde,
    She low let fall, that flowd from her lanck syde
    Downe to her foot, with carelesse modestee.

(3.9.21)

In this simple revelation, as in her fully earned possession of chivalric gifts, the woman is acknowledged as willingly disclosed rather than opaque, and this acknowledgment obviates all earlier need for defensiveness.

What has this lovely and happy vignette to do with the story of Malbecco, or for that matter with shame and exposure? The brief episode of Britomart's revelation in companionship, in the context of the knights' easy graciousness in Malbecco's unwelcoming home, is an icon of everything that is inaccessible to Malbecco in spite of (or perhaps because of) his own hunger: social camaraderie, candor, the pleasure of revelation, an openness to marvel, the very possibility of satisfaction. (These points hold despite the fact that Malbecco is nominally included among Britomart's admirers; in any case the passage about her revelation may be a late interpolation, since Malbecco is jealous of her, taking her to be a male knight, at 3.9.27. If this is the case, Spenser may hardly be distinguishing Malbecco as an independent character in these stanzas.)[22] Malbecco's existence is characterized by candor's opposites, compulsive secrecy and sexual shame; by the torment of constant suspicion of and efforts to control others, figured as imprisonment and as continual watching; by the fear of contempt if any aspect of his life is exposed. All of these torments unite to crush him in the second great moment of sexual vision in his story, his fascinated view of Hellenore mating with the satyr (3.10.44–52), an Ovidian passage in which are represented human capacities the very opposite of those in Britomart's revelation: capacities not for bliss and awe but for shame, suffering, and extinction. To this episode we will turn, after some remarks on the structure of the whole story.

That structure adapts to Chaucerian fabliau the sensibilities of Ovidian elegy; the coarse, vivid, and earthy attitudes of fabliau's bourgeois characters are replaced by the elegant cynicism, urbanity, and manipulations of the *Amores* as more suitable expressions of courtly characters' decadent eros. The marks of Ovid's elegies are everywhere. Paridell is the flippant *amator*, interested in the trivialized frissons of seduction, tantalization, playfully calculated contempt for and cruelty toward the cuckolded husband, and the pleasures of deceit. He and Hellenore play the coy game with spilled wine, drawn from *Amores* 2.5 and *Heroides* 17, less for the pleasure of communication than for the pleasure of risking and evading Malbecco's notice, a larger game that controls the action of both cantos as it does many of Ovid's elegies. And the mating of the satyr with Hellenore nine times is one of several overt allusions to the *Amores* (*Am.* 3.7).

The decadent frivolity and cruelty of Spenser's expanded erotic

---

[22]For this point, see Rudolf B. Gottfried, "Spenser Expands His Text," *Renaissance News* 16 (1963), 9–10. But see *Variorum* 3.278–79, for a note by H. E. Cory (1917) to the effect that Spenser delays Britomart's revelation "until she sits down in this larger and lewder company [lewder, that is, than Malecasta]: with the half-barbarous Sir Satyrane, with a rake, a wanton wife, and a miser."

elegy are broken periodically by moments of Vergilian nobility, in which the ironies of Vergilian pathos and suffering are transformed into momentary achievements of reliable happiness or hope. This is true of the Vergilian revelation of Britomart; it is also true of Britomart's exalted response to Paridell's cynical narrative of the Troy story. Her intertwined erotic and imperial hopes, blessed rather than thwarted by the transcendent powers of Spenser's providential cosmos, lead to her identification with Brutus, whose heroic expansion she describes as the emergent revelation of internal forces pressing outward:

> So huge a scope at first him seemed best,
> To be the compasse of his kingdomes seat:
> So huge a mind could not in lesser rest,
> Ne in small meares containe his glory great.

> (3.9.46)

In the character and history of Britomart, Spenser sketches the capacities of a Vergilian identity, first by focusing on Britomart Vergilian motifs and issues (the revelation of the numinous, the relation of individual destiny to *imperium*, the importance of the city), and second by inflecting the motifs away from Vergilian doubt and pathos, in the direction of happiness and fulfillment. The Vergilian self in this episode of *The Faerie Queene* is an image of desire in the process of being gratified, an expansive and expanded selfhood that embraces figures of its history and of its future. Identity emerges from hiddenness to full view, as Britomart's glory literally emerges from her armor and Brutus's greatness of mind emerges from his civic mission.

This notion of identity contrasts not only with the evident triviality of Paridell's eroticism, but also and more especially with the notions of identity underlying Malbecco's shame and metamorphosis, in Spenser's darkest interpretation of Ovid's work. For if Malbecco is treated by Paridell as the contemptible cuckolded husband of the *Amores*, his sexual shame and secrecy exposed by the shamelessness of the lovers, his torment aligns him also with the wish for secrecy found in various forms in the *Metamorphoses*. His closest Ovidian analogue from that work is Aglauros.

In Chapter One I said that Aglauros's confused desire exemplifies the desire of the have-not to be privy to, to have access to, others' happiness; she expresses wishes both for money and for the sexual happiness of her sister, whose liaison with Mercury she cannot stop imagining. Her cupidity seems to emerge from an inner economy of privation; her infection by the allegorical Invidia suggests that her own identity is emptied (or perhaps has always been empty, given her earlier role in spying out Minerva's secret) of any substance except the growing fascination with others' happiness, perceived as secrets from which she is excluded. Looking becomes both a compulsion and a torment for a character whose greed and whose acts of spying are rooted in interior privation. An analogous understanding of the relationships among spying, *cupiditas*, malice, fascinating secrets, the envy of happiness, and the privation of being is at work in Spenser's treatment of Malbecco, whose allegorical transformation into Gealosie more closely resembles Aglauros's metamorphosis than it does any other kind of metamorphosis in Ovid's poem.

Both Malbecco and Aglauros are the kinds of character which Harry Berger describes as the have-not, to which he ascribes a condition articulated by Kierkegaard: "To despair over oneself, in despair to will to be rid of oneself, is the formula for all despair." The spiritual and psychic movements of such characters begin "in absence of spirit" and move "through privation to inward pain"; these characters are characteristically restless, driven by a hunger created by interior emptiness, and are able neither to "rest in themselves nor ease the pain of being themselves."[23]

Though Berger ascribes the condition of the have-not to more Spenserian characters than I would (he suggests Lucifera, Duessa, Archimago, Occasion, Furor, Braggadochio, Malbecco, among others), I take his description as an acute and useful key to Ovid's Aglauros (though Berger's derivation of the condition in the "Christian metaphysic of evil as nonbeing" would not apply to her) and to Spenser's Malbecco, whose despair over himself appears in his typical acts of hoarding and hiding. The objects of these actions are multiple: he hoards and hides his treasure, his household, himself, his wife, in strenuous and futile efforts to hold on to things and relations that he never experiences as truly his. Interior privation makes him fear deprivation at others' hands: he cannot bear to be perceived by the outside world because of the shame of his secret. But the exposure of secrets

[23]Harry Berger, "The Prospect of Imagination: Spenser and the Limits of Poetry," *Studies in English Literature* 1 (1961), 93–120 at 105–7.

is one of the great themes of the *Metamorphoses*, and a recurrent one in Spenser's poetry; sexuality constantly risks becoming the salacious gossip of an invasive and inescapable social world, both the pleasures and sufferings of erotic privacy trivialized by exposure:

> . . . warily he watcheth euery way,
> By which he feareth euill happen may:
>
> . . . . .
>
> So doth he punish her and eke himselfe torment.
>
> . . . . .
>
> False loue, why do men say, thou canst not see,
> And in their foolish fancie feigne thee blind,
> That with thy charmes the sharpest sight doest bind,
> And to thy will abuse? Thou walkest free,
> And seest euery secret of the mind;
> Thou seest all, yet none at all sees thee.
>
> (3.10.3–4)

This threat of exposure is for Malbecco permanent misery, a state of perpetual shame, and it locates his gross inhospitality to the knights as an act of defensiveness, analogous to Aglauros's truculent attempt to bar the door to Mercury in the *Metamorphoses*.

Aglauros sits tormented and fascinated at the threshold of the room where Mercury and Herse find their erotic happiness between god and human; Malbecco's torment and fascination come from seeing his wife's erotic happiness with beasts, which he experiences as a spectacle both shameful for her and shaming to himself (3.10.44–52):

> Yet afterwards close creeping, as he might,
>   He in a bush did hide his fearefull hed,
> The iolly *Satyres* full of fresh delight,
>   Came dauncing forth, and with them nimbly led
> Faire *Hellenore*.
>
> (3.10.44)

> The silly man that in the thicket lay
>   Saw all this goodly sport, and grieued sore,
> Yet durst he not against it doe or say,
>   But did his hart with bitter thoughts engore,
> To see th'vnkindnesse of his *Hellenore*.
>
> (3.10.45)

> At night, when all they went to sleeepe, he vewd,
>   Whereas his louely wife emongst them lay,
>   Embraced of a *Satyre* rough and rude.

(3.10.48)

The depiction of Hellenore's actions is delicately sensitive to her liberation from the deadening confines of her marriage but remains an expression of natural erotic joy unsuitable for human beings.[24] Still, Spenser takes pains to emphasize the spectacle of happiness and potency presented to Malbecco's vision, and to contrast the satyrs' natural abundance of energy with his deprivation. He creeps and hides in the Ovidian woods, latent with erotic energy, while the satyrs come "dauncing forth," "full of fresh delight"; their sexual force and openness is an added misery, taken as a rebuke by natural vigor to human incapacity. Such "goodly sport" exacerbates his shame, and the very act of spying is another manifestation of his inward emptiness. Significantly for a hoarder, his sexual shame is intensified by the loss of his buried treasure, and this double exposure of his secrets triggers not merely embarrassment's temporary desire to hide but a panicky need to be rid of the burden of his selfhood, to annihilate himself.

> With extreme fury he became quite mad,
>   And ran away, ran with himselfe away:
>   That who so straungely had him seene bestad,
>   With vpstart haire, and staring eyes dismay
> From Limbo lake him late escaped sure would say.

(3.10.54)

In Malbecco's final metamorphosis we see an example of that despair at being oneself which Berger describes: Malbecco's shame, self-loathing, and shocked awareness have all been heightened by an enforced confrontation with the realities of his erotic life made public.

---

[24]On Hellenore's "comic liberation," see Donald Cheney, "Spenser's Hermaphrodite and the 1590 *Faerie Queene*," *PMLA* 87 (1972), 192–200 at 198; Harry Berger, "The Discarding of Malbecco: Conspicuous Allusion and Cultural Exhaustion in *The Faerie Queene* 3.9–10," *Studies in Philology* 66 (1969), 135–54 at 144. For the Ovidian indebtedness of Hellenore's story, see Helen Cheney Gilde, "Spenser's Hellenore and Some Ovidian Associations," *Comparative Literature* 23 (1971), 233–39.

Griefe, and despight, and gealosie, and scorne
Did all the way him follow hard behind,
And he himselfe himselfe loath'd so forlorne,
So shamefully forlorne of womankind;
That as a Snake, still lurked in his wounded mind.

(3.10.55)

The sentence structure that places side by side the intensifier *himselfe*
and the direct object *himselfe* underscores the paradoxy of shame.
The "selfe-murdring thought" (stanza 57) which had begun as a desire
to hoard and to hide, thus to protect a precarious privacy masking
interior lack, becomes a vain flight from selfhood. The paradox is
reinforced with the line describing Malbecco's allegorization of himself: he "forgot he was a man, and *Gealosie* is hight." This distillation
of his identity into the pure essence of jealousy suggests that he loses
his full and potentially complex identity as a human being; on the
other hand, he becomes what his inner impulse has most truly been.
He "himselfe himselfe" flees, but finally encounters only himself and
has only himself to live with. Stanza 58 links Malbecco's nightmarish
seclusion with the restlessness of the have-not. The constant laceration
of shame becomes self-perpetuating; it "doth with curelesse care con-
sume the hart":

...at the last he found a caue with entrance small.

Into the same he creepes, and thenceforth there
Resolu'd to build his baleful mansion,
In drery darkenesse, and continuall feare ....
...he dare neuer sleepe, but that one eye
Still ope he keepes.

(3.10.57–58)

The "joylesse dread" (3.11.1) which is one result of excessive solitude has intensified throughout Malbecco's story until his deadly life
transforms itself into a living death characterized by that never-resting
eye guarding against all observation by the outside world, that eye
representing the tormented self-consciousness of abashment in its ex-
tremest form. Malbecco's shame is an abiding condition of internalized exposure, his desire an impossible wish to hide from the audience
of himself. The easy candor, splendor, and camaraderie of idealized
Vergilian vision and the secrecy, closeness, and isolation of Ovidian

sexual exposure between them shape the ethos of the tale and allow
Spenser the rich mix of generic elements within his fabliau.

The Ethics of Ceremonial Display:
Exposure and Abashedness in Wedding

We think of Spenser, rightly, as our greatest poet of wedding. He
is so not only because his wedding poems and passages celebrate the
ceremonial dignity, the elegance, the pomp, the sensuous opulence,
and the erotic promise of marriage, but also because they acknowledge
the anarchic forces that threaten marriage.[25] I want to trace in the
following pages one of those dark forces. Spenser's wedding pieces
are crossed by an anxiety that attends the ceremonial pageantry, the
sheer visibility and even publicity of wedding's display. This display
may take the shape of a procession, a masque, a dance, a blazon of
the bride. The anxiety may appear in diction, in similes, in plot situations, in the writer's analyses of wedding's ethics and conventions
or in the writer's analysis of character; the tone and degree of this
anxiety vary considerably from piece to piece.

In all cases, it is specifically the bride who is vulnerable to the
potential hurtfulness of display. Spenser understands the ceremonies
and festivities of his cherished weddings as (among many other things)
cultural conventions, like those of love poetry, which are capable not
only of celebration and praise but also of undermining the interior
affective life and the subjectivity of the beloved woman. In the following discussion of weddings in *Epithalamion* and in *The Faerie
Queene*—those of Amoret and Scudamour, Florimell and Marinell,
the Thames and the Medway—and of the betrothals of Una and
Redcrosse, my chief argument is that wedding in the publications of
1595 and 1596 is the locus of a tension between two understandings
of ceremonial display and the function of individual persons in cer-

---

[25]See Thomas M. Greene, "Spenser and the Epithalamic Tradition," *Comparative
Literature* 9 (1957), 215–28 at 227; Douglas Anderson, " 'Vnto My Selfe Alone':
Spenser's Plenary Epithalamion," *Spenser Studies* 5 (1985), 149–66; Joseph Loewenstein, "Echo's Ring: Orpheus and Spenser's Career," *English Literary Renaissance*
16 (Spring 1986), 287–302. Heather Dubrow, *A Happier Eden: The Epithalamium
in Stuart England* (Ithaca: Cornell University Press, 1990), discusses darker aspects
of a wider range of poems; see especially chapter 1.

emony.[26] Ceremony can be understood to celebrate the participants'
identities as they are manifested in social roles and relationships
(bride, daughter, bearer of dowry, potential mother; groom, potential
father, and so on). Or ceremony can be understood to strain and
threaten the authenticity of an interior selfhood, which is represented
as reticence and the desire for freedom from the gaze of others.

This tension exists in *Epithalamion*, where the degree of anxiety is
relatively light; anxiety about the display of the bride and her abashment is a mere shadow passing over the dominant tone of jubilation:

> Loe where she comes along with portly pace,
> Lyke Phoebe from her chamber of the East,
> Arysing forth to run her mighty race,
> Clad all in white, that seemes a virgin best.
>
> . . . . .
>
> Her modest eyes abashed to behold
> So many gazers, as on her do stare,
> Vpon the lowly ground affixed are.
> Ne dare lift vp her countenance too bold,
> But blush to heare her prayses sung so loud,
> So farre from being proud.
> Nathlesse doe ye still loud her prayses sing,
> That all the woods may answer and your eccho ring.
>
> (*Epith.* 148–66)

The narrator-bridegroom acknowledges the bride's bashfulness before
the staring gazers and tries in various ways to improve the delicate
social situation. First, Spenser's splendid revision of the epithalamic
norm, making narrator and groom one person, has the consequence
of countering the lover's desire to display the bride with his eager
solicitude for her discomfort. Attention is drawn to the bride's

---

[26]Stephen Greenblatt, "Psychoanalysis and Renaissance Culture," in *Literary The-
ory/Renaissance Texts*, ed. Patricia Parker and David Quint (Baltimore: Johns Hopkins
University Press, 1986), 210–24, discusses a tension in Renaissance culture between
the two understandings of identity that I address in Spenser's weddings, via the story
of Martin Guerre: "At issue is not Martin Guerre as subject but Martin Guerre as
object, the placeholder in a complex system of possessions, kinship bonds, contractual
relations, customary rights, and ethical obligations.... Martin's subjectivity... does
not any the less exist, but it seems peripheral, or rather, it seems to be the *product*
of the relations, material objects, and judgments exposed in the case rather than the
producer of these relations, objects, and judgments" (216).

abashedness, so the tiny efforts he makes to accommodate her bashfulness take on a touching, dramatic urgency. Second, as always in Spenser's work, mythic creatures both natural and divine are less rigorously subject than humans to the psychology and decorums of reticence, reserve, and shame. Sun and moon in particular are the exemplary figures for whom jubilant display is the very essence of identity; comparing the bride to Phoebe is a way of assimilating the beauty of natural spectacle to the human bride.[27] Third, the speaker begins the refrain of this stanza with the concessive "Nathlesse"—as if the bride's bashfulness *could* be a cogent reason for the singers to silence their praises—and then encourages them to sing "still": her abashedness is a matter worth attention, but the celebration of wedding is a greater priority.

The same priority emerges at the very heart of the ceremony, when the bride and groom make their vows at the altar; it is significant that the bride's blush takes up nearly the whole of this stanza:

> Behold whiles she before the altar stands
>
> . . . . .
>
> How the red roses flush vp in her cheekes,
> And the pure snow with goodly vermill stayne,
> Like crimsin dyde in grayne,
> That euen th'Angels which continually,
> About the sacred Altare doe remaine,
> Forget their seruice and about her fly,
> Ofte peeping in her face that seemes more fayre,
> The more they on it stare.
> But her sad eyes still fastened on the ground,
> Are gouerned with goodly modesty,
> That suffers not one looke to glaunce awry,

---

[27]The finest example in *The Faerie Queene* of Spenser's treatment of the sun as appropriate mythic figure of gorgeous display is the sunrise on the day that Redcrosse is to fight Sansjoy; it is a companion piece to the simile comparing the bride to Phoebe in *Epithalamion*:

> At last the golden Orientall gate
>   Of greatest heauen gan to open faire,
> And *Phoebus* fresh, as bridegrome to his mate,
> Came dauncing forth, shaking his deawie haire:
> And hurld his glistring beames through gloomy aire.
>
> (1.5.2)

Which may let in a little thought vnsownd.
Why blush ye loue to giue to me your hand,
The pledge of all our band?

(*Epith.* 223–239)

This is a remarkable choice of subject for the stanza we expect to depict the speaking of the vows. The groom hopefully interprets the blush as a mark of conventional modesty, of the bride's purity and guard over her thoughts. But this will not sufficiently account for the bride's blushing, because Spenser goes out of his way to amplify the blush and to complicate its motives and the responses that it evokes in observers.

The two similes for the blush—"the pure snow with goodly vermill stayne, / Like crimsin dyde in grayne"—are attenuated versions of ancient and venerable similes of human reddening taken from Homer, Sappho, Vergil, and Ovid and used so plentifully by Renaissance writers. Spenser is relatively uninterested, here, in the historical interactions of these similes within his poem or in their potential implications about erotic drives. We might almost consider them conventional in the worst sense—as automatic and unexamined filler—were it not for the stanza's continued and odd emphasis on the blush. The following lines, about the relationship between the angels and the bride, are *not* conventional; they acknowledge that the bride's blush is not simply charming but also arousing to observers, regardless of the bride's own will. To blush is a natural response (one might speculate) to angels "ofte peeping" in one's face; but the blusher, so far from being able to protect herself, only attracts more appreciative gazing, and also desire, by blushing: her face "seemes more fayre, / The more they on it stare." These angels' happy amazement is a gentle, echoing transformation of those ancient literary blushes, using identical allusive similes, which arouse more violent desires—in Vergil's Turnus when he sees Lavinia's blush, in Ovid's Salmacis when she sees Hermaphroditus blush, in the lover of *Amores* 2.5 who responds with both tenderness and violence when his lover blushes. Given this allusive context, it will hardly do to attribute the bride's abashedness to "goodly modesty," as the narrator does. At the very least, we must say that her abashedness seems less a sign of her heavenly purity than of her vulnerable humanity.

In the other wedding pieces published in 1595 and 1596, Spenser resists what he depicts as wedding's risky exposure of interior reticence. This is so in Amoret's eerie adventures with Busyrane in *The Faerie Queene* 4.1. A good deal has been made of the grotesquerie of the heart cut from Amoret's body and what this might signify in terms of some inability, failure, or lack on her part.[28] But her suffering may perhaps be a legitimate response to the public exposure that she suffers during her boisterous wedding day. Busyrane's Petrarchan masque first appears on that "very selfe same day," and the masque's externalization of the forces of love, together with the coarse publicity of the festivities, has some causal relationship to her disappearance:

> For that same vile Enchauntour *Busyran*,
>   The very selfe same day that she was wedded,
>   Amidst the bridale feast, whilest euery man
>   Surcharg'd with wine, were heedlesse and ill hedded,
>   All bent to mirth before the bride was bedded,
>   Brought in that mask of loue which late was showen:
>   And there the Ladie ill of friends bestedded,
>   By way of sport, as oft in maskes is knowen,
> Conueyed quite away to liuing wight vnknowen.
>
> (4.1.3)[29]

The consequence is an ordeal in which the woman's heart, one elemental organ of interior life, is carved out and exposed in a violation of the interiority and secrecy of bodily life and affect:

> Her brest all naked, as net iuory,
>
>   . . . . .
>
> Of her dew honour was despoyled quight,
> And a wide wound therein (O ruefull sight)
> Entrenched deepe with knife accursed keene,

---

[28]See the survey of criticism by Helen Cheney Gilde in "The Sweet Lodge of Love and Deare Delight: The Problem of Amoret," *Philological Quarterly* 50 (1971), 63–74. Thomas P. Roche's *The Kindly Flame: A Study of "The Faerie Queene" 3 and 4* (Princeton: Princeton University Press, 1964), 72–88, helpfully describes the masquers as love-sonnet metaphors personified.

[29]Spenser's emphasis on the very public mirth "before the bride was bedded" has an analogue in George Puttenham's *The Arte of English Poesie* 1.26, "The manner of reioysings at mariages and weddings," in which he describes the vigorous epithalamic music, noise, and bustle provided by the throng of well-wishers outside the bedchamber as cheerful efforts intended to overwhelm the "skreeking and outcry of the young damosell" (51). I cite the edition of Gladys Dodge Willcock and Alice Walker (Cambridge: Cambridge University Press, 1936).

Yet freshly bleeding forth her fainting spright,
  (The worke of cruell hand) was to be seene,
That dyde in sanguine red her skin all snowy cleene.

At that wide orifice her trembling hart
  Was drawne forth, and in siluer basin layd.

                                          (3.12.20–21)

Britomart's rescue of Amoret from her nightmare in Busyrane's house can be understood as Spenser's indictment of wedding conventions' rough handling of the bride's reticent identity. But the most curious, oblique, and extensive treatment of wedding's exposure of the bride occurs in the narrative of Florimell's wedding day (5.3.1–40). In this wedding, as in that of Amoret, Spenser pays close attention to the bride and almost none to the groom.

Florimell has been the elusive embodiment of beauty since her first appearance in the poem: she first appears like a shooting star (3.1.16), a blaze of gold and white, as she dashes on her palfrey past the disguised Britomart, Arthur, Timias, and Guyon, forever fleeing the desire she awakens simply by being both beautiful and elusive. Her marriage might be an apt point in the narrative for Spenser to allow her to stop being elusive. He might, for example, indulge in a blazon of the bride, as he so beautifully does elsewhere. Or he might sketch out a new step of Florimell's erotic maturity, thus giving us a fuller sense of her presence and her subjectivity, as he periodically does with Britomart. But in fact, the great poet of wedding apparently goes out of his way to avoid describing the wedding itself except for a cursory stanza mentioning the splendors that he intends not to dwell on:

To tell the glorie of the feast that day,
  The goodly seruice, the deuicefull sights,
  The bridegromes state, the brides most rich aray,
  The pride of Ladies, and the worth of knights,
  The royal banquets, and the rare delights
  Were worke fit for an Herauld, not for me.

                                          (5.3.3)

What Spenser describes instead is an extraordinary interruption in the tournaments and competitions that accompany the wedding, competitions attended by characters from throughout the epic. Artegall is there, for instance. Like many knights in tournaments, he enters the lists disguised—but by the shield of Braggadochio, of all people. The potential for comedy ensuing from this situation might be considerable, if Braggadochio himself were not transformed from the puffed-up, harmless buffoon of Book 2 who lacks all sense of his disproportion to Belphoebe into a real threat to genteel society, now with a streak of surliness. When Braggadochio predictably comes forth to claim the victory and the congratulations of Florimell, he turns on her with gross and unnecessary social insult, and by this act even more than by falsely claiming victory he shows himself to the others as unfit, unworthy of toleration, and deserving of his eventual disgrace:

> To whom the boaster, that all knights did blot,
>   With proud disdaine did scornefull answere make;
>   That what he did that day, he did it not
>   For her, but for his owne deare Ladies sake,
>
>   .   .   .   .   .
>
> And further did vncomely speaches crake.
>
> (5.3.16)

Braggadochio is devoid of the social instincts that allow others to preserve face; his failure of deference is a failure of self-presentation, too, though he seems unaware that he has thus betrayed himself. His crudity could hardly light upon a better target, though, for Florimell is one of the two most reticent and authentic sensibilities present (Guyon is the other), and she movingly responds with a shame that seems to be partly humiliation at Braggadochio's rough usage, partly embarrassment for him: "Much did his words the gentle Ladie quell, / And turn'd aside for shame to heare, what he did tell" (5.3.16).

   This crass degradation of Florimell is the outcome of only the first of a series of competitions in which Braggadochio's refusal to recognize that he is outclassed is treated by the narrator and by other characters less as comical than as threatening to each new competitor. He claims Artegall's victory with an outrageous sense of entitlement like that which had prompted him to offer Belphoebe the privilege of ravishment in Book 2. His demeanor, as he brandishes the shield with which Artegall had earned his victory, seems to invite an effortless and unthreatened rebuke of the kind Belphoebe had administered to comic effect; but in Book 5 the upstart's claim is more dangerous, and Artegall attacks verbally with a speech of more than twenty-one lines, with rhetorical insistence on the display of bodily proofs of identity:

> For proofe shew forth thy sword, and let it tell,
> What strokes, what dreadfull stoure it stird this day:
> Or shew the wounds, which vnto thee befell;
> Or shew the sweat, with which thou diddest sway
> So sharpe a battell, that so many did dismay.
>
> But this the sword, which wrought those cruell stounds,
> And this the arme, the which that shield did beare,
> And these the signes, (so shewed forth his wounds)
> By which that glorie gotten doth appeare.
>
> (5.3.21–22)

Braggadochio's hollow display is, to use Artegall's word, a *defacing* of others' worth, as is his boorishness to Florimell. (We might contrast the happier dynamics between Hal and Falstaff when Falstaff tells the story of Gads Hill, and when he claims the honor of Hotspur's death: Hal's easy confidence and security of place make possible both his noblesse oblige toward Falstaff and the canny improvisatory displays of the braggart soldier's self-aggrandizements which could never be welcome in Artegall's world.) Filled with rage against "graceless guyle," the hero of justice is driven to display himself directly. And this righteous exhibition of his sword, wounds, and sweat points to a problem central to life lived as a performance—one of the problems in Book 5. Artegall's initial disguise at the tournament is not any kind of legitimate Spenserian reserve or hiddenness, but a technique for winning personal glory and astonishing an audience, and it finds itself stymied when Braggadochio knows too little to play by the rules that honor such finesse. It is a rhetorical technique, and the threat to its success can be met only with more of the rhetoricity of display.

Braggadochio's next competitor is Florimell: he astonishes everyone by bringing out the false Florimell and claiming her as the true one. The problematic nature of display crops up again: the false Florimell ("snowy," all white and incapable of blushing because she has no interiority) melts like a doppelgänger upon contact with her double, and the true Florimell demonstrates both her shock and her authenticity by blushing, in a "bashfull" resistance to display, to the very necessity of making "paragone, / And triall" (5.3.24) by exhibition. Display in Book 5 bears a contradiction that does not attend it elsewhere in the poem: display has shown the truth of both Artegall's and Florimell's identities, yet it has also shown the onlookers the deceptiveness of their former judgments, equally based on display. Display is unreliable as a bearer of truth (largely because it intends an effect, unlike accidental revelation), and yet truth value hinges on it insofar as it is a form of unmasking or "vncasing" the bogus:

> So forth the noble Ladie was ybrought,
>   Adorn'd with honor and all comely grace:
>   Whereto her bashfull shamefastnesse ywrought
>   A great increase in her faire blushing face;
>   As roses did with lillies interlace.
>   For of those words, the which that boaster threw,
>   She inly yet conceiued great disgrace.
>
>   · · · · ·
>
> Then did he set her by that snowy one,
>   Like the true saint beside the image set,
>   Of both their beauties to make paragone,
>   And triall, whether should the honor get.
>   Streight way so soone as both together met,
>   Th'enchaunted Damzell vanisht into nought:
>   Her snowy substance melted as with heat,
>   Ne of that goodly hew remayned ought.
>
>   (5.3.23–24)

Braggadochio is daunted by his Florimell's unforeseen evaporation, but only momentarily. He recovers to face his next competitor, Guyon. Having lost victory, lady, and magic girdle, he is determined to hang on to Guyon's horse, Brigadore, whom he had stolen in Book 2. The evidence of rightful possession depends, crucially, not on domination (a natural possibility for a tale of horsemanship) but on the intimacy of horse and master, the interiority of the horse's body, and the failure of others' attempts to master Brigadore by force. Only Guyon knows the secret of the black mark in the horse's mouth, and only Guyon can quiet him, instantly, with love:

> Ne he his mouth would open vnto wight,
>   Vntill that *Guyon* selfe vnto him spake,
>   And called *Brigadore* (so was he hight)
>   Whose voice so soone as he did vndertake,
>   Eftsoones he stood as still as any stake,

> And suffred all his secret marke to see:
> And when as he him nam'd, for ioy he brake
> His bands, and follow'd him with gladfull glee,
> And friskt, and flong aloft, and louted low on knee.

> (5.3.34)

This tiny recognition scene is one of the few episodes in Book 5 which can justly be called moving, and one of the few in which justice depends on the witness of love. Such witness, moreover, is interpretable: Artegall has no trouble in judging Guyon the true owner. The intimacy between horse and master is candid, without opacity; this non-rhetorical, spontaneously expressive relation beheld by Artegall is evidence as clear and telling as the identifying mark itself.

Braggadochio's anger at Artegall's judgment against his ownership of Brigadore marks his distance from the blustery character that he was in Book 2. There he had simply tried to soothe his ruffled feathers with self-flattery; here he poses a nastier threat, as he "gan... vpbrayd" and "reuil'd, and rated, and disdayned." This aggressiveness is of a piece with the rest of his behavior; throughout he shows himself crude in the management of his own demeanor and of deference to others, important elements of courtesy. The have-not aspirant to a circle of privilege and civilized behavior cannot simply be dismissed and transcended, as the celestial Belphoebe could afford to do in Book 2; he must be exposed, degraded, disgraced, and made an object of ridicule. That Spenser wishes to register some degree of unease with the extremity of this display is clear from his giving the job to Talus, and having it done out the back door; yet the narrator's own remark is notable for its zealous satisfaction:

> So ought all faytours, that true knighthood shame,
> And armes dishonour with base villanie,
> From all braue knights be banisht with defame:
> For oft their lewdnes blotteth good deserts with blame.

> (5.3.38)

Talus's violence, in this one instance, is actually the foundation of laughter: not the laughter that the braggart soldier of Book 2 might elicit, nor the harsher laughter that satire might produce (say, in Jonson's characterizations of Politic Would-bes and other pretenders), but the refined, self-congratulatory laughter of a social circle that has just had its privilege reinforced by uncasing a counterfeit:

Ladies can laugh at Ladies, Knights at Knights,
To thinke with how great vaunt of brauerie
He them abused, through his subtill slights,
And what a glorious shew he made in all their sights.

(5.3.39)

Spenser seems to approve this entertainment and to acknowledge social differentiation as an essential art of government; yet one cannot help wondering whether Spenser misses the comic energy of his original miles gloriosus, and whether Florimell had much fun at her own wedding.

This is a remarkable wedding story, for a variety of reasons. A conspicuous lack of attention is paid the wedding itself. Braggadochio levels realistic and embarrassing social insult at the bride. The bride is challenged by a double of herself to prove her very identity. Spenser places an extraordinary emphasis upon the "uncasing," the exposure and humiliation of Braggadochio. The dynamics of this startling episode I take to be as follows. The lyric utterance of wedding's celebration which we might expect from Spenser is aborted by the satiric mode of the exposure, shame, and humiliation of the aspirant to noble circles. Both the disgraced character and the bride's double have a scapegoating function; by accruing to themselves the potentially hostile motivations that can spur display, they allow Spenser to protect and affirm the interiority of the true bride. Anxiety about display as exposure of the authentic, inward self is deflected into accusation of wicked characters, who clearly deserve exposure. Hence the glide from Florimell's wedding, which Spenser declines to dilate, to the tournament; it is as if Spenser himself insists on the testing of the bride's authenticity. Furthermore, if we recall the hollow void around which the false Florimell has been built, we can say that Spenser identifies the true Florimell's authenticity with an interior life that is her subjectivity.

The two Spenserian marriage ceremonies in which the problematic display and abashedness of the bride do not arise are worth looking at, in order to consider why they are exceptions to my argument. One is the marriage of the Thames and the Medway (4.11.8–53), in which Spenser fully indulges his love of the sensuous beauty of ceremonial pageantry; we are presented with an enormous procession depicting only a riot of happiness and exuberant energy. One reason that Spenser can enjoy this wedding so purely, without anxiousness about display, is that it is comprised of those mythic and natural creatures who—like Phoebe in the *Epithalamion* simile—do not fully share the Spenserian human psychology of reticence.[30] Among the noble creatures who assemble for this great festivity are Britain's rivers, which are simultaneously anthropomorphized dignitaries; their processions are simply the flowings of which they consist in nature:

> There was the speedy Tamar, which deuides
>   The Cornish and the Deuonish confines;
>   Through both whose borders swiftly downe it glides,
>   And meeting Plim, to Plimmouth thence declines:
>   And Dart, nigh chockt with sands of tinny mines.
>   But Auon marched in more stately path,
>   Proud of his Adamants, with which he shines
>   And glisters wide, as als' of wondrous Bath,
> And Bristow faire, which on his waues he builded hath.
>
> (4.11.31)

It is during the marriage of rivers that Florimell and Marinell are finally brought together, in the realm of Proteus (4.11.1–7, 4.12.3–35). Gordon Braden links Florimell's erotic vicissitudes to the river marriage: "The whole [river] marriage is bracketed by the case of Florimell, for whom the polymorphous perversity of water is a prison. ... The marriage festival in a roundabout way occasions Florimell's release from this state."[31] And Barbara Lewalski has made the fine suggestion that the river marriage might be understood as a surrogate for Florimell's diminished and troubled wedding.[32] The river marriage complements Florimell's in its mythic participants' ease as visible creatures, in its unabashed pageantry, in the abundance of its descriptive rhetoric. If Spenser gives to his river wedding the ease, the rhetorical plenitude and the fluency that he withholds from Florimell's wedding, then the results are to underscore the unhappier display of the human bride who is forced to defend the legitimacy of her own

[30]More precisely, Spenser's mythic creatures move fluidly in and out of this psychology as it suits Spenser's purposes: Diana shows plenty of abashedness when Venus enters her grove (3.6.18–19); Phoebus blushes in the "Aprill" eclogue and when he sees Sansloy's attempt on Una's chastity (1.6.6).

[31]Gordon Braden, "riverrun: An Epic Catalogue in *The Faerie Queene*," *English Literary Renaissance* 5 (Winter 1975), 25–48 at 47–48.

[32]Barbara Lewalski's suggestion came in the course of a discussion after a paper that I gave at the Renaissance Society of America Conference, 1989.

identity and to underscore the troubling aspects of the human urge to display, expose, or uncase.

Una's betrothal to Redcrosse (1.12), the second exception to my argument, is simply without anxiety about the ethics of ceremonial display. Una's distress as she attempts to save her parents and her kingdom has been a chief plot element of the book, and the success of her and Redcrosse's combined efforts leaves no room in her for anything but triumphant love. This triumph is especially well marked by her discarding of the veil that has covered her face throughout Book 1; no obstacles now stand between her and the world. Una comes forth

> So faire and fresh, as freshest flowre in May;
>   For she had layd her mournefull stole aside,
>   And widow-like sad wimple throwne away,
>   Wherewith her heauenly beautie she did hide,
>   Whiles on her wearie iourney she did ride;
>
>   .   .   .   .   .
>
> The blazing brightnesse of her beauties beame,
>   And glorious light of her sunshyny face
>   To tell, were as to striue against the streame.
>   My ragged rimes are all too rude and bace,
>   Her heauenly lineaments for to enchace.
>
>   (1.12.22–23)

The clarity and simplicity of Una's radiant glory revealed to the world's gaze occur in a wedding piece published in 1590. It is no accident that the wedding works that show more unease with display occur in the poems published in 1595 and 1596, for throughout the work of these later years Spenser contemplates a good many disquieting aspects of vision and display. They are the subject of the next chapter.

Chapter Five

The Invidious Eye:
Spenser's Publications, 1595–1596

Throughout his work, I have been arguing, Spenser values candor for its pristine naturalness, for the ease of social relations that it allows—for instance, between Diana and her nymphs, or between Britomart and her companions in Malbecco's castle—and for its unintentional and consistent revelations. The concomitant principle is an aversion to display, the consciousness of the observed inherently sullied by awareness of a watcher, whose mere presence controls or alters the observed character. But participants in courtly life generally grasped the value and uses of its theatrical nature, and of flamboyant and ostentatious display. For Spenser, with his bias against theatricality in nontheatrical contexts, the 1590s brought a problem in depicting praiseworthy members of courtly and ruling groups, and characters who are in various ways figures for the Queen, who use display in the arts of government. Spenser had depicted court characters from very early on in his career, of course. The fox and the ape of *Mother Hubberds Tale* are courtiers; Elizabeth is honored with fictional analogues from the beginning. But in the depictions of those analogues to Elizabeth, the problem of their control over vision and visibility did not arise, although Elizabeth herself seems always to have understood what she articulated in 1586: "[W]e princes are set on stages in the sight and view of all the world duly observed," a fact that complicated her decisions about Mary, Queen of Scots.[1]

Intentional display becomes a problem in different ways, and on a larger scale, in the works published in 1595 and 1596 than it had been in earlier works. (These are the marriage volume of 1595, containing the *Amoretti* and the *Epithalamion*, the volume joining *Astrophel* and *Colin Clouts Come Home Againe*, published the following year, and Books 4 through 6 of *The Faerie Queene*. The *Fowre Hymnes* and the *Prothalamion*, also published in 1596, have no part in my argument.) Purposive display arouses Spenser's suspicions and caution, but it is also an effective and perhaps necessary instrument in good government. The depiction of women beheld can best guarantee the integrity of both observer and observed if the woman's candor is preserved via her unawareness of a watcher, and if the watcher brings to the scene a Homero-Vergilian capacity for awe. But in the works of 1595–96, female characters may show the will to control the visible and to direct the response of the viewer. Management of the visible becomes a prerogative of authority figures, female as well as male, good as well as wicked, in love as well as in politics. The aim of what follows is to detail some of these problems and their larger consequences, and to describe Spenser's resourcefulness in negotiating them.

The Mythologizing of Ralegh's Marriage

I that was wount to behold her ridinge like Alexander, huntinge like Diana, walkinge like Venus, the gentle winde blowinge her faire heare about her pure cheekes, like a nimph, sumetyme sittinge in the shade like a goddes, sumetyme singinge like an angell, sumetyme playinge like Orpheus. Behold the sorrow of this worlde. Once amiss hath bereved mee of all.[2]

[1]Elizabeth's speech replying to a petition urging execution for Mary, presented 12 November 1586. The text, along with selections from others of Elizabeth's speeches, is found in George P. Rice, Jr., *The Public Speaking of Queen Elizabeth: Selections from Her Official Addresses* (New York: Columbia University Press, 1951), 90.

[2]The introduction to Agnes Latham's edition of the *Poems* (Cambridge: Harvard University Press, 1951), xliv–xlv, cites a portion of Ralegh's letter with original orthography. Edward Edwards's two-volume *Life* publishes all extant letters in vol. 2, with spelling modernized and punctuation silently altered (New York: Macmillan, 1868).

Sir Walter Ralegh's lament about his estrangement from the Queen after the discovery of his marriage resonates with the same literary and mythic understanding of access to a revered woman which occurs throughout Spenser's work. Spenser's wish is always to transcend the social estrangements that require defense, and one important figure for this transcendence is depicted in a male character's easy, unthreatened, and unthreatening proximity to a woman who elicits wonder—a woman who often has a happy and fertile mythopoeic kinship to Ovid's nymphs or to Vergil's Venus and Dido, both of whom bear the combined glory of the goddess of love and the goddess of chastity. But the attempt to establish this proximity is often strained in the late works. The paradigmatic instance is Belphoebe's rebuff of Timias after she discovers him with her twin, Amoret, "that new louely mate" (4.7.35):

> Which when she saw, with sodaine glauncing eye,
>   Her noble heart with sight thereof was fild
>   With deepe disdaine, and great indignity,
>
>   .   .   .   .   .
>
>   Is this the faith, she said, and said no more,
> But turnd her face, and fled away for euermore.
>
> (4.7.36)

The shock to Belphoebe is one that is meant to elicit the reader's sympathy, for Spenser has taken pains to sketch, once again, her eager absorption in the hunt, in the society not only of her companion nymphs but also of Timias. Their tentative relationship has clearly been a factor in the development of her history beyond what is possible for Ovid's nymphs, but her persistence as virginal nymph and her historical link with Queen Elizabeth mean that she cannot have

---

Ralegh's own epistolary and poetic practice after Elizabeth's discovery of his marriage exhibits not only his efforts to reconcile with her but also—especially in *The Ocean to Cynthia*—an equivocal near-acknowledgment of the worship of Cynthia as a social utility, and a bitter, grieving awareness of the gap between the hierarchic mystery of the divine mistress and his recent experience of her tyranny. See Stephen Greenblatt, *Sir Walter Ralegh: The Renaissance Man and His Roles* (New Haven: Yale University Press, 1973), 75–98, and Robert Stillman, "'Words cannot knytt': Language and Desire in Ralegh's *The Ocean to Cynthia*," *Studies in English Literature*, 27 (Winter 1987), 35–52.

strayed far from the same kind of innocent immersion in the hunt which preceded her surprised discovery of the wounded Timias:

> It fortuned *Belphebe* with her peares
> The woody Nimphs, and with that louely boy,
> Was hunting then the Libbards and the Beares,
> In these wild woods, as was her wonted ioy,
> To banish sloth, that oft doth noble mindes annoy.
>
> (4.7.23)

This innocence might arouse reader sympathy for Belphoebe, but the abject misery of Timias also elicits sympathy—for his vulnerability to her wrath and disdain:

> He seeing her depart, arose vp light,
> Right sore agrieued at her sharpe reproofe,
> And follow'd fast: but when he came in sight,
> He durst not nigh approch, but kept aloofe,
> For dread of her displeasures vtmost proofe.
>
> (4.7.37)

The story, as Upton noted in 1758, is a fictive version of Ralegh's estrangement from Queen Elizabeth when his marriage to Elizabeth Throckmorton was discovered.[3] In the passage that begins this section, from a letter addressed to Robert Cecil from the Tower, Ralegh elegantly articulates his own sense that he has lost both Venus and Diana, lost his access to nymph and goddess, in the person of the Queen whom he regularly addressed in the rhetoric of Petrarchan love and service.

In a discussion of biographical and autobiographical fictions in Spenser's poetry published in 1595–96, Donald Cheney mentions Ralegh's marriage crisis in terms that suggest how Spenser might fictionalize it in his poetry: "In the 1590s, it seems, to cling to the dream or the memory of a lost or inaccessible lover is to be held in

---

[3]Upton mentions the "secret piece of history . . . delicately touched" in Belphoebe's discovery of Timias with Amoret in his running commentary as well as in his preface to *The Faerie Queene*. See *John Upton: Notes on "The Faerie Queene,"* ed. John G. Radcliffe, 2 vols. (New York: Garland, 1987), 1.33–34 and 2.858. See also Walter Oakeshott, "Carew Ralegh's Copy of Spenser," *Library*, 5th ser., 26 (March 1971), 1–21, on notations apparently made by Ralegh's family indicating points in Spenser's work which the family understands to refer to Ralegh.

thrall to a fairy queen who increasingly takes on the aspect of a belle dame sans merci; yet to seek fulfillment with her earthly sister is to risk the wrath of Belphoebe."[4] It would not be surprising if many of the issues addressed in the works of these years, including Spenser's depictions of desire and volition in vision, emerge in part as figurations and analyses of Ralegh's marriage. It may further be that Ralegh's marriage crisis becomes not only an event allegorically described in the story of Belphoebe and Timias, but one important source of invention in much of Spenser's later work.[5] Ralegh's marriage and its discovery (no cause for rejoicing in themselves) fuel Spenser's resources in allowing him to develop a series of related story motifs variously linked to aspects of the historical event. Certainly the poetry grapples more directly than before with the problem of an admired or inspiring woman as invidious intruder into the affairs and the consciousness of her beholder, and with the problem of volition in the Petrarchan beloved, conceived as the woman's will to control visibility and display. Spenser uses, for instance, the courtly and Petrarchan motif of the power possessed by the beloved's eye to fix and slay, but he expands the power to abilities to spy, envy, invade. It seems a reasonable possibility that Spenser's understanding of the events of Ralegh's marriage coalesces with his poetic efforts to depict

[4]Donald Cheney, "Spenser's Fortieth Birthday and Related Fictions," *Spenser Studies* 4 (1983), 3–31 at 9. The evolution of criticism on Ralegh's relation to the Queen can be seen in the following works: Allan Gilbert, "Belphoebe's Misdeeming of Timias," *PMLA* 62 (1947), 622–43; Walter Oakeshott, *The Queen and the Poet* (London: Faber and Faber, 1960) and "Carew Ralegh's Copy of Spenser"; Hugh English, "Spenser's Accommodation of Allegory to History in the Story of Timias and Belphoebe," *Journal of English and Germanic Philology* 59 (160), 417–29; Greenblatt, *Sir Walter Ralegh*; James Bednarz, "Ralegh in Spenser's Historical Allegory," *Spenser Studies* 4 (1983), 49–70. Questions of dating Ralegh's marriage and its possible role in *Colin Clouts Come Home Againe* are discussed in the *Variorum* 7 (pt. 1), 450–51.

[5]Throughout this chapter, in support of the proposal argued variously by Cheney, Bednarz, and others about the function of Ralegh's trouble with Elizabeth in Spenser's poetry, I follow Annabel Patterson's model of what she names the hermeneutics of censorship. The author who wishes to raise issues that may provoke the censors proceeds partly by an equivocal use of criticism through a redistribution of problematic elements of historical events in narrative. Her example is *Lear,* which is "a play so deeply ambiguated, so clearly referential in some way to the Union debate, but so utterly resistant to assimilation by either side in the controversy, that it could safely take its place in a theater unusually vulnerable at that moment to state interference" (*Censorship and Interpretation: The Conditions of Writing and Reading in Early Modern England* [Madison: University of Wisconsin Press, 1984], 71).

feminine consciousness, and leads him from his analyses of masculine visual power to a consideration of both masculine and feminine visual invasiveness in the later works.

The unease that Spenser expresses with the invidious eye of an authoritative or revered figure (of either gender) varies in tone and treatment from work to work. At the start of the story of Timias's alienation from Belphoebe, moral sympathy is about equally balanced between the squire and the nymph, and Spenser shows Belphoebe's discovery of Timias with Amoret as an accident that unsettles them both, in a reversal of the Actaeon story pattern: a Diana figure accidentally intrudes on the secret intimacy of a male hunter. In *Epithalamion*, the jealous Cynthia is conceived in an Ovidian-neoteric way as simultaneously the moon shining in the lover's chamber window and a peeping goddess who may begrudge newly wedded privacy and happiness.

> Who is the same, which at my window peepes?
> Or whose is that faire face, that shines so bright?
> Is it not Cinthia, she that neuer sleepes,
> But walkes about high heauen al the night?
> O fayrest goddesse, do thou not enuy
> My loue with me to spy:
> For thou likewise didst loue, though now vnthought,
> And for a fleece of woll, which priuily,
> The Latmian shepherd once vnto thee brought,
> His pleasures with thee wrought.
>
> (*Epith.* 372–81)

Cynthia's envious spying and her threat to the happiness of lovers may suggest reverberations of Ralegh's troubles with *his* Cynthia, but in Spenser's wedding poem the troubling implications of a feminine will to control vision are easily subordinated to a dominant jocundity.

Certain poems among the *Amoretti*, published together with *Epithalamion* in 1595, focus the problems of feminine powers of the eye more strongly, in terms of Petrarchan conceits about the eye. The dazed viewer and lover stands amazed at the beloved's beauty and goodness in sonnets 3 and 17, and is smitten by the loveliness of her eyes, "no eies but ioyes," in sonnets 8 and 9. But more often those eyes, apparently invulnerable to the intromissive kind of sight suffered by the lover, emit death, as in sonnets 7, 10, 12, 16. An imputation of the lady's ill will enters with the figure of the cockatrice, in sonnet 49:

> But if it be your pleasure and proud will,
>   to shew the powre of your imperious eyes:
>   then not on him that neuer thought you ill,
>   but bend your force against your enemyes.
> Let them feele th'utmost of your crueltyes,
>   and kill with looks, as Cockatrices doo.

And malice compounded with deceit, coercive power, and display triumphs in the brilliant sonnet 53, in which Petrarchan and Neoplatonic conflicts about the relation between beauty and goodness emerge in the problem of display:

> The Panther knowing that his spotted hyde
>   Doth please all beasts but that his looks them fray:
>   within a bush his dreadfull head doth hide,
>   to let them gaze whylest he on them may pray.
> Right so my cruell fayre with me doth play:
>   for with the goodly semblant of her hew,
>   she doth allure me to mine owne decay,
>   and then no mercy will vnto me shew.
> Great shame it is, thing so diuine in view,
>   made for to be the worlds most ornament:
>   to make the bayte her gazers to embrew,
>   good shames to be to ill an instrument.
> But mercy doth with beautie best agree,
>   as in theyr maker ye them best may see.
>
>   (*Amor.* 53)

Bad faith and mystification are explicitly attributed to the beloved here: in the form of feminine consciousness of beauty displayed, in the purpose of display to ensnare or control the Petrarchan servant, and in the new use of the motif of hiding one's head in the bushes as an act attributable to the mystifier's malice. The two earlier appearances of this motif, in 1590, were the comic hiding of Braggadochio from Belphoebe, and the comic-grotesque hiding of Malbecco as he watches Hellenore with the satyrs. Not only has the tone departed from Spenser's comic range altogether, but the purposes of hiding the visage have moved toward tactical coercion and have been transferred to the woman, who hides the face as an exercise of power rather than of self-protection. The display of feminine beauty is understood as an instrument of control over victims who respond with reflexes only, like animals, to visual stimuli; the panther and the woman use their apparently ornamental passivity in active aggression. Spenser's lovely overcomings of Petrarchan limitations (e.g., sonnets 40, 64, 67, 75, 81) notwithstanding, the *Amoretti* also succeed in recapitulating, intensifying, personalizing certain risks and dangers of Petrarchan amorous relations.[6] Traditionally enough, imperiousness emanates from the lady's eyes. Less traditionally, sonnets of defensiveness against the hierarchical superiority of the beloved jostle with sonnets that seek to preserve such superiority; guile and predation are ascribed to the lady; display is shown to be an instrument of control or, at best, one interpretation by the victim of the lady's destructively ambiguous behavior, as when sonnet 61 reinterprets her scorn as sublimity.

The interpretation of the putatively tyrannical woman's role in the *Amoretti* is deeply ambivalent, necessarily poised between adoration and resentment, leading the lover to the edge of articulating the social mystification of the lady's elevation.[7] Sonnet 61 is a defense of hierarchic mystery and a defensive argument for retaining the perception

---

[6]On the *Amoretti*, I am indebted to Louis Martz, "The *Amoretti*: 'Most Goodly Temperature,' " in *Form and Convention in the Poetry of Edmund Spenser*, ed. William Nelson (New York: Columbia University Press, 1961), 146–68 and 180 (notes); Donald Cheney, *Spenser's Image of Nature: Wild Man and Shepherd in "The Faerie Queene"* (New Haven: Yale University Press, 1966), 111–16; Joseph Loewenstein, "Echo's Ring: Orpheus and Spenser's Career," *English Literary Renaissance* 16 (Spring 1986), 287–302, in which he argues that the sequence's movement toward a transformation of Petrarchan affective structure "is followed by a reversion toward the fallen, idolatrous Petrarchanism, towards that embittered psychic world with which the sequence opened" (294–95).

[7]In this chapter I adopt Kenneth Burke's terms from *A Rhetoric of Motives* (New York: Prentice-Hall, 1950) as the best crystallizations of Spenser's working concepts in these years. The following passage can be taken to describe what I understand to be Spenser's practice: "We should be on the lookout for occasions when expressions for motives on their face 'divine' are better explained as stylizations of motives belonging to the social hierarchy.... We are looking for elements of 'social mystery' rather than of 'celestial' mystery, hence our term, 'socioanagogic.'... Allegorical and moral senses lead into the socioanagogic insofar as the emphasis is placed upon the hierarchic mystery (the principle of secular divinity, with its range of embarrassment, courtship, modified insult, standoffishness...). In brief, the socioanagogic sense notes how the things of books and of the book of Nature 'signify what relates to worldly glory' " (215, 220).

of this hierarchy as divine rather than social, regardless of the toll taken in sustaining the perception:

> The glorious image of the makers beautie,
>> My souerayne saynt, the Idoll of my thought,
>> dare not henceforth aboue the bounds of dewtie,
>> t'accuse of pride, or rashly blame for ought.
> For being as she is diuinely wrought,
>> and of the brood of Angels heuenly borne:
>> and with the crew of blessed saynts vpbrought,
>> each of which did her with theyr guifts adorne;
> The bud of ioy, the blossome of the morne,
>> the beame of light, whom mortal eyes admyre:
>> what reason is it then but she should scorne
>> base things, that to her loue too bold aspire?
> Such heauenly formes ought rather worshipt be,
>> then dare be lou'd by men of meane degree.
>
> (Amor. 61)

To comply with his own debasement is this Petrarchan lover's way of sustaining the elevation of the loved woman; the poem describes a process of altering the apprehension of the lady's behavior from pride and hardness to divinity. The Petrarchan poem allows the lover to lower himself in the hierarchy, thus retaining the mystery of the lady's adornment and preserving some dignity to himself.

In Burkean terms, we can say that Spenser wishes to trust a purely moral or tropological interpretation of social intercourse and wonders beheld, in which the perception of celestial mystery is an adequate interpretation of woman viewed. But he finds himself faced with literary and political models of intercourse in which celestial mystery is one instrument of social hierarchy, a rhetorical self-presentation intended to control others' interpretative reading of objects beheld. When visibility is controlled and intentional rather than accidental, it demands interpretation not as the revelation of celestial mystery but as social mystification. Much of the ambivalence or corrosiveness of tone and incident in parts of *The Faerie Queene* 4 and 5 can be attributed to the fact that Spenser's effort to articulate courtly social reality and necessities puts at risk all idealist perception and all projection of wish in eikastic images.

The plot motif of a threat to a union of lovers intersects with the theme of hierarchic superiority and its control of the visible in a brief Ovidian mythic foray of *Colin Clovts Come Home Againe*, one in which the source of the threat is no virgin queen, goddess, or nymph but an irate *senex*. *Colin Clovt* is a poem that struggles throughout with the asserted superiority of a beloved woman, Colin's adored Rosalind, and with the allure, the glamor, and the dangers of court life, dominated as it is by vying and envy. Both of these are problems of hierarchy—one amorous, one political—faced by Colin, who creatively adapts to Rosalind's unresponsiveness by devoting himself to her superiority and his own inferiority, and who defends against both the attractiveness and the corruption of court life with a grasp of the inevitability of aspiration and envy there.

Another of the poem's defenses is a turn to comedy, in the brilliant story of the marriage of the Mulla and Bregog rivers. Mulla's father, in spite of the apparently ubiquitous power of his gaze, is initially incapable of forcing his will:

> But for her father sitting still on hie,
> Did warily still watch which way she went,
> And eke from far obseru'd with iealous eie,
> Which way his course the wanton *Bregog* bent,
> Him to deceiue for all his watchfull ward,
> The wily louer did deuise this slight:
> First into many parts his streame he shar'd,
> That whilest the one was watcht, the other might
> Passe vnespide to meete her by the way;
> And then besides, those little streames so broken
> He vnder ground so closely did conuay,
> That of their passage doth appeare no token,
> Till they into the *Mullaes* water slide.
> So secretly did he his loue enioy.
>
> (*Colin Clovt* 132–45)

Bregog simply disperses himself, in an Ovidian play on his fluvial capacity for division and his human capacity for sexual pleasure, and slides into the Mulla underground, in a place of real hiddenness and freedom from the gaze of coercive authority. But, predictably in this Irish-Ovidian nature fantasy, intimate secrets are revealed, and the father's rage leads to a landslide destroying the river: "so deare his loue he bought" (*Colin Clovt* 155). The comic subversion of invidious authority and the futility of such repression before the stronger powers of hiddenness adumbrate the historical fate of Ralegh and his family. As Cheney argues,

Spenser's celebration of his Irish countryside hints at an eroticized land-scape which the poet dreams of possessing in secure anonymity, far from the envious court where Elizabeth views her courtiers' marriage as threats to her sovereignty.

Colin's hopeful identification with the watery fluidity of "my riuer Bregog" is set against the experience of the Shepherd of the Ocean whose relationship with Cynthia is deeply troubled, as the chaste but ever-changing moon exerts her power over the waves.[8]

Opacity of Countenance and Control of the Body: Book 5 of *The Faerie Queene*

In Book 5 of *The Faerie Queene*, Spenser perceives the maintenance of power as being partially dependent upon continuous display, upon using occasions as assertations of visibility and its capacity to warn, threaten, control. Ideally, in Spenser's work, invisibility aspires to relief from the burden of control potentially inherent in both seeing and being seen. Yet power relies upon the publicity of the visible, and it implies the constantly rhetorical *aims* of visibility. Publicity of this kind intends to persuade, threaten, or coerce the witness. The non-intentional self-expressiveness of Belphoebe is innocent precisely in-sofar as it is not rhetorical: it has no aims directed toward a witness. But the various defenders of justice in Book 5 (a group including Mercilla and Zele, Arthur, Artegall, and Britomart) and their antag-onists (Radegund, Grantorto, Geryoneo) cannot often rely on such unpredictable revelations in their defense; they must create and con-trol visible spectacles. The necessity for this pervasive display makes Spenser uneasy. He has consistently tried to acknowledge the possible assertion of power in social acts of sight, and then to circumvent or transcend such assertions; he tries to make possible a non-rhetorical interpretation of persons viewed. This is to say: in making possible the candor of the observed, Spenser is also at pains to make available to the observer a legitimate idealist hermeneutics. This possibility is drastically reduced if a character intentionally displays signs of iden-tity or affect and asserts control over others with such display. Pub-licity as the manipulation of the visible for rhetorical ends can only

[8]Cheney, "Spenser's Fortieth Birthday," 18. On the folk-tale motif of "the escaping couple and pursuing father," see Roland M. Smith, "Spenser's Irish River Stories," *PMLA* 50 (1935), 1047–56.

elicit resistance from a writer who profoundly mistrusts display but who has ambivalently sought to align himself with court and Queen throughout his career. In the discussion of Book 5 which follows, I want to consider, first, display as the control of self-presentation and demeanor; next, the use of display of the body as institutional signs and warnings by governmental representatives, and the problems of interpretation which accompany this kind of display; and, finally, some aspects of the story of Radegund.

In Spenser's earlier treatments of a beheld woman there has been only glancing acknowledgment that she sees all, and no acknowledgment that her being seen by all is problematic; this is the case in the "Aprill" eclogue, as we have seen. But in *The Faerie Queene* 5 it becomes clear that the Queen is so frequently enjoyed as the cynosure of all eyes partly because she has a political will to be seen and partly because she is the center of a socio-political structure that uses visibility as an instrument. Spenser tentatively accepts the necessity of display, as in Mercilla's court, where her placement as the book's structural analogue to the goddess Isis helps to legitimize her superior powers, but where her historical analogy to Elizabeth, a queen but also mortal, allows Spenser to articulate problems of social encounters and decorums which would hardly arise for Isis.

Candor is impossible for the beheld object in the diverse displays of Mercilla and her servants; interpretation is at best difficult for the viewer. It is the very object of the display of the ruler set in the "view of all the world" to refuse the clarity of candor, and to retain the prerogative of limiting or occulting interpretation of the display. Unlike any other admirable woman in *The Faerie Queene*, Mercilla intentionally "sate on high, that she might all men see, / And might of all men royally be seene" (5.9.27). Her full awareness in the control of the visible and in the management of demeanor ("A chearefull countenance . . . let fall") are apparently praised when Arthur and Artegall are brought to her:

> So sitting high in dreaded souerayntie,
>   Those two strange knights were to her presence brought;
>   Who bowing low before her Maiestie,
>   Did to her myld obeysance, as they ought,
>   And meekest boone, that they imagine mought.
>   To whom she eke inclyning her withall,
>   As a faire stoupe of her high soaring thought,

A chearefull countenance on them let fall,
Yet tempred with some maiestie imperiall.

. . . . .

So did this mightie Ladie, when she saw
Those two strange knights such homage to her make,
Bate somewhat of that Maiestie and awe,
That whylome wont to doe so many quake.

(5.9.34–35)

The very concept of this self-aware, carefully directed display is antithetical to other Spenserian values that I have been describing. Countenance, demeanor, face—these are now valuable not for their unintentional and accidentally observed aspects, but for their presentational force and their capacity to direct the perceptions of viewers.[9] Mercilla's change of countenance controls the definition of the knights' behavior: by acknowledging their honorific rituals, she receives their regard as deference. Spenser thus seems simultaneously to recognize that the mystery of hierarchy is handled quite consciously as an instrument and to accede to the perception of Mercilla's place in the hierarchy as all but divine, for the woman condescends from her height to notice the knights. Spenser's precise understanding of Mercilla, and his moral position in relation to her and to Elizabeth, are tantalizingly difficult to articulate.[10] But that is just the problem of display, given its previous treatment in the epic and Spenser's anti-

[9]Erving Goffman usefully isolates and defines these phenomena in *Interaction Ritual: Essays on Face-to-Face Behavior* (New York: Doubleday, 1967). Goffman, Burke, in *Rhetoric of Motives*, and Frank Whigham, in *Ambition and Privilege: The Social Tropes of Elizabethan Courtesy Theory* (Berkeley and Los Angeles: University of California Press, 1984), focus on "the performative life as *predicament*" (Whigham, 37).

[10]I take this difficulty as an intentional caginess on Spenser's part; the depiction of Mercilla's court, like the depiction of Radegund, is a meditation on the woman ruler which is ultimately "resistant to assimilation" by any political ideology. Patterson, *Censorship and Interpretation*, 71.

Many commentators have articulated many forms of dissatisfaction with the tone and ethos of Book 5. See, e.g., Michael O'Connell, *Mirror and Veil: The Historical Dimension of Spenser's "Faerie Queene"* (Chapel Hill: University of North Carolina Press, 1977), 125–60; Angus Fletcher, *The Prophetic Moment: An Essay on Spenser* (Chicago: University of Chicago Press, 1971), 136, 189, 216; Judith Anderson, " 'Nor Man It Is': The Knight of Justice in Book 5 of Spenser's *Faerie Queene*," PMLA 85 (1970), 65–77, rpt. in *Essential Articles for the Study of Edmund Spenser*, ed. A. C. Hamilton (Hamden, Conn.: Archon Books, 1972), 447–70.

theatrical bias: by making candor impossible, display complicates interpretation, because of the endlessly reflexive awareness of the performer before her audience. Government requires both the equity of Isis and the skills of the panther.

Disruptions in *The Faerie Queene* 5 emerge from a variety of sources: aspirants to the privilege of tyranny over their local domains, ideologues like the Giant, foreign adversaries, lower classes that can be swayed to alternative visions of the distribution of wealth, upstarts aspiring to place and recognition. Representatives of all these types clamor against the order of good government. Most of the actions of court representatives serve to challenge, limit, control, or destroy the agents of disruption, and thus to preserve civilized order in the face of aggressive envy. The bullying behavior of Sir Sanglier and Munera, the combat of ideologies between the Giant and Artegall, Radegund's degradation of men, the larger bids for power of Geryoneo—all of these express an invidious desire by the wicked character to wield power or to have access to privilege, rank, and wealth; the courtly agents act to prevent any of these would-bes and have-nots from gaining such access.

Envy is not always a bad thing in Spenser's work, certainly not always a monstrous thing. In the 1590 *Faerie Queene*, Britomart knows envy at seeing Scudamour and Amoret reunited (3.12.46). In Book 4, Poeana envies the love and camaraderie of Aemylia, Placidas, and Amyas (4.9.9), and Scudamour envies the frank lovers of the Garden of Venus (4.10.28). But envy in these characters is largely the acknowledgment of a wish for love and belonging, the acknowledgment of unhappiness when excluded from others' private happiness, and the prelude to their own fulfillment in love. Further on in the work, especially in Book 5, envy becomes a more dangerous and unappeasable thirst to bully or degrade others in order to feel the thrill of domination; to aspire to the closed circles of privilege; or to expose and humiliate competitors. It becomes a ubiquitous and destructive force, exhausting or destroying aspirants and defenders alike.

Of the arts that sustain government in this book, a crucial one is the discernment and weeding out of bogus or unsuitable aspirants to nobility. One means to this end is to expose and disgrace, by making the politic would-be an object of "iest and gibe" (5.3.39). The curious dynamics of this righteous display of counterfeits Spenser details in the tournament and contest of Florimells which dominate the account of Florimell's wedding (5.3), as we have seen. Uncasing, which is the making visible of the fraudulent, merges into the rage of dismemberment, one logical limit of imposed exposure. In Book 5, dismemberment is often associated with the institution of warning displays or "moniments" by the representatives of justice or good government, spectacles intended to discourage wrongly aspiring behavior by an untrustworthy society (generally specified only as "all" or "all men"). The first instance occurs when Artegall chops off Munera's hands and feet, and nails them "on high, that all might them behold" (5.2.26). A slightly more complicated instance occurs when, after the death of the Soldan, Arthur displays his armor, "That all men which that spectacle did see, / By like ensample mote for euer warned bee" (5.8.44). The battle preceding this action is long and indecisive until Arthur unveils his magic shield, panicking the Soldan's horses and sending his chariot careening out of control.

Spenser's two mythic similes for the careening chariot draw on the *Metamorphoses*: the story of Phaeton (*Met.* 1.747–79, 2.1–400) and that of Hippolytus (*Met.* 15.497–545). Both tales, as Ovid tells them, give a good deal of attention to the grief of the dead youth's loved ones. Hamilton notes that Spenser uses Phaeton's story also at 1.4.9 and 3.11.38, and that his witty variation here is to make the horses his subject; this choice effectively deflects emphasis from the pathos of Ovid's tale and reminds us of the Soldan's hubristic rebellion against legitimate authority, similar to that of Sol's son. But in the Hippolytus simile, Spenser goes out of his way to evoke such pathos:

> Like as the cursed sonne of *Theseus*,
>> That following his chace in dewy morne,
>> To fly his stepdames loues outrageous,
>> Of his owne steedes was all to peeces torne,
>> And his faire limbs left in the woods forlorne;
>> That for his sake *Diana* did lament,
>> And all the wooddy Nymphes did wayle and mourne.
> So was this Souldan rapt and all to rent,
>> That of his shape appear'd no litle moniment.

(5.8.43)

The contribution of this stanza to the tonal effect of the tale is odd. In a passage depicting a villain who represents a Spanish king defeated in a representation of the scattering of the Armada, we might not be entirely surprised if an English author were to indulge in nationalistic fervor over his defeat. But the simile of stanza 43 seems to curb any

potentially uncritical enthusiasm, and to suggest that even in the allegorization of a historical episode so powerful in the imagination
and culture of the English, Spenser is drawn to the pathos in the
mythic tale itself of the dismemberment of a lovely youth who is a
votary of Diana's.

If the dominant tone and ethos are disturbed by this simile within
the conflict between Arthur and the Soldan, they are all but inscrutable
in the narrator's stance toward the bad poet in Mercilla's palace. The
bad poet is charged with slandering the celestial mystery of the monarch and making of her a mortal involved in social mystification: "For
that therewith he falsely did reuyle, / And foule blaspheme that Queene
for forged guyle" (5.9.25). The difficulties of interpreting the display
of the poet, his tongue nailed to a post, himself identified by a humiliating inscription, are abundant even without the added compli-
cation of Spenser's offering elements of interpretations other than the
single clear one he voices. The legend over the poet's head is a palimpsest, "Mal Font" or "Malfont" replacing "Bon Font" or Bon Fons.
The source of this message is unclear; its rhetoric, if it issues from
the poet, is wildly different in meaning and tone than if it issues from
the judicial system. "Malfont" might mean "wicked fount" or "evil
maker" or even "they do evil," in which case the identification of
"they" becomes the next question. And yet, as in a literal palimpsest,
attention remains directed to the original level of inscription and to
the act of erasing as a gesture designed to show the power of the
government. The narrator's own interpretation of this "moniment"
remains difficult. It may be that Spenser's hostility extends to the bad
poet for defying poetry's function of identifying and praising true
celestial mystery: such glory remains true and unthreatened in the
blazon of Belphoebe and in the epiphanic career of Britomart, but,
as in *Colin Clout* and in *Amoretti* 61, Spenser treads a very fine line
between true mystery and mystification in objects beheld. This interpretive vertigo is built into the episode; its frustration is implicit
in the very act of display. "Few could rightly read," the narrator says,
and no wonder: display is designed to be all but opaque to the viewer.
Yet this spectacle obviously also intends some clear rhetorical aim,
some message, and the one irreducible and unambiguous element of
the display is the violence done to the body, the nailed tongue an
immediately visual, nonverbal sign of judiciary power.

This exposure and mutilation of the body occurs with a disquieting
frequency in Book 5. It is the more remarkable given Spenser's at-

tention to the integrity and tenderness of the body elsewhere in the poem. It is often the result of a righteous zeal, which Spenser first depicts in the stripping of Duessa in Book 1; because of her biblical prototype, her fate there is to escape into the "wastfull wildernesse apace, / From liuing eyes her open shame to hide" (1.8.50; compare Rev. 12.6). But she and many other characters in Book 5 find the secrecy of the body stripped more violently, as though the zeal to expose the counterfeit becomes an uncontrollable and violent urge to make visible, on the part of both the adversaries and the allies of justice. One way to see this violence is as an inscription of the sovereign's power on the body of the subject, as Foucault and others working his vein have argued.[11] Within the context of Spenser's depictions of the body in its vulnerability, its fleshly delicacy, and its harboring of treasures, this violence and the zest for it—sometimes on the part of the narrator as well as of the characters—are worth considering in another episode.

The violence and sexual explicitness of attack in the battle between Britomart and Radegund strenuously reverse the values and perception patterns that I have been arguing for Spenser's work. Until this book, most of Spenser's depictions of feminine life have as their fundamental model the Ovidian nymph, with her qualities (divided among various characters) of bodily tenderness, pristine intimacy with nature, the strength of originary earliness, a capable athleticism, a wish for candid privacy in her sylvan setting, a sense of feminine camaraderie. All of these features vanish in the conflict of Britomart and Radegund; indeed, both the skills and the reticences that mark the Ovidian nymph in Spenser's apprehension of her give way to the grossness of exposure and to distortions of the mythic feminine. In a battle in which love, domination, and justice are all at stake for the combatants, neither combatant retains the skill of her training in arms, at all times praised by Spenser; both attack the privy parts, more often represented as vulnerable and deserving of the greatest discretion. Instead of displaying feminine camaraderie, woman turns on woman as though they are of different species:

---

[11] For example, Jonathan Goldberg, *James I and the Politics of Literature* (Baltimore: Johns Hopkins University Press, 1983), 2: "Public dismemberment...is congruent with numerous actions that occur in Book 5 of *The Faerie Queene*. It was one way in which the power of the monarch was displayed, inscribing itself on the body of the condemned."

> But through great fury both their skill forgot,
> And practicke vse in armes: ne spared not
> Their dainty parts, which nature had created
> So faire and tender, without staine or spot,
> For other vses, then they them translated;
> Which they now hackt and hewd, as if such vse they hated,
>
> As when a Tygre and a Lionesse
> Are met at spoyling of some hungry pray.
>
> (5.7.29–30)

The inevitability of this battle in the establishment of justice and in Britomart's victory over the violent, Amazonian, inequitable qualities in herself Spenser does not question. Indeed, the very creation of Radegund seems to be Spenser's own act of violence against that model, insofar as his turn from Ovidian nymph to Amazon is not neutral but consequential in its wrenching of Spenser's own expressed values. The aggression and ferocity of Amazonian life, for instance, elicit an opposing notion of shamefastness substantially different from reticence as desire for hiddenness, which I discussed in Chapter 3:

> Such is the crueltie of womenkynd,
>   When they haue shaken off the shamefast band,
>   With which wise Nature did them strongly bynd,
>   T'obay the heasts of mans well ruling hand,
>   That then all rule and reason they withstand,
>   To purchase a licentious libertie.
>   But vertuous women wisely vnderstand,
>   That they were borne to base humilitie,
> Vnlesse the heauens them lift to lawfull soueraintie.
>
> (5.5.25)

Such a definition is doubly defensive, in a way that the conception of shamefastness as a wish for inner solitude or reticence is not. It identifies women as ideally subordinated to "mans well ruling hand," identifies them, that is, not by freedom from masculine desires but by submission to them; and it suggests shamefastness as a defense for men against the feared aggressions of women. The final line is an oddly hasty bow to the Queen and to the prudent position on the controversy over feminine rule, one that does not fully disguise Spenser's resistance to feminine tyranny in the 1590s.[12] The tone of the stanza, like the initial representation of Radegund as monstrous, shows more defensive resentment toward female rule and its potential will to domination than Spenser could have felt when the feminine inspirer of order, in "Aprill" or in the 1590 Proem to Book 2, was a relatively static presider over the expansive, trustful vision of admirer, explorer and reader. Such resistance on Spenser's part toward the domination of the female ruler—Elizabeth, who threatens private sexual choice; the jealous Belphoebe of Book 4; Radegund, who threatens gender identity—helps to account for the turn from Ovidian-nymph to Amazonian qualities, and for the turn against the vulnerable integrity of the body throughout Book 5.

Yet, in spite of Spenser's apparent anxiety about the feminine ruler whose will it is to spy out all hiddenness, to control display and its interpretation, he cannot forbear a tempering of Radegund's monstrosity. He does this by giving her unexpected, hidden motives of vulnerability, as if he does not simply dislike the Queen's harshness to her Petrarchan servant but also wants, in justice, to acknowledge its internal springs—her vulnerability to betrayal and her need for love. There is no single stance toward the political and hierarchic issues; rather, there are diverse meditations upon them. The story of Radegund's nascent love for Artegall, although it comes after her violence and after her imprisonment of him and other men, is offered as a reason for her hardness, as her way of struggling with the pressures of desire. The narrative turns away from the establishment of institutional monuments of justice, toward forces and secrets hidden within the body, toward blushes and other accidental revelations of interior affective movements in face and countenance of kinds that we have seen before:

---

[12]The data on this controversy are provided in James Phillips's essays "The Background of Spenser's Attitude toward Women Rulers," *Huntington Library Quarterly* 5 (1942), 5–32, and "The Woman Ruler in Spenser's *Faerie Queene*," ibid., 211–34. See also Winfried Schleiner, "Divina virago: Queen Elizabeth as Amazon," *Studies in Philology* 75 (1978), 163–80; Rosemond Tuve, "Spenser and Some Pictorial Conventions, with Particular Reference to Illuminated Manuscripts," ibid. 37 (1940), 149–76, rpt. in *Essays by Rosemond Tuve: Spenser, Herbert, Milton*, ed. Thomas P. Roche, Jr. (Princeton: Princeton University Press, 1970), 112–38 at 120–27; Constance Jordan, "Woman's Rule in Sixteenth-Century British Political Thought," *Renaissance Quarterly* 40 (1987), 421–51.

> And still the more she stroue it [her love-sickness] to subdew,
> The more she still augmented her owne smart,
> And wyder made the wound of th'hidden dart.
>
>
> With that she turn'd her head, as halfe abashed,
>   To hide the blush which in her visage rose,
>   And through her eyes like sudden lightning flashed,
>   Decking her cheeke with a vermilion rose:
>   But soone she did her countenance compose.
>
>
> Yet durst she [Clarin] not disclose her fancies wound...
>   For feare her mistresse shold haue knowledge gayned,
>   But to her selfe it secretly retayned,
>   Within the closet of her couert brest.
>
>
> Therewith she [Clarin] gan at first to change her mood,
>   As one adaw'd, and halfe confused stood;
>   But quickly she it ouerpast, so soone
>   As she her face had wypt, to fresh her blood.
>   (5.5.28, 30, 44, 45)

In the first two passages here, Radegund's spontaneous manifestations resemble the manifestations of earlier books in their innocence of rhetorical motive, though they differ from the revelations of Belphoebe or Britomart in their relative lack of access to transcendence. Radegund reveals no celestial Beauty, but she does movingly reveal her own drama of desire; this shift in interpretation of the woman observed, from the celestial to the dominantly social, is one of the qualities that occasionally encourage readers to remark on the novelistic bent of this episode.

The gradually increasing emphasis on secrets as a deceitful form of the hidden is another quality by which this episode presages the later novel of manners. Composure of countenance grows to be all-important, not just in order to save face but in order to conceal self-interest and to betray others; the rhetorical management of countenance returns. So Radegund's blush is an unwilled, moving expression of her abashedness and a revelation of her secret love. But Clarin's abashedness, more culpable, is followed by the deceptive turn to wipe her face as cover for her confusion. A. C. Hamilton's commentary says that this is a " 'realistic' detail almost without precedent in the poem"; its presence is a mark of the new imperative for secrets characterized by deception rather than by candor in social relations.

But Spenser never fully suffers the circumscription of privacy by controlled visibility. There is a handful of incidents in Book 5 in which the hiddenness of bodily life or of solitude flashes out briefly, often poignantly. Candid, unintended revelations persist, revealing themselves accidentally and authentically, as in Guyon's identification of Brigadore, in Radegund's visage as it surprises Artegall in battle, in her later blush. Such moments elude the effort to control the availability of display and to control the responses of viewers. Artegall might be wrong to succumb to Radegund when already betrothed to Britomart, as Spenser suggests with Artegall's overly easy promise of "seruice" as the prize of battle. But the willingness to risk the sufferance of radically unforeseeable visions is his strength, as it is Aeneas's; it is the single quality that can temper his *salvagesse sans finesse.*

This innocence of candor is what saves Britomart's vision in Isis Church from the interpretive corrosions elsewhere in the book, and distinguishes her vision from the displays that it resembles: the necessarily equivocal self-presentations of Mercilla's royalty and the idol set up by Geryon.[13] Britomart's experience occurs in two stages, both of them important for the development of her perception and for the problems of vision and display in Book 5. In Busyrane's house (3.11) she had stared, puzzled but uncomprehending, as at a riddle:

> Tho as she backward cast her busie eye,
>   To search each secret of that goodly sted,
>   Ouer the dore thus written she did spye
>   *Be bold:* she oft and oft it ouer-red,
>   Yet could not find what sence it figured.
>
> (3.11.50)

The pageants and pictures of Busyrane fascinate the eye but repel the understanding; the secrets seen there remain alien and opaque to Britomart. But her envisionings in Isis Church are more resonant with her awareness. Spenser uses his characteristic diction in speaking of her amazement at the craftsmanship evident in the temple, diction

---

[13]The best analysis of Britomart in Isis Church remains Fletcher's, in *Prophetic Moment,* 259–76; I rely on it in the paragraphs that follow.

like that of Vergil's in depicting Aeneas in the temple of Juno, but without Vergil's ironies:

> She wondred at the workemans passing skill,
> Whose like before she neuer saw nor red;
> And thereupon long while stood gazing still,
> But thought, that she thereon could neuer gaze her fill.
>
> (5.7.5)

The long duration of Britomart's gaze, and the assumptions about filling a space within herself with what she sees, are not surprising. But, as Angus Fletcher finely notes, the greater awareness of this watcher, conveyed unobtrusively and simply in the phrase "But thought," sets her apart from other marveling heroes in the poem.[14] She also shows a departure from her usually cautious behavior: after her open awe, after the gesture of approval bestowed by the statue of the goddess, Britomart trustingly surrenders herself to sleep under the aegis of this protective patron:

> To which the Idoll as it were inclining,
> Her wand did moue with amiable looke,
> By outward shew her inward sence desining.
> Who well perceiuing, how her wand she shooke,
> It as a token of good fortune tooke.
>
> . . . . .
>
> her helmet she vnlaste,
> And by the altars side her selfe to slumber plaste.
>
> (5.7.8)

The next stage of her act of vision is a dream identification with this august figure—a ruler who blesses rather than condemns the private sexual choice of her votary, unlike Elizabeth; a goddess who blesses rather than persecutes, unlike Vergil's Juno—through a metamorphic coronation. Britomart's unexpected dream elevation is a received manifestation of the destiny into which she is growing, rather than an institutional display of justice like Mercilla's. The dream coronation extends Britomart's awe, which resembles that of Vergil's Aeneas before his mother's epiphany, to her own epiphanic transformation into an Isis figure. She fuses the role of beholder and beheld,

---

[14]Ibid., 266.

and reaps, as it were, both the pleasure of beholding and the pleasure of being beheld as a goddess:

> Her seem'd, as she was doing sacrifize
>   To *Isis,* deckt with Mitre on her hed,
>   And linnen stole after those Priestes guize,
>   All sodainely she saw transfigured
>   Her linnen stole to robe of scarlet red,
>   And Moone-like Mitre to a Crowne of gold,
>   That euen she her selfe much wondered
>   At such a chaunge, and ioyed to behold
> Her selfe, adorn'd with gems and iewels manifold.
>
> (5.7.13)

Britomart's response of amazement to her elevation through these cosmic symbols of coronation aligns the dream not with those episodes of a troubling will to control vision, expose secrets, and determine display, but with the book's fleeting episodes in which hidden intimacies, unexpected sights, and the non-intentional expressiveness of candor preserve the possibility of interpretive freedom to the viewer. We have already mentioned Guyon's claiming of Brigadore, Radegund's face revealed to Artegall, her later blush. The Isis Church episode, documenting both Britomart's waking wonder and her dreaming joy and expansiveness, is the largest and most substantial of these moments, and one of the most important conceptually, since Spenser stakes on the episode his hopes of benignly uniting political and private.

The episode can support these hopes partly because the idealist basis of authority is preserved in the episode. Never in danger of being a mere mystifier, Britomart bears from earlier books her essence and her destiny as a part of providential hierarchy. Her elevating metamorphosis, a reflective as well as an enabling image of what she will be, excludes the interpretive threat that all marvels beheld must be taken equivocally, as elements in a process of mystification. When Britomart enters Radegund's story in the second half of canto 7, battling fiercely, ruling and then restoring male rule, she also enters the sphere of Spenser's ambivalence about those matters and his resistance to the Queen's management of herself displayed for political purposes. But one function of the Isis Church episode is to preserve the possibility of reliable vision and reliable interpretation of marvels beheld. Britomart's blessing by the maternal goddess and her lying down to sleep by the altar preserve the germ of the epic's wish for proximity to feminine life and its mysteriousness.

Social Decorum: Tact and the Liberation from the Tyranny of the Public Gaze in Book 6 of *The Faerie Queene*

One more unexpected expression of candor occurs very near the end of Book 5. Artegall has arrived to champion Irena against Grantorto. Irena has no knowledge of his arrival, and while the sun "did to the world display / His chearefull face" (5.12.11), she prepares to present herself suitably "to receiue the doome of her decay" (5.12.12):

> Then vp she rose, and on her selfe did dight
>   Most squalid garments, fit for such a day,
>   And with dull countenance, and with dolefull spright,
>   She forth was brought in sorrowfull dismay.
>
>   · · · · ·
>
> Like as a tender Rose in open plaine,
>   That with vntimely drought nigh withered was,
>   And hung the head, soone as few drops of raine
>   Thereon distill, and deaw her daintie face,
>   Gins to looke vp, and with fresh wonted grace
>   Dispreds the glorie of her leaues gay;
>   Such was *Irenas* countenance, such her case,
>   When *Artegall* she saw in that array,
> There wayting for the Tyrant, till it was farre day.
>
>   (5.12.12–13)

The problematic image of the concealing and opening rose finds its appropriate topic in the bodily manifestation of joy here, in the finest example of this rose so far in *The Faerie Queene*. It is part of the cluster of unintentional wonders beheld and countenances met in Book 5 which I have been sketching. It is also a signal of things to come in Book 6, for these unintended and moving visibilities help to make possible the poise of Book 6, which acknowledges but also transcends the more fracturing threats of Book 5. Book 6 shifts its emphasis from force, monarchic politics, and the skills of the panther to the arena of courtly manners, especially in the context of that frequent story motif, the intrusion on privacy. It was Ralegh's dilemma that his relationship with the Queen and the royal intolerance of his marriage were alike understood and articulated with a Petrarchan rhetoric of abject servant and adored mistress which blurred any possible boundaries between monarchic politics and private intimacies, so that both the Elizabeths and Ralegh himself understood betrayal in one sphere as equivalent to betrayal in the other—though Ralegh struggles, in letters, poetry, and action, to transcend this bind. In Book 6, Spenser voices a need more clearly to demarcate boundaries between political and private, in what may be further inflections on Ralegh's marriage crisis, and to mediate these two spheres with a more subtle and delicate practice of courtly manners than was available in much of Book 5. Gradually he restores the possibility of a fragile but harmonious presence of men and women to one another, in the vision on Mt. Acidale.

The route to that fleeting moment of release lies through a new attentiveness to social demeanor and tact, which is to say ways of witnessing, acknowledging, or refusing to acknowledge privacies observed, in the way that Alma feigns to overlook Guyon's awkwardness with Shamefastnesse. As in Book 5, Spenser faces the fundamental and insistent publicity of courtly life. But now such publicity is not inevitably a threatening pressure on the desired solitude of characters. Although it is patently so in the well-known episodes of intrusion, such social density can also make possible an acknowledgment and liberation of a character's unperceived prowess or interiority, if skill in social and class decorums guides face-to-face encounters.

Characters in *The Faerie Queene* seek, as we have repeatedly seen, a solitude that permits candor. It is in this form that hiddenness is the object of a strong wish in the poem: characters desire a solitary, protected or reliable setting in which to be openly themselves, like the Hermit who happily lives "like carelesse bird in cage" (6.6.4). But there is also the kind of hiddenness in which internal forces or processes are kept contained within the formal container of the body: Britomart's early experience of love, Timias hiding his love from Belphoebe while she nurses him, Serena and Timias festering "priuily" as their "inner parts now gan to putrify" (6.6.5). A primary and benign instance is the body of the virginal Queen, "In whose chast breast all bountie naturall, / And treasures of true loue enlocked beene" (4.Proem.4), as we saw in Chapter Three. Most often such energies within characters move naturally toward emergence. Such energies will out, and with them the full range of risks attending defense and defenselessness.

Book 6 opens with a proem the Paradise of which is characterized precisely as free from the issues of defense and defenselessness and so permitting the full process of emergence of virtue. This Paradise is the setting for a fine reworking, the first of two in this book, of the unfolding flower image that had proved troublesome as a figure for the virginity of Belphoebe in Book 4 but that works so beautifully at the end of Book 5, as an image of Irena's movement to joy. Belphoebe's stanzas are both descriptive and epideictic, intended to glorify the Queen and her court as well as Belphoebe; the combination of Spenser's ambivalence about the value of virginity, the conflicting literary Ovidian and patristic traditions of virginity, and the connotative tensions between purity and fertility in the flower image creates a fascinating but impossible tangle of contradictions. The Proem to Book 6, differentiating between the generative processes of Paradise and the sterile seemings of this imperfect world, removes the qualities of defensiveness and vulnerability without limiting the tenderness of the spreading flower; Paradise is a sanctuary that guarantees the flower's purity and its eventual strength by keeping it hidden from view:

> Reuele to me the sacred noursery
> Of vertue, which with you doth there remaine,
> Where it in siluer bowre does hidden ly
> From view of men, and wicked worlds disdaine.
> Since it at first was by the Gods with paine
> Planted in earth, being deriu'd at furst
> From heauenly seedes of bounty soueraine,
> And by them long with carefull labour nurst,
> Till it to ripenesse grew, and forth to honour burst.
>
> Amongst them all growes not a fayrer flowre,
> Then is the bloosme of comely courtesie,
> Which though it on a lowly stalke doe bowre,
> Yet brancheth forth in braue nobilitie,
> And spreds it selfe through all ciuilitie:
> Of which though present age doe plenteous seeme,
> Yet being matcht with plaine Antiquitie,
> Ye will them all but fayned showes esteeme,
> Which carry colours faire, that feeble eies misdeeme.
>
> (6.Proem.3–4)

The logical and temporal distinctions between Paradise and earth, Antiquitie and this "present age," are not tightly consistent here—is "vertue" hidden in Paradise's "siluer bowre" or "planted in earth," or both at once? Still, it is possible to say that the separation of Paradise from this world in its "present age" is more happily made than the parallel separation in Book 5, where it is defined negatively by the departure of Astraea. The imagery here suggests not a divorce of the gods' blessings from this world, and no retreat like Astraea's, but Paradise's fertile nurturance and the gods' bringing to birth of a blessing for the world. This birth is described as an emergence or thrust from the small, enclosed, protective spaces of "heauenly seedes" to a bowering and thence to the braver actions of branching and spreading.

The diction and tone established in the Proem make possible a happier and less tense analysis of social relations than in the previous book, one pitched toward a series of individuals' relations rather than toward the unwieldy social structures and the darker vision of Book 5.[15] It is through the aggregate of many individual encounters in Book 6 that Spenser is able to depict not political structures but the social premises and relations that underlie those structures. The modes of courtly and pastoral romance allow a depiction of the aristocratic world that Spenser has also contemplated in Book 5, but with the conventions of pastoral and folk tale, which allow more obliquity of representation than in the more realistic court and political contexts of Book 5. Both books embroil their characters in the profound publicity of aristocratic life; as in most of Ovid's work, there is scant escape from the constant visual witness of characters to each other. But Book 6 offers the possible relief of this pressure through the exercise of tact. Furthermore, social visibility and tact are bound up with social class, as in Calidore's fortuitous encounter with Tristram.

Calidore spends a good deal of time and attention in his visual survey of the young Tristram when they meet: "Him stedfastly he markt" (6.2.5); "Whom *Calidore* a while well hauing vewed, / At length bespake" (6.2.7); "when he long had him beholding stood" (6.2.24). Calidore's attentiveness is partly perceptive admiration, partly concern as he tries to decipher Tristram's social class from his appearance. For Tristram has courted shame by fighting the boorish knight:

[15]For fine comparisons of the structure and ethics of Books 5 and 6, see Cheney, *Spenser's Image of Nature*, 176–96; Humphrey Tonkin, *Spenser's Courteous Pastoral: Book 6 of "The Faerie Queene"* (Oxford: Clarendon Press, 1972), 35–40.

> ...What meanes this, gentle swaine?
> Why hath thy hand too bold it selfe embrewed
> In blood of knight, the which by thee is slaine,
> By thee no knight; which armes impugneth plaine?
>
> (6.2.7)

The urgency of determining class in order to determine the possibility of dishonor sanctions Calidore's long and beautiful contemplation of Tristram, whose appearance hints at nobility but also confounds it. His "woodsmans iacket" of Lincoln green marks him as an English pastoral swain—albeit a wealthy and stylish one—in the line of Robin Hood. But his literary affiliation is with Belphoebe and the Ovidian sylvan hunters of the poem:

> Buskins he wore of costliest cordwayne,
>   Pinckt vpon gold, and paled part per part,
>   As then the guize was for each gentle swayne;
>   In his right hand he held a trembling dart,
>   Whose fellow he before had sent apart;
>   And in his left he held a sharpe borespeare,
>   With which he wont to launch the saluage hart
>   Of many a Lyon, and of many a Beare
> That first vnto his hand in chase did happen neare.
>
> (6.2.6)

It is the costliness of these appurtenances that provides an initial clue that Tristram is aristocratic. More important, once Calidore decides that Tristram's answers and actions confirm his nobility, he hastens to identify Tristram as Ovidian. On Spenser's part, the thematic interest in Ovidian solitude is evident; but even Calidore places Tristram in an Ovidian world as part of his tactful effort both to acknowledge what he himself is witness to and to allow Tristram the privilege of hiding his identity in the woods if he chooses:

> Faire gentle swayne, and yet as stout as fayre,
>   That in these woods amongst the Nymphs dost wonne,
>   Which daily may to thy sweete lookes repayre,
>   As they are wont vnto *Latonaes* sonne,
>   After his chace on woodie *Cynthus* donne:
>   Well may I certes such an one thee read,

> As by thy worth thou worthily hast wonne,
>   Or surely borne of some Heroicke sead,
> That in thy face appeares and gratious goodlyhead.
>
> But should it not displease thee it to tell;
>   (Vnlesse thou in these woods thy selfe conceale,
>   For loue amongst the woodie Gods to dwell;)
>   I would thy selfe require thee to reueale,
>   For deare affection and vnfayned zeale,
>   Which to thy noble personage I beare,
>   And wish thee grow in worship and great weale.
>
>   (6.2.25, 26)

Such tact is, in this instance, a direct result of Calidore's perception of class and a living literary world where tact is always a problem. Visual tact resides, as throughout Book 6, not in averting the gaze, as Alma so graciously does, but in fully and eloquently acknowledging what has been witnessed.

This kind of tact we see also when Calidore interrupts the intimacy of Calepine and Serena (the latter Ralegh's name for his wife),[16] who imagine that they are "far from enuious eyes that mote [them] spight" (6.3.20):

> To whom Sir *Calidore* approaching nye,
>   Ere they were well aware of liuing wight,
>   Them much abasht, but more him selfe thereby,
>   That he so rudely did vppon them light,
>   And troubled had their quiet loues delight.
>   Yet since it was his fortune, not his fault,
>   Him selfe thereof he labour'd to acquite,
>   And pardon crau'd for his so rash default,
> That he gainst courtesie so fowly did default.
>
>   (6.3.21)

Calidore has often been accused of a gaucherie here, and the intrusion ultimately leads to Serena's abduction by the Blatant Beast—but this is something for which Calidore cannot be said to bear responsibility. In fact, his handling of this small contretemps is a paradigm for Spenser's resolutions of large and important tensions in the work of this period. Calidore's intrusion is accidental, and so releases Spenser

---

[16]See Oakeshott, *Queen and the Poet*, 98.

from making judgments against the invidious eye which it is possible to make against Malbecco or against Ovid's Aglauros. The invader of love's solitude has the grace to be abashed at his own interruption of secret sights—a crucial capacity and value in Spenser's work. And Calidore channels his abashedness into eloquence and tact, accepting responsibility for the intrusion but also treating it lightly.[17] His speech admits the value and the privacy of the witnessed activity, so that it is no cause for shame on the part of the witnessed individuals, but also it implicitly acknowledges that persons witnessed might be abashed, and with that act of acknowledgment lessens the need for such a reaction. In the *Metamorphoses*, Ovidian secrets are cheapened into gossip, sullying those who wish not to display; Spenser redefines secrecy in his Ovidian woods as privacy, with the greater dignity of that concept. The invasive threat of Cynthia's jealous eye in the *Epithalamion*, or of the father river in *Colin Clout* who wishes to prevent the marriage of the Mulla and the Bregog, is transcended here with social skills that recognize rather than evade the social density of courtly life.

Frank Whigham argues, apropos of Elizabethan courtesy theory: "If all utterance in this context comes to have primarily epideictic force; if the manifestation of style transcends issues of substance; if subjects of conversation increasingly become querelles; if conversation is not listened to but watched; then the power relation between speaker and hearer becomes skewed normatively toward the audience. Speech and other significations reveal not power but powerlessness, a pleading with the audience for a hearing, for recognition, for ratification."[18] This is a fine formulation with which to articulate personal relations in a variety of Renaissance works; it has obvious applications for the relations between audience or watcher and the viewed object of attention. In the meeting of Calidore and Tristram, for instance, the

---

[17]For a point of view contrary to mine—one that has wide currency today—about Calidore's behavior at 6.3.21, see Richard Neuse, "Book 6 as Conclusion to *The Faerie Queene*," *English Literary History* 35 (1968), 329–53 at 343, rpt. in *Critical Essays on Spenser from ELH* (Baltimore: Johns Hopkins University Press, 1970), 222–46. On Calidore's intrusions, see Cheney, *Spenser's Image of Nature*, 198; Tonkin, *Spenser's Courteous Pastoral*, 289; Harry Berger, "A Secret Discipline: *The Faerie Queene*, Book 6," in *Form and Convention in the Poetry of Edmund Spenser*, ed. William Nelson (New York: Columbia University Press, 1961), 35–75 at 40; Dorothy Culp, "Courtesy and Fortune's Chance in Book 6 of *The Faerie Queene*," *Modern Philology* 68 (1971), 254–59.

[18]Whigham, *Ambition and Privilege*, 38–39.

importance of the "audience" is clear, though "witness" might better be substituted because of the different implications of audience in this episode. Spenser obviously understands the potential imbalance of power in such a meeting; he admits this when Calidore assumes the right to intervene and judge the circumstances. But Spenser also shows both characters at pains to acknowledge the separate, Ovidian life and the solitude, hence the dignity, of Tristram, through Calidore's scrupulous politeness and his literary allusiveness, forms both of tact and of decorum. Tristram is dependent upon Calidore only for the privilege of being made squire; otherwise both characters explicitly avoid either pleading or powerlessness. It is the intricate social relation itself, a fictive reflection of courtly complexities, which underscores the notion of Tristram's autonomous selfhood, because Calidore acknowledges the independent life that Tristram lives as Ovidian hunter and romance prince. He is momentary witness to Tristram's identity, but not creator and cause of that identity, as Whigham's "audience" can be. Tristram is born to the nobility, but he has also earned his grace, as his history shows; this earned identity lessens the ascriptive power of the audience and increases the value of achieved mastery.

The consummation of Tristram's revelation is Calidore's dubbing him a squire, a longstanding wish of Tristram's which he voices as a transition from the childhood world of Ovidian hunter to the masculine adulthood of epic chivalry:

> Ne is there hauke, which mantleth her on perch,
> > Whether high towring, or accoasting low,
> > But I the measure of her flight doe search,
> > And all her pray, and all her diet know.
> > Such be our ioyes, which in these forrests grow:
> > Onely the vse of armes, which most I ioy,
> > And fitteth most for noble swayne to know,
> > I haue not tasted yet, yet past a boy,
> And being now high time these strong ioynts to imploy.
>
> (6.2.32)

When Calidore agrees, naming him with the ideals of courage, fidelity, and truth which he already possesses independently of outside witness, Tristram unfolds his joy in this book's second reworking of the opening flower image, a vehicle that Spenser uses as elegantly here as in the Proem and in the description of Irena's countenance:

Full glad and ioyous then young *Tristram* grew,
Like as a flowre, whose silken leaues small,
Long shut vp in the bud from heauens vew,
At length breakes forth, and brode displayes his smyling hew.

(6.2.35)

This is a joy achieved only because the delicate balances of Tristram's social instincts and of Calidore's visual tact complement each other. The deference of Calidore's intentional divestment of power is possible in the first place because Tristram appears as a romance marvel, his path as an Ovidian sylvan youth accidentally crossed by events that reveal him, rather than appearing in the postures of self-assertive display that necessarily characterized real-life courtiers and the characters of Book 5. Their unexpected meeting transcends defense by acknowledging it, making possible the full witness and the radiant disclosure of identity.

Calidore, who is not always given credit for subtlety, regularly reveals a tact that acknowledges the possibility of abashedness, shame, or defensiveness, and then transcends it; he defines the circumstances of an event so as to make this transcendence possible, in adventures that parallel those of Artegall but in ways that Artegall never does. In the story of Artegall and Munera, for instance, conflict is defined so starkly as mutual assault, and the threat of the enemy is so strong, that the only solution is the suppression of pity in Munera's dismemberment and drowning:

Yet for no pitty would he change the course
    Of Iustice, which in *Talus* hand did lye;
    Who rudely hayld her forth without remorse,
    Still holding vp her suppliant hands on hye,
    And kneeling at his feete submissiuely.
    But he her suppliant hands, those hands of gold,
    And eke her feete, those feete of siluer trye,
    Which sought vnrighteousnesse, and iustice sold,
Chopt off, and nayld on high, that all might them behold.

(5.2.26)

The parallel story in Book 6 edges toward such violent antinomies; Briana, far from taking a suppliant posture and begging mercy, seems the more dangerous evil for her rhetorical attack on Calidore. She tries the extraordinary social tactic of turning the moral tables on the hero, hoping to preserve innocence to herself by making *him* ashamed for killing her men:

> False traytor Knight, (sayd she) no Knight at all,
>   But scorne of armes that hast with guilty hand
>   Murdred my men, and slaine my Seneschall;
>   Now comest thou to rob my house vnmand,
>   And spoile my selfe, that can not thee withstand?
>
> (6.1.25)

But Calidore, at first abashed, recovers his poise and simply refuses to be put in the defensive position:

> Much was the Knight abashed at that word;
>   Yet answerd thus; Not vnto me the shame,
>   But to the shamefull doer it afford.
>   .   .   .   .   .
> Then doe your selfe, for dread of shame, forgoe
>   This euill manner, which ye here maintaine.
>
> (6.1.26–27)

Briana here begins to lose the scornful superiority that force had allowed her to assume; she gives it up freely when Calidore, having conquered her champion, Crudor, in battle, treats her with a generosity that Artegall could conceptualize only as the weakness of pity:

> So all returning to the Castle glad,
>   Most ioyfully she them did entertaine,
>   Where goodly glee and feast to them she made,
>   To shew her thankefull mind and meaning faine,
>   By all the meanes she mote it best explaine:
>   And after all, vnto Sir *Calidore*
>   She freely gaue that Castle for his paine,
>   And her selfe bound to him for euermore;
> So wondrously now chaung'd, from that she was afore.
>
> (6.1.46)

This change in her is not purely an unmotivated response to generosity. Briana's villainous career has consisted of degrading knights by bearding them because she herself has been degraded by Crudor, whose unbending pride makes him humiliate her, demanding a price for his love, by humiliating others. Shame is the central motive in this episode; the cycle of degradation is more effectively broken by Calidore's tactful refusal to enter its defensive maneuvers, and his concomitant recognition of Briana's shame, than by Artegall's undiscriminating ferocity. Briana and Crudor are liberated from the services, tyrannies, and humiliations of traditional courtly love. This is the book's first instance of new access by a man and a woman to each other's presence, transcending defense.

I said in Chapter Three that it would be necessary to consider further how Spenser arrives at the resolutions of Mt. Acidale through the issue of defensiveness and through the disenchantments of Book 5. We have now come some way toward that end. One of the fundamental tensions of Book 5 lies in Spenser's struggle with the fact that feminine consciousness, which he has been showing with increasing clarity throughout his work, may have to encompass not only feminine will but, more precisely, feminine envy, coerciveness, tyranny, and spying; in this, Ralegh's Cynthia is no superior to Ovid's predatory gods or their descendants, Spenser's lecherous knights. Woman beheld may herself wilfully control both vision and interpretation; the wish for proximity to feminine life can be fulfilled only if the tyranny and the hunger of the gaze are abandoned by feminine as well as by masculine will.[19] In Book 5 there is little possibility of these surrenders. The requirements of governmental theatricality, the control of signs' interpretation, and the rhetorical balances by which Elizabeth's female rule survived so long are all predicated on the will of the woman who can no longer be beheld "huntinge like Diana, walkinge like Venus." Worse, there is little desire for access to feminine life in Book 5, except briefly in the Isis Church episode; there is instead resistance to it, shying away from it. But Vergil's and Ovid's goddesses and nymphs are restored in Book 6, and this reappearance is specifically a release of *wish,* in the depiction of female characters who once more evoke a desire in the beholder for access to them:

[19]Britomart's releasing surrender to sleep near Isis generalizes Spenser's depiction of the usually masculine wish for proximity to the healing mysteriousness of a feminine being. Britomart's trust is childlike, and in that limited sense not determined by gender; but it also culminates in her sexual maturity and consciousness, and in that sense transcends the atavism of the preconscious Chrysogonee, who had also entrusted herself to a mysterious, sexually transforming sleep.

Much wondred *Calidore* at this straunge sight,
  Whose like before his eye had neuer seene,
  And standing long astonished in spright,
  And rapt with pleasaunce, wist not what to weene;
  Whether it were the traine of beauties Queene,
  Or Nymphes, or Faeries, or enchaunted show,
  With which his eyes mote haue deluded beene.
  Therefore resoluing, what it was, to know,
Out of the wood he rose, and toward them did go.

(6.10.17)

If Chrysogonee, in Book 3, represents a relatively early and problematic effort to acknowledge the otherness of feminine bodily life
and to enjoy proximity to it legitimately, then Calidore's visual bliss
on Mt. Acidale boldly articulates the strength of the wish and its
poignance—both the stronger for having faltered in Book 5—and
resolves some of the ethical problems of representation that we saw
in the Chrysogonee episode. Schooled by the realities depicted in Book
5, Spenser no longer finds it difficult to depict feminine consciousness,
and so the nymphs and graces on Mt. Acidale can be urbane, aware,
even powerful. But Spenser's redefinition of the fiction of Ralegh's
marriage crisis as an issue of courtly manners, unintentional encounters, demeanor and tact rather than as the threat of an invidious eye
allows him to transcend the inherently defensive postures before the
agents and signs of justice of Book 5. Calidore's intrusion on Mt.
Acidale is a large-scale version of his intrusion on Calepine and Serena
earlier in the book, and the narrative line avoids the hostilities that
accompany both masculine and feminine consciousness in Book 5.

Calidore is one of the two male observers who have access to this
scene of the feminine; his poignant question "But why when I them
saw, fled they away from me?" (6.10.19) marks both the central issue
of plot and theme and the tone of yearning for the elusive fulfillment
of his wish. Both of these are centered in the problem of the male
viewer. He functions to underscore the ungratifiable yearning of the
solitary male watcher not simply for erotic satisfaction but for the
fulfillment of dominantly feminine society, not only for a vision of
cosmic harmony but for the delight-filled intimacy of the dance's
intercourse, emphasized by the generous but closed circuit of its movement: "All raunged in a ring, and dauncing in delight" (6.10.11).

This male wish for access to self-contained feminine life is one rhetorical motive in the Chrysogonee episode, as it is more lightly in Guyon's meeting with the nymphs of the fountain, but the blocking of its full expression makes those two episodes problematic. In Books 3 and 4 Spenser casts a male desire for absorption into feminine autonomy in the form of a Petrarchan love story between the imperial votaress Belphoebe and her servant Timias, but from the start this story involves notions of sustained frustration—notions that finally elude Spenser's efforts to resolve the tale happily and that were, in any case, the chief reason for his shying from Petrarchanism and its modes of regard between men and women. The problems of these kinds of regard are highlighted again in the *Amoretti* and in Colin Clouts's late defense of his inferior's worship of Rosalind, in *Colin Clovts Come Home Againe*; male access to feminine life is still frustrated and compromised, and neither male nor female lover in the Petrarchan system of affects awakens the *reader's* wish for their company. But in Book 6 the wish for proximate feminine society embodies itself in Calidore and his vision of the dance on Mt. Acidale. In creating this episode Spenser once more acknowledges the charisma that Elizabeth's feminized court might exert on its courtiers—did exert on Ralegh, as his marriage showed—and, in Calidore's graceful regret and search for the meaning of the vision, Spenser provides the courtier with an alternative to Timias's "dismay" (3.5.43) before the vision of beauty hierarchically elevated. In Calidore's presence on Mt. Acidale Spenser resolves this problem of the arresting, debilitating power of woman viewed by modulating the bliss of vision into the pleasure of knowing. This pleasure of conceptual structure is clearly not ample recompense for Colin's sense of loss, a sense that gently tinges the joyousness of the episode with a sad awareness of the limits of human experience and of the artist's recognition of the ultimate impossibility of subjecting even one's own creations to one's knowledge. But the pleasure of knowledge—specifically knowledge of the facts that Colin gives Calidore—is one means by which the arresting power of beauty may be overcome, and is one way to preserve something of a transcendent vision within quotidian reality.

Moreover, it is possible for Calidore to achieve this preservation, with Colin's help, partly because he has already shown himself to be capable of transforming the initial visual arrest of eros. When he had first beheld Pastorella, garlanded and seated on a "litle hillocke" and admired by the shepherd swains "As if some miracle of heauenly hew

/ Were downe to them descended in that earthly vew" (6.9.8), he too
had admired, "markt her rare demeanure," and evaluated her social
standing as making her worthy to be "a Princes Paragone" (6.9.11).
He feeds his hungry gaze on her, and notoriously suspends his quest
(6.9.12). But then he stirs himself to action, in graceful and eager
efforts to win her: he embraces the pastoral ethos of simplicity, labor,
and retirement from the courtly world (though his destiny and his
love will lead him back to his quest), and he labors at humble tasks
for her (6.9.37).[20] His love is worked out in quotidian actions, in a
sequence of unglamorous days, among family members and neigh-
bors—including his luckless rival in love, Coridon, with whom he
must establish workable relations because Coridon is part of his beloved's social world.

The kind of arrest which undid Artegall and his heroic ethos when
surprised by Radegund's beauty is considerably gentler and less trau-
matic in Colin's pastoral piping to his beloved on Mt. Acidale. Still,
Colin is understandably irritated at Calidore's interruption of the
Grace's dance, and Spenser takes pains to detail Calidore's negotiation
of this difficult social encounter before turning to Colin's dilation on
the vision's significance:

> But *Calidore*, though no lesse sory wight [than Colin],
> For that mishap, yet seeing him to mourne,
> Drew neare, that he the truth of all by him mote learne.

> And first him greeting, thus vnto him spake,
> Haile iolly shepheard, which thy ioyous dayes
> Here leadest in this goodly merry make,
> Frequented of these gentle Nymphes alwayes,
> Which to thee flocke, to heare thy louely layes;

---

[20]Calidore's assumption of pastoral labor and of "shepheards weed" (6.9.36) is
not without its risks to the heroic ethos; Spenser conveys this risk with direct criticism
("Who now does follow the foule *Blatant Beast*...?" 6.10.1) and with a disquieting
analogy with the uxorious Paris, at 6.9.36. (For the complications and possible confusions of allusion in this stanza, see *Variorum* 6.243.) Still, Calidore's decorous
pastoral behavior, born of love, and his subsequent courtesies and chivalric rescues,
together suggest that the heroic norm can expand to accommodate his diplomatic
gifts and even to accommodate a truancy that may be an extension and not an
abandonment of the heroic quest.

Tell me, what mote these dainty Damzels be,
Which here with thee doe make their pleasant playes?
Right happy thou, that mayst them freely see:
But why when I them saw, fled they away from me?

                                        (6.10.18–19)

Hamilton remarks of stanza 19 that "in his affability, [Calidore] is less than honest: he knows that they fled because they saw him. In reply, Colin Clout exposes his duplicity." Surely "duplicity" is a bit strong for the affability that characterizes Calidore's attempt to establish friendly relations before apologizing; he momentarily "fayns to ouersee" his own intrusion in order to obviate awkwardness in his initial greeting of a stranger, and he begins with the complimentary assumption, with its hint of admiration, that Colin's musical skills make him the daily intimate of such lovely creatures. His presentation of amiable demeanor prevents the need for beginning with abject apologies and makes the apology for his intrusion appropriately delicate when it does come. He neither overstates his regret nor ascribes to himself more blame than his accidental intrusion requires: "Right sory I.../ That my ill fortune did them hence displace" (6.10.20). Then, in what may be as much a tactful gesture of acknowledging Colin's chagrin as a function of his own desire to know more, Calidore urges Colin to talk about it, with a graceful reminder that the observers must take what they can of the lost vision into their own, more quotidian lives: "But since things passed none may now restore, / Tell me, what were they all, whose lacke thee grieues so sore" (6.10.20).

These suggestions presuppose some subtle rhetorical aims on Calidore's part. But I have already proposed that rhetorical intention in visual encounters is one thing that can corrupt them—hence Spenser's negative ethical evaluations of the nymphs met by Cymochles and Guyon in the Bower of Bliss, and his unease with the harsh "moniments" of Munera's hands and feet and with the Soudan's arms, displayed as admonitions to society at large. Intentions controlling encounters in Book 6, however, are more benign, issuing from Calidore's fundamental respect for those whom he sees and his efforts to be courteous, to appreciate their gifts, and to draw out their special strengths, one effect that he has on both Tristram and Colin. Fully capable of physical combat when necessary, he prefers to assume that people might be good if they are treated well, as in his generosity with Briana. In this he contrasts with the champions of justice in Book

5, who must often assume that evil characters will persist in their evil and that the members of society require visual warnings that are little less than threats. He also contrasts with other characters in his own book, as James Nohrnberg notes: "Spenser's stories all insist that contempt is opposed to courtesy, as pride to holiness. The 'difficult' person is often a case of embittered self-love, and there are many difficult persons in the sixth book, though frequently what we see of them is their envy. Both arrogance and envy make one want to shame others. . . . The attempt to shame other persons in this legend is symbolized by various kinds of exposure." In this context Nohrnberg cites Briana and Crudor (whom we have already seen), Turpine, Despetto and Fefetto, Mirabella, Coridon, Maleffort.[21] We may say that Spenser has gone some way toward resolving the problem of intentional display or intentional control of demeanor: it is reprehensible when its aim is to control, subdue, or humiliate others, when, in Nohrnberg's terms, it is grounded in contempt; it is a happier quality, even a virtue, when its aim is to elicit the *virtù* and grace of persons encountered.

Colin's long explanation of the Graces (6.10.21–28) does both himself and Calidore good. Colin benefits from a second, extended, and gracious apology from Calidore, who now shoulders the blame for cutting short Colin's bliss, though with a passing acknowledgment that it was bad luck and not malice that led him to "this luckelesse breache." Calidore shows again his delicate ability to refuse an inappropriate sense of shame. And he has the pleasure of lingering in these "discourses," feeding his "greedy fancy" with "delight" (6.10.30).

I have referred loosely to "what Calidore learns," and it is worth trying to say more exactly what that is. To begin with, it is better to speak of what he experiences or understands, first because these are more inclusive verbs and do not risk the implication that a verbal, conceptual moral or lesson sums up the significance of the vision, and second because they are less active verbs, and more appropriate for what Calidore undergoes on Mt. Acidale, than the more focused verb *to learn*.

Calidore understands, then, at least two things, and one is a good deal easier to articulate than the other. He understands the mythic

[21]James Nohrnberg, *The Analogy of "The Faerie Queene"* (Princeton: Princeton University Press, 1976), 706–7.

and iconographic information that Colin gives him about the Graces. But as I said, this information, fine as it is, is not sufficient recompense for the loss of the vision and the loss of bliss for its beholders, as both of them acknowledge. The second thing that Calidore understands and experiences is the elusiveness of bestowed presence, the limits of mortal access to divine epiphanies, and the painfulness of acknowledging these limits. This is why his poignant question "But why when I them saw, fled they away from me?" parallels and distantly echoes Aeneas's question to his mother, "cur dextrae iungere dextram / non datur ac veras audire et reddere voces?" (Aen. 1.408–9). The answer to Aeneas's question about the Acidalian vision, near the very start of the Vergilian epic, lies in the fickleness and wilfulness of his mother. But the answer to Calidore's question about his Acidalian vision, coming as it does so near the end of Spenser's epic, is that Spenser can now both depict a momentary, blissful access to feminine life observed and insist on the separateness, the integrity, the otherness of that life, allowing it to protect itself by becoming invisible. The poise between these two conditions is a new thing in Spenser's work.

Gerald Bruns, discussing hermeneutical experience in a meditation on certain ideas of Gadamer's, suggests that "one would say that in understanding one encounters the other in its otherness, not as an object in a different time and place but as that which resists the grasp of my knowledge or which requires me to loosen my hold or open my fist. It is that which will not be objectified before me.... What happens in understanding is that I ... experience the refusal of the other to be contained in the conceptual apparatus that I have prepared for it."[22] This model of understanding can contribute a good deal to our understanding of Calidore, who "wist not what to weene" and fears that he is deceived by his senses, and therefore resolves to know, with a human hunger for conceptual knowledge which unhappily dissolves the very object it would know. This feminine dance is "that which will not be objectified," either before Calidore or before the artist.

If Spenser's effort here is to acknowledge that feminine life is autonomous, and will not be objectified, then perhaps we might also account for the extremely delicate handling of feminine consciousness

---

[22]Gerald Bruns, "On the Tragedy of Hermeneutical Experience," *Research in Phenomenology* 18 (Fall 1988), 191–201, at 193–94.

in the episode. These hundred naked damsels and the Graces contained in their circle are an elegant expansion and rectification of Cissie and Flossie's playfulness, a decorously erotic venerean troop of ladies. That Venus presides here, and not Diana (compare Diana's parallel episode on Arlo Hill, in the *Mutabilitie Cantos*) is important: it is a development from the Temple of Venus in Book 4, in which we find the rare circumstance of Venus in the company of women. (Venus is accompanied by a flock of nymphs as well in *Muiopotmos* 113–20.) The transfer of Diana's typically female consorts to Venus (more regularly depicted throughout her history with a single male companion) allows Spenser to dissolve the problem that we saw in the middle books—that the attractive qualities of virginal life preclude full sexual consciousness. Here the society of the feminine not only allows but essentially *is* an emblem of feminine sexual awareness, neither infantile nor maternal, urbane yet innocent. Chrysogonee all but lacks mortal consciousness, Britomart is Spenser's splendid depiction of a complex, developing, and individual psychological consciousness; the dance of these damsels *emblematizes* consciousness. It embraces the mysterious intelligence implicit in the harmony of the dance and in the iconographic erudition surrounding the Graces; it embraces female society, whose members regard each other (compare Chrysogonee's solitude, underscoring the simple-mindedness of her faint verbal protests). This use of emblem is, among other things, an extension of Spenserian acknowledgment, in this case an openhanded understanding that "the presentness of other minds is not to be known, but acknowledged."[23]

The split of the watching male consciousness between Colin and Calidore also helps partially to resolve this complicated problem of feminine consciousness and consciousness of a watcher (a solution perhaps suggested by the sustained discrepancies between Arthur's and Artegall's responses to the signs of justice in Book 5). Calidore's famous *faux pas* is a matter of becoming visible to the dancers; his watching, his pleasure, and his desire are all sanctioned as long as the women are free of the knowledge of his gaze. But this unawareness no longer extends in any degree to feminine consciousness as a whole. This is so because we are shown that the feminine circle is, finally,

[23]Stanley Cavell, "The Avoidance of Love: A Reading of *King Lear*," in *Must We Mean What We Say? A Book of Essays* (Cambridge: Cambridge University Press, 1969), 267–353 at 324. Cavell's discussion of acknowledgment and the tragic in *Lear* is addressed at length by Bruns in "On the Tragedy of Hermeneutical Experience."

aware of the male presence of Colin Clout—aware of him, allied with him, benignly disregardful of him. The "Ciuility" that the dancers represent may or may not be summoned by the Orphic poet—he is graceful enough to demur on this point—but it is clear that he is there on the sufferance of the feminine, which can afford to be heedless of him. It is the female gaze that we see here: not, as in Book 2, primarily intromissive, sight as a matter of appetitive ingestion, but imagined as the very essence of generosity, as Colin explains of the Graces and as we see in their focus on the damsel at the center:[24]

> And euer, as the crew
> About her daunst, sweet flowres, that far did smell,
> And fragrant odours they vppon her threw;
> But most of all, those three did her with gifts endew.
>
> (6.10.14)

This generosity extends to Colin insofar as we have the sense that Graces *permit* him to be there and to share their focus on his beloved. (Compare Cymochles' nymphs, who solicit his gaze rather than permit it, in an act that is simply more vulgar than the splendid and gracious accommodations of the maidens on Acidale.) The Petrarchan gaze of the male viewer—potentially arrested, frustrated, greedy—gives way to, or is transformed by, the benign female gaze, as if the presence of the maidens chastens male wish by absorbing it. Candor becomes not unconsciousness of male presence but an inclusive disregard of it, within the limits of a caution that dispels the dancers when candor's open secrecy is threatened. Feminine presence is imagined not as the power to coerce male servitude through a Petrarchan hardness of heart, but as an interior authority that allows love and allows the male gaze in circumstances where all viewing imaginations grant to women viewed both an innocent candor and an inner privacy that allows for consciousness. On Mt. Acidale, feminine life can trust at least one beholder, briefly.

---

[24]Feminine generosity is not *entirely* triumphant in the episode, however; at 6.10.28 Colin addresses to Gloriana an apology for having sung of her "poore handmayd" and assuring her that he intended only a coattail effect: he has sung of her "That when thy glory shall be farre displayd / To future age of her this mention may be made." Perhaps the invidious eye of Cynthia still intrudes on secluded lovers here. See Seth Weiner, "Minims and Grace Notes: Spenser's Acidalian Vision and Sixteenth-Century Music," *Spenser Studies* 5 (1984), 91–112, for explication of the technical and symbolic aspect of the minim, and, at 106, a discussion of the syntactic ambiguity of stanza 28.

Conclusion

Faune, nympharum
fugientum amator

Both of the episodes from *The Faerie Queene* about which I raised questions in the Introduction—Una's encounter with Sansloy, Sylvanus, and satyrs (1.6.4–19) and the encounter of Diana and her nymphs with Faunus (7.6.40–55)—demonstrate the ubiquity of vision and its social decorums, even in remote and wild settings, in Spenser's fictive world. Between them, they exemplify most of the concerns that I have been arguing as being central to Spenser's artistry and ethics. Both depict marvels beheld; both imitate and develop the dynamics of vision in the *Metamorphoses* and (more distantly in the cases of these two episodes) the Aeneid. Both raise in particular the question of how male characters regard female; in Spenser's poem as in ancient optics, this question includes consideration of the nature of desire—or, more precisely, the range of possible kinds of desire.

Sansloy's wish to "feed his fyrie lustfull eye" (1.6.4) by attacking Una, for instance, presupposes a traditional optics in which sight immediately inflames aggressive desire, but Sansloy's desire remains uninteresting when compared to that of Sylvanus. Spenser acknowledges Sylvanus's initial sexual interest when he remarks that Sylvanus "burnt in his intent" (1.6.15). But desire moves immediately into diverse and complex forms when Spenser allows Sylvanus, in his homely and gentle way, to echo Aeneas's wonder before the Venus-within-a-Diana figure of his mother in *Aeneid* 1, and when Spenser describes Sylvanus's memory of Cyparissus, a memory the substance of which is an allusion to Ovid's *Metamorphoses* 10.106–42. Vision awakens not a simple drive, but a Vergilian constellation of wonder, memory, painful loss, revival of love. For Sylvanus, a mythic nature spirit who has lost a loved boy, this response to the sight of Una is a passing poignance, less radically painful than Aeneas's human response to the elusiveness of his mother, but it is from Vergil's poem that Spenser develops his tone.

Other decorums of vision are honored in this episode, through other imitations. In response to Sansloy's nasty transgression, Phoebus "His blushing face in foggy cloud implyes, / And hides for shame" (1.6.6). This blush is not a sign of abashedness about his own exposure or visibility, but an embarrassment for Una. His blush is an act of generosity for her sake, and in this regard it is a moving transformation of the Ovidian sun, who similarly exists as natural object and anthropomorphic god at once, but whose reddenings most often represent sexual boldness and arousal, not gentlemanly modesty for a lady. Spenser thus makes Vergil and Ovid allies in this episode, through his adaptations of their treatments of myth and vision; the effects are to emphasize the episode's unexpected move from violence to marvelling tenderness in the behaviors directed toward Una, to underscore the diversity of responses to sights seen, and to imagine one way in which the hungers of the eye might be sanctioned and satisfied.

The greater number of these hungers and satisfactions is masculine in Spenser's work; most of the watchers of *The Faerie Queene* are males, the Queen-as-reader and courtly ladies excepted. (The facts that the Queen is the poem's arch-reader, and that ladies are often addressed as readers and viewers, complicate matters, but not impossibly so. Spenser clearly expects characters like Belphoebe and landscapes like the Bower of Bliss to evoke desire from readers of both genders, at the same time that he images men as most immediately subject to desire aroused through the eyes and women as a relatively more stable source of desired presence.) But from the beginning there have been brief instances of feminine watching. Nymphs joyfully celebrate Eliza in "Aprill," although their sisters in Book 1 of *The Faerie Queene* are envious and spiteful when they see Una. When Britomart looks into Merlin's magic glass, Spenser is reminded of a tower

Wherein th'Aegyptian *Phao* long did lurke
From all mens vew, that none might her discoure,
Yet she might all men vew out of her bowre.

(3.2.20)

The happy groom of the *Epithalamion* asks the girls of the village, perhaps with some comic tactlessness, whether they have ever seen such beauty as that of his bride. In *The Faerie Queene* 6 the lady whose bullying knight has been seized with desire for Priscilla describes the latter as fair enough for a heart "not carried with too curious eyes" (6.2.16—"a bitchy remark," comments Hamilton). These emulous or secretive acts of observation give way to the large-scale feminine celebration of Colin's lass on Mt. Acidale, at the end of Book 6. Britomart proves a relatively complex watcher: she feels both envy and yearning when she sees Amoret and Scudamour embrace (3.12, 1590 ed.). She has the strength to consider and to resist the blandishment of erotic art in Busyrane's tapestries, and she is capable of an exaltation amounting to sublimity in her Isis Church transformation.

This is a small list of female viewers, compared to the large supply of male viewers. Moreover, it shows no consistent patterns of the kind that Spenser usually builds among related episodes. To imagine women as gazers—which is to say, as possessors of autonomy and will, and as agents within visual acts—is difficult or uninteresting for Spenser until the works published in 1595 and 1596, and then the pride, touchiness, and hostility of his chief female pryer into mysteries arouse defensiveness and anxiety. Nor does the Mt. Acidale episode fully master these conflicts. Feminine presence there is granted consciousness of certain kinds and degrees, but the assertiveness of will so problematic in Spenser's Cynthia is evaded altogether. The feminine still relies on hiddenness—or magic disappearance—as its safeguard against the male intruder, even the well-disposed one. Hence the need for yet another treatment of the story of beholder and beheld, in what becomes a brief resolution through comedy, in the episode of Faunus and Diana. In this episode, Spenser faces the threat of Cynthia and uses it to make of women's autonomy something both comic and creative.

We need to clarify at once that Cynthia's authority *is* one of the issues of this story. First, Diana is called by her name of Cynthia early in the episode (*FQ* 7.6.38); she may thus be linked with the threatening Cynthia in the works of 1595–1596 and with the Cynthia whose courtly reign in the circle of the moon is threatened by the aspiring observer Mutabilitie earlier in the canto. Second, the Molanna who arranges Faunus's peep-show is, not coincidentally, the sister of Mulla, the river nymph who together with the river Bregog briefly outfoxed the eye of authority in *Colin Clout*. Finally, although the male viewer obviously dominates certain stanzas, the real danger of inviting feminine scrutiny and action by spying on it and being caught is acknowledged when Faunus is discovered and punished by Diana and her nymphs.

Kenneth Gross makes a strong argument for Faunus as iconoclast of pagan divinity. His claims for Spenser's "founding skepticism" are greater than any that I would argue for, but he aptly perceives Faunus's laugh as "an attack on the divine authority of a chaste, queenly goddess"—a laugh less at Diana herself, isolate in this story, than at the Elizabethan and Spenserian Cynthia who fuses qualities of Diana and qualities of Elizabeth.[1] Faunus is clearly an inadequate, disgraceful, and voyeuristic observer, akin to the Braggadochio of Book 2 in his complacence. But he is also a figure of Spenser's liberation from profound burdens in his work: the burden of anxiety about Cynthia's imperious eye, the burden of loss and its pathos and grief, the burden of the inaccessibility of feminine life.

My sense of this liberation might be clarified in a number of ways. For example, the narrative at first follows the line of emphases and values that I have been describing throughout this book, and these are worth reviewing briefly. Diana's independent athleticism and the pure, expansive, sensory pleasure of privacy in the groves are presented as her reasons for settling on Arlo Hill as her getaway:

> But mongst them all, as fittest for her game,
>   Either for chace of beasts with hound or boawe,
>   Or for to shroude in shade from *Phoebus* flame,
>   Or bathe in fountaines that doe freshly flowe,
>
>   . . . . .
>
>   She chose this *Arlo*. . . .
>
>   . . . . .

---

[1] Kenneth Gross, *Spenserian Poetics: Idolatry, Iconoclasm, and Magic* (Ithaca: Cornell University Press, 1985), 234–45 at 243.

In her [Molanna's] sweet streames, *Diana* vsed oft
(After her sweatie chace and toilesome play)
To bathe her selfe; and after, on the soft
And downy grasse, her dainty limbes to lay
In couert shade, where none behold her may:
For, much she hated sight of liuing eye.

(7.6.39, 42)

Scenes of ongoing feminine life emerge easily from descriptions of nature; although the nymphs consort openly with satyrs, we are led into the ambience of a self-contained feminine world. The corruption of the maid and the surreptitiousness of secrecy-as-betrayal are present here as in the story of Radegund and Clarinda, but again in ways more comic and distanced, less fraught with the weight of Queen Elizabeth's and Elizabeth Throckmorton's real-life experience, than in the episode of the Amazon queen's betrayal by her maid. Diana, bathing, is said to be "for *Ioue* a likely pray" (7.6.45), an assertion that, because it is so patently untrue of Diana herself, can be meant only to recall Ovid and the paradigm of nymphs exposed to greedy eyes. Finally, Faunus is easy to identify as the grossly inadequate viewer, unaware of the splendor that he beholds:

There *Faunus* saw that pleased much his eye,
    And made his hart to tickle in his brest,
    That for great ioy of some-what he did spy,
    He could him not containe in silent rest;
    But breaking forth in laughter, loud profest
His foolish thought. A foolish *Faune* indeed,
    That couldst not hold thy selfe so hidden blest,
    But wouldest needs thine owne conceit areed.
Babblers vnworthy been of so diuine a meed.

(7.6.46)

These repeated patterns are both pleasant and witty. But Spenser's every repetition is a generic or linguistic experiment, a working out of possibilities in the narrative plenitude that grounds each use of an iconographic pattern. Why exactly do we need Faunus and Diana if we already have Braggadochio and Belphoebe?

Faunus is not only insensitive to the privacy and the divinity of the woman beheld; he is also oblivious to any potential desire for proximity to the feminine. This is as much as to say that Faunus is oblivious to the pathos of the viewer. Such obliviousness to the ungraspable otherness of the beheld person is evidently a lack, given Spenser's Vergilian values about responsiveness to vision; hence his rebuke of Faunus for the crudity of laughter rather than awe as a response.

But we cannot do justice to the tone of this episode if we do not also grant that Faunus's obliviousness is a liberation for Spenser. Faunus simply laughs—with delight in his own successful machinations, at nakedness and at the goddess's sexual parts, in a simple glee unburdened by the elusiveness of feminine life and by the possibilities of loss haunting Spenser's own consciousness. It is the narrator, not Faunus, who laments the subsequent loss of Diana's divinity from Arlo Hill, and the decline of its natural splendor. Kenneth Gross reminds us that "what Spenser retains from Ovid...is his habit of parodying etiological myth. For as a fable of iconoclasm, the Faunus episode presents us not so much with sacred history as with an etiology of disenchantment, a myth of demythologization. It tells a story not of the origins of nature or the gods but of the degradation of both."[2] It is remarkable, considering the force of Spenser's sense of mutability as decline, that this tale of a degradation should seem so full of energy, assertiveness, and exuberance. The eloquent grief of the end of the tale is balanced by the comic energy of the voyeur. (Contrast the languorousness of Cymochles in the Bower of Bliss.) This energy was incipient in Braggadochio's response to Belphoebe, but it blossoms here with Faunus's greater intelligence, self-awareness, and relish of his own active viewing.

The same point applies to the response of the beheld goddess and her nymphs. Female characters and lovers exposed have typically responded with defensiveness and abashedness; feminine anger has typically been depicted as an overbearing tyranny. But in the Faunus episode, the pressure of feminine anger is a new response to exposure, and it turns against an object deserving of it. Faunus, who thinks himself protected and privileged by his hiding place, finds himself exposed as the new cynosure of all eyes; Diana runs straight at the territory of the intruder, overwhelming him through his own desire to see, like the lark of the simile:

> The Goddesse, all abashed with that noise,
>   In haste forth started from the guilty brooke;

2 Ibid., 238.

And running straight where-as she heard his voice;
Enclos'd the bush about, and there him tooke,
Like darred Larke; not daring vp to looke
On her whose sight before so much he sought.

(7.6.47)

The anger of Diana and the nymphs liberates the goddess (compare her withdrawal and defensiveness with Venus in *Faerie Queene* 3.6) and liberates female will. This anger has real effects—the terror of Faunus, the stoning of Molanna—but they are effects in a comic tale, in which the nymphs simply stop chasing Faunus and Molanna is united with her beloved river. Feminine anger is freed to be apt, vigorous, and direct rather than burdensome and ominous; Spenser's own response is freed from defensiveness when he depicts virginity as revolt rather than as vulnerability.[3] This conception too was incipient in the competence and independence of Spenser's earlier nymphs, but it blossoms here with their comically aggressive response:

So did *Diana* and her maydens all
Vse silly *Faunus*, now within their baile:
They mocke and scorne him, and him foule miscall;
Some by the nose him pluckt, some by the taile;
And by his goatish beard some did him haile.

. . . . .

Some would haue gelt him . . .

. . . . .

Others would through the riuer him haue driue,
And ducked deepe: . . .

[3]The terms of this contrast are taken from Richard Halpern, "Puritanism and Maenadism in *A Mask*," in *Rewriting the Renaissance: The Discourses of Sexual Difference in Early Modern Europe*, ed. Margaret Ferguson, Maureen Quilligan, and Nancy J. Vickers (Chicago: University of Chicago Press, 1986), 88–105 at 94: "... the maenad was not the only figure for the fierce virgin available to Renaissance poetry. Amazons and the nymphs of Diana also withold their sexuality in ways that make them independent, strange, and frightening to men. All of these figures mark the point at which virginity ceases to denote submission and begins to denote revolt, at which purification becomes danger. In all of these cases, moreover, active virginity is marked by wandering, which contrasts with the stasis of domestic space."

> But most agreed and did this sentence giue,
>   Him in Deares skin to clad; and in that plight,
> To hunt him with their hounds, him selfe saue how hee might.
>   (7.6.49–50)

This slapstick violence we might understand equally as a version of medieval dramas' high-spirited punishments of Vice or Satan (similarly derived punishments occur in Marlowe's *Faustus* and in *The Merry Wives of Windsor*) or as a parody of the Orpheus story: the nymphs are comic cousins of the maenads, and they pummel their victim rather than tear him to pieces.

The simile of the housewife, with which Spenser describes the nymphs' anger, may indeed seem more appropriate to the world of *The Merry Wives* than to this Ovidian world. It is oddly bourgeois in this mythic landscape, a quotidian scene set within the glamorous leisure of nymphs and goddesses:

> Like as an huswife, that with busie care
>   Thinks of her Dairie to make wondrous gaine,
>   Finding where-as some wicked beast vnware
>   That breakes into her Dayr'house, there doth draine
>   Her creaming pannes, and frustrate all her paine;
>   Hath in some snare or gin set close behind,
>   Entrapped him, and caught into her traine,
>   Then thinks what punishment were best assign'd,
> And thousand deathes deuiseth in her vengefull mind.
>   (7.6.48)

Why this sudden appearance of the domestic and of the hope of gain, when Diana and Ovidian nymphs are marked by their avoidance of the household as the paradigmatic feminine sphere? It is, after all, one sphere of feminine life to which Spenser has paid scant attention— with the vital exception of Pastorella's simple housekeeping before Calidore's gaze, a gaze that expresses his hunger both for her and for the domestic stability she represents to a tired knight errant (6.9.13– 37). The household enters Spenser's work in Book 6 of *The Faerie Queene* laden with the pathos of Colin's desire; it reappears without pathos in the dairy simile describing the anger of the nymphs. Moreover, in Gerald Bruns's formulation, "the household is the region of comedy, where everything is up close and familiar, not distanced.... So these [characters in the Faunus episode] are demystified creatures.

Our fear of castration is dispelled; we're all at home."[4] In the description of the dairy, Spenser is free to imagine the feminine presence, still competent and vigorous, of the domestic sphere, of the ordinary world, without the Vergilian loss implicit in visions of more numinous women. It also seems possible that the class distinction between Diana and her nymphs, on the one hand, and the bourgeois housewife, on the other, allows Spenser a figurative relief from the domination of the imperial votaress while still allowing access to feminine energy and anger.

The horned god begins his Spenserian career in his Greek incarnation as Pan, in the "Aprill" eclogue. In the pursuit of Syrinx there (to recapitulate briefly), neither god nor author shows any significant interest in the nymph's Ovidian desire for solitude, or in her loss. Nor does the woman placed at the center of a ring and the joyous celebration of her in "Aprill" raise any questions of feminine will or abashedness; as I said at the beginning of this book, the poem raises no questions about social decorums between beholder and beheld. When the horned god next appears, in the person of Sylvanus in *Faerie Queene* 1, some of these matters interest Spenser more, as we have seen; but the treatment of Una is perfunctory and conventional compared to the development of the beholders. Sometime after 1590, when Spenser must have been working on the poems to be published in 1595 and 1596, he works out certain apprehensions of feminine will to which he had given little attention in his early poems and in the first three books of the epic. The female viewer and the beloved, elevated woman who uses the skills of the panther to control her lover or her courtiers become crucial figures in these later works. Women are increasingly understood as possessors of volition and autonomy, and as agents within visual acts, but their actions are often understood as threatening and dangerous.

Book 6 of the epic begins a recovery from these disenchantments. Recovery is made possible by a shift away from gender in relation to vision and a new attentiveness, instead, to social demeanor more broadly. The expanded anatomy of face-to-face encounters and of tact, as in Calidore's meeting with Tristram, allows Spenser to re-

---

[4]Gerald Bruns's comment in conversation, in response to the question I posed about the simile of the housewife and her dairy. I am grateful to him and to Stephen Fallon, who helped me think through some of the points of this conclusion.

construct some ideals of mutual human presence, and eventually to return to large-scale depictions of men's and women's presence to each other, most notably in the Mt. Acidale episode. But the Acidalian vision is fragile and tentative and, as I said, does not fully master the epic's conflicts about sight, will, desire, and mutual presence. Neither Mt. Acidale nor Arlo Hill alone suffices to resolve the difficulties of seeing and being seen. Together, they offer Spenser's readers a moment of poise in the human struggle to gratify the hungers of the self while acknowledging the independent life of the other.

Index of Episodes from Epics

General Index

Library of Congress Cataloging-in-Publication Data

Krier, Theresa M., 1953
  Gazing on secret sights : Spenser, classical imitation, and the decorums of
vision / Theresa M. Krier.
    p. cm.
  Includes bibliographical references.
  ISBN 0-8014-2345-7 (alk. paper)
  1. Spenser, Edmund, 1552?–1599—Knowledge—Folklore, mythology.
2. Spenser, Edmund, 1552?–1599—Knowledge—Literature. 3. Ovid, 43
B.C.–17 or 18 A.D.—Influence—Spenser. 4. Virgil—Influence—Spenser. 5.
Classicism—England—History—16th century. 6. Mythology, Classical, in literature. 7. Latin poetry—History and criticism. 8. Imitation (in literature) 9. Secrecy in literature. 10. Vision in literature. I. Title.
PR2367.M83K75 1990
821'.3—dc20   89–28299